Cuba at a Crossroads

Cuba
at a Crossroads

———■———

Politics and Economics after

the Fourth Party Congress

Edited by

Jorge F. Pérez-López

University Press of Florida
Gainesville/Tallahassee/Tampa/Boca Raton
Pensacola/Orlando/Miami/Jacksonville

Copyright © 1994 by the Board of Regents of the State of Florida
Printed in the United States of America on acid-free paper
All rights reserved

99 98 97 96 95 94   6 5 4 3 2 1

An earlier version of chapter 2, by Juan M. del Aguila, was originally published as "The Party, the Fourth Congress, and the Process of Counter-Reform" in *Cuban Studies* 23, edited by Jorge F. Pérez-López, Reprinted by permission of the University of Pittsburgh Press. Copyright 1993 by University of Pittsburgh Press.

An earlier version of chapter 4, by Archibald R. M. Ritter, was originally published as "Exploring Cuba's Economic Futures" in *Cuban Studies* 23, edited by Jorge F. Pérez-López. Reprinted by permission of the University of Pittsburgh Press. Copyright 1993 by University of Pittsburgh Press.

An earlier version of chapter 7, by Maria Dolores Espino, was originally published as "Tourism in Cuba: A Development Strategy for the 1990s?" in *Cuban Studies* 23, edited by Jorge F. Pérez-López. Reprinted by permission of the University of Pittsburgh Press. Copyright 1993 by University of Pittsburgh Press.

Library of Congress Cataloging-in-Publication Data

Cuba at a crossroads: politics and economics after the Fourth Party Congress/Jorge F. Pérez-López, editor.
p.   cm.
Includes bibliographical references and index.
ISBN 0-8130-1310-0
1. Cuba—Economic conditions—1959–   2. Cuba—Economic policy.
3. Cuba—Politics and government—1959–   I. Pérez-López, Jorge F.
HC152.5.C7972   1994
330.97291—dc20   94-16203

The University Press of Florida is the scholarly publishing agency for the State University System of Florida, comprised of Florida A & M University, Florida Atlantic University, Florida International University, Florida State University, University of Central Florida, University of Florida, University of North Florida, University of South Florida, and University of West Florida.

University Press of Florida
15 Northwest 15th Street
Gainesville, FL 32611

CONTENTS

Tables	ix
Introduction *Cuban Politics and Economics in the 1990s* JORGE F. PÉREZ-LÓPEZ	xi
Chapter One *Leadership Strategies and Mass Support: Cuban Politics before and after the 1991 Communist Party Congress* JORGE I. DOMÍNGUEZ	1
Chapter Two *The Party, the Fourth Congress, and the Process of Counterreform* JUAN M. DEL AGUILA	19
Chapter Three *Continuity and Change in Cuba's International Relations in the 1990s* DAMIÁN J. FERNÁNDEZ	41
Chapter Four *Cuba's Economic Strategy and Alternative Futures* ARCHIBALD R. M. RITTER	67
Chapter Five *Reflections on Economic Policy: Cuba's Food Program* SERGIO G. ROCA	94
Chapter Six *Cuba's Labor Adjustment Policies during the Special Period* SERGIO DÍAZ-BRIQUETS AND JORGE F. PÉREZ-LÓPEZ	118

Chapter Seven
   Tourism in Cuba: A Development Strategy for the 1990s?   147
   MARÍA DOLORES ESPINO

Chapter Eight
   *Cuban Biotechnology: A First World Approach to
      Development*   167
   JULIE M. FEINSILVER

Chapter Nine
   *Islands of Capitalism in an Ocean of Socialism:
      Joint Ventures in Cuba's Development Strategy*   190
   JORGE F. PÉREZ-LÓPEZ

Chapter Ten
   Reforming Cuba's Economic System from Within   220
   ANDREW ZIMBALIST

Chapter Eleven
   Economic Reform in Cuba: Lessons from Eastern Europe   238
   JORGE F. PÉREZ-LÓPEZ

Contributors   264

Index   265

TABLES

2-1.	Members Elected to the Political Bureau of the Cuban Communist Party during the Fourth Congress	31
4-1.	Major Cuban Macroeconomic Indicators, 1987–92	70
4-2.	Cuban Foreign Exchange Earnings by Commodity or Service, 1988–92	71
4-3.	Some Alternative Scenarios for Cuba's Economic Future, 1993–95	80
5-1.	Cuban Annual Per Capita Food Consumption, 1982–89	97
5-2.	Cuban Food Production, 1980–92, and Food Program Targets, 1993–95	98
5-3.	Cuba's Food Sector: State Sales, 1980–90, and Food Program Targets, 1993–95	101
5-4.	Selected Cuban Imports, 1958–89	104
6-1.	Objectives and Key Concepts Relating to Principal Cuban Emergency Labor Resolutions, 1990–92	122
6-2.	Emergency Labor Measures in Effect in Cuba in Late 1992	133
7-1.	International Visitors to Cuba, 1982–91	150
7-2.	International Visitors to Cuba through Travel Agencies, by Area of Origin, 1980–89	151
7-3.	Cuba's Capacity for International Tourism, 1989–91	153
7-4.	Cuba's Hard Currency Visitors' Expenditures and Gross Revenues from Visitors, 1977–91	156
7-5.	Visitors' Arrivals from Capitalist Nations and Hard Currency Expenditures in Cuba, 1982–91	157

9-1. Partial List of Foreign Joint Ventures with Cuban Partners	198
9-2. Other Arrangements with Foreign Entities	203
9-3. Numbers of Cuban Joint Ventures with Foreign Investors, 1990–92	207
10-1. Application of Material Incentives, 1985–90	227
11-1. Cuban State Budget, 1985–90	246
11-2. Number of Cuban Industrial Enterprises according to Value of Output, 1988	250

INTRODUCTION

Cuban Politics and Economics in the 1990s
JORGE F. PÉREZ-LÓPEZ

Cuba is at a crossroads. Some thirty-five years after the triumph of a popular revolution, the winds of change blow over the island. The pursuit of socialism by a small, developing island nation in an increasingly capitalist world poses tremendous challenges for the Cuban leadership and for the nation.

A strong case can be made that at no time has the survival of the Cuban revolution been under more severe challenge than in the 1990s. Not only is the leadership confronted by a severely hostile external economic environment, but it also faces autochthonous pressures for political and economic change unmatched in the last three and one-half decades.

In power longer than any regime in modern Latin America with the exception of the Stroessner regime in Paraguay—but closing in quickly on that dubious record and likely to surpass it by the time this book is published—the Cuban ruling elite has aged, leadership renovation has been stunted, and the political system has increasingly lost touch with the population, particularly with the young. Economic hardships have intensified, bringing widespread pessimism among the population about the economic future of the nation.

The first few years of the 1990s already have been difficult. The economy has been undergoing a prolonged recession, which began in the mid-1980s. In 1986, the Cuban leadership embarked on a so-called rectification process (*proceso de rectificación de errores y tendencias negativas*), which centralized economic policy making and largely eliminated existing market-oriented mechanisms. Political and economic changes in Eastern Europe and the former Soviet Union that began in 1989–90 have had a devastating impact on Cuba's external sector and on overall economic performance. In 1990, Cuba announced that it had entered a period of severe economic austerity, the "special period in time of peace" (*período especial en tiempo de paz*).

Cuba's recession has deepened in the 1990s, and the prospects for a turnaround in the foreseeable future appear dim. Between 1989 and 1992, the global social product has contracted by at least 40 percent, exports have fallen by more than 70 percent, and so have imports (including foodstuffs, consumer goods, and energy). The average Cuban citizen has experienced a significant reduction in standard of living, not only because of the lesser availability of consumer goods but also because of inconveniences associated with the lack of such basic services as electricity, running water, and public transportation. Cubans have also begun to experience, for the first time, actual or impending cutbacks in education and public health services, achievements of the revolution to which the citizenry had grown accustomed and which it took for granted.

Despite the deteriorating economic situation, the Cuban leadership has succeeded in keeping the potential opposition in check, openly repressing emerging dissident groups. At the same time, the leadership has stepped up the pressure to extract even more sacrifices from the population in an all-out campaign to preserve one of the last bastions of socialism.

Perhaps as important, the end of the Cold War has left Cuba without major foreign allies or benefactors, alone for the first time in more than three decades. The crumbling of the socialist bloc has forced Cuba to depend exclusively on its own resources for economic growth and development. At a time when many developing countries—and the former socialist countries as well—are actively restructuring their economies and racing to insert themselves into the world economic system, so is Cuba. However, saddled with a legacy of three decades of inefficient central planning, a high foreign debt, virtually no access to financial markets, and an economy that continues to be heavily dependent on sugar, Cuba enters the race from the back of the pack and with a severe handicap.

In the 1990s, Cuba stands at the intersection of several roads, each associated with alternative models of political and economic organization. One of these roads is the intransigent pursuit of socialism at any economic and social cost, making good on the slogan "Socialism or Death." Another is the pursuit of a set of policies conducive to economic reform and marketization, along the lines of the Eastern European example, accepting the attendant political changes. A third might be the path of "market socialism" being pursued by China. There might also be indigenous trails to be blazed, as well as crossways from one road to another. One or more of these paths might lead to political stability, sustainable economic development, and social and economic well-being, others might be false starts or cul-de-sacs, and still others might lead to dead ends.

This book brings together eleven essays by a dozen specialists who explore key issues related to Cuban politics and economics in the 1990s. Most of the essays were prepared for a conference sponsored by the Cuban Studies Institute (Instituto de Estudios Cubanos) held at Rollins College, Winter Park, Florida, in June 1992. The essayists endeavored to examine the current situation in Cuba and prospects for the 1990s in their areas of expertise. Where appropriate, the writers also attempted to evaluate the likelihood of success of strategies that the Cuban leadership is pursuing.

The Fourth Congress of the Cuban Communist Party (Partido Comunista de Cuba, PCC), held in October 1991, is a focal point of the analyses. Originally scheduled to take place at the end of 1990 and postponed several times, the congress was awaited in Cuba with a heightened degree of anticipation. Communist Party congresses were held in the former Soviet Union and Eastern European nations at five-year intervals; emulating this practice, Cuba began to hold such gatherings in the 1970s, during the so-called period of institutionalization of the revolution. The First Congress of the PCC was held in December 1975; congresses were also held in December 1980 and February 1986.

In Cuba, as in other socialist countries, the Communist Party congresses served multiple purposes. Through the lens of domestic politics, a party congress was a major event that allowed the ruling party to project an image of orderly governance and stability. Preparations for the congresses normally involved intensive—or at least frequent—meetings at workplaces, schools, and neighborhoods to discuss the main agenda items, under the close tutelage of party cadres. The vast number of meetings and the high attendance (attendance typically was compulsory) were trumpeted by the government-controlled media as evidence of public participation in decision making and of representative democracy at its best. Meanwhile, the process of selecting delegates provided an opportunity for limited renewal of leadership and the showcasing of rising stars.

At another level, the party congresses also provided the leadership of the ruling PCC with an opportunity to bask in the limelight, as accomplishments since the last congress were presented in minute detail. PCC congresses offered Fidel Castro a platform from which to report fully on the successes of his administration. His "Central Reports," extremely detailed and chock-full of statistics, touched on essentially all areas of governance: international relations, economic development, foreign trade, education, defense, culture, sports, and so on.

But party congresses were not only reflective and self-congratulatory events. They also served the purpose of setting out the party's vision of the future and a general program of action for the upcoming five-year period. In fact, adoption of such a five-year program was perhaps the principal concrete accomplishment of the congresses. Because the entire community of socialist countries held their party congresses at about the same time, there was also an opportunity to coordinate programs across countries—bilaterally and within the Council for Mutual Economic Assistance—factoring external resources, in the form of foreign trade and assistance, into each country's medium-term economic and social development plans.

The high level of anticipation associated with the Fourth Congress arose from the expectation—perhaps more accurately, the hope—on the part of many that the congress might approve concrete steps to begin a genuine process of democratization and economic liberalization. Although it did bring about some minor changes in the political and economic arenas, it is fair to say that the changes fell far short of the expectations of those with a reformist agenda.

These essays examine issues of relevance to Cuba after the Fourth Congress of the Cuban Communist Party in the political and economic arenas. The first part of the volume explores issues related to domestic politics and international relations. In chapter 1, Jorge I. Domínguez examines two important dimensions of Cuba's political system: the ruling institutions and mass support. He argues that since the mid-1980s, Cuba's political institutions, such as the PCC and the mass organizations, have lost prestige and effectiveness while Fidel Castro's personal leadership role has risen. He concludes that the Fourth Congress only intensified this trend.

These judgments are supported by Juan M. del Aguila in chapter 2. He posits that there has been a move to downsize the Communist Party bureaucracy and to centralize administrative and ideological controls at the top. He associates this counterreform with the broader rectification process and sees it culminating at the Fourth Congress. While downsizing and cleansing the party through the removal of cadres shored it so that it would not drift and decay—as had its counterparts in the former communist world—it also eliminated potential sources of disagreement and reform within the ruling elite.

At the same time that the political institutions have weakened, Domínguez contends that the frequency and intensity of opposition to the regime have intensified. More so than ever before, Cuban citizens have begun to demonstrate a willingness to speak up and resist government economic policies and engage in behavior at odds with regime preferences. Especially since the fall of 1991, the government has pursued an aggressive repression campaign against opposition groups, deploying gangs to harass and intimidate them and jailing their leaders.

Turning to international relations, Damián J. Fernández holds in chapter 3 that Cuban foreign policy in the 1990s is driven primarily by economic pragmatism: a pressing need to find trading partners to replace the ubiquitous former Soviet Union and Eastern European nations. This economic imperative explains, in part, Cuba's revitalized relations with China, an intense public relations campaign in Latin America and Western Europe (particularly Spain) to promote Cuba as a trade and investment partner, and efforts to cultivate other oil-exporting nations. Cuba's new foreign policy, in his view, raises important opportunities and challenges. On the one hand, enhanced international transactions might have a salutary effect on the economy, but, on the other, the establishment of economic enclaves operating with dollars or other hard currencies and not open to the population might have a negative effect on the social fiber.

The second part of the volume concentrates on economic issues. In chapter 4, Archibald R. M. Ritter assesses Cuba's current economic strategy and explores possible economic futures. According to Ritter, Cuba's economic crisis is probably the most severe the nation has faced since the nineteenth century: a sharp decline in export earnings has generated serious energy and food crises and an investment decline.

The lack of flexibility of economic institutions will make sustained recovery most difficult in the longer term.

Ritter touches briefly on Cuba's economic strategy for the 1990s, developed in response to the current economic crisis and ratified by the Fourth Congress. The main strands of this strategy are (1) a program of import substitution, including a food production program (*programa alimentario*, PA) aimed at achieving self-sufficiency in foodstuffs; (2) energy substitution, replacing oil use with animal (ox carts) and human (bicycles) power, as well as the reduction of output in oil-intensive lines of production; (3) a major effort at export promotion, including the development of markets for traditional exports (especially sugar), and the development of new sources of foreign exchange, in particular biotechnology exports and tourism; (4) a greater effort to attract foreign investment; (5) some management reforms to increase efficiency and productivity; and (6) toleration of a higher degree of decentralization, autonomy, and improvisation in the actual functioning of enterprises.

In analyzing Cuba's alternate economic futures, Ritter identifies certain key factors which, in his view, will shape the course of events. Based on these factors, he develops a continuum of scenarios for Cuba's economic future (from optimistic "best case" to pessimistic "worst case") and distills them into five likely outcomes or models, ranging from the status quo to a full-blown market economy. He concludes that the most attractive model to many Cubans would be a "social economy of the market" model that blends market behavior and distributional equity while preserving some public sector involvement in the economy.

The rest of the chapters in the second part deal with more discrete issues affecting the Cuban economy in the 1990s raised in summary fashion by Ritter. Chapters 5 through 10 concentrate on specific aspects of the economic strategy that Cuba is pursuing in the 1990s, while chapter 11 touches on key issues that would have to be addressed in creating a market economy in Cuba.

Sergio G. Roca focuses in chapter 5 on perhaps the highest short-term economic priority of Cuba's revolutionary government: increasing the output of agricultural products to feed the population and generate exports. Roca sees the PA not as an ad hoc response to the economic crisis of the 1990s but rather as part of a broader strategy, which began to be implemented in the mid-1980s, to reinstitute economic centralization and the return to the mobilization model of the 1960s. Although data are not available to carry out a comprehensive evaluation of the results of the PA, fragmentary information from different sources collated by Roca points to mixed effects on production: for example, output of tubers and vegetables has risen, but output of beef and milk has declined.

Perhaps more interesting, Roca suggests that the PA might perform the role of a laboratory to test certain market-oriented policies that later could be expanded to the economy at large. Examples are the authorization of individual and community garden plots to promote self-sufficiency in food consumption and the decision by the leadership (publicly supported by Fidel Castro, who earlier had opposed it) to increase prices of selected agricultural commodities to cover production costs, stimulate output, reduce subsidies, and support increases in worker salaries. The extent of success of elements of the PA in which market criteria are prevalent could well influence how widely such methods are diffused.

In chapter 6, which Sergio Díaz-Briquets and I coauthored, we examine Cuba's response to worker dislocations. The nature, severity, and length of labor dislocations in Cuba, and therefore the public policy response—in terms of type and modalities of adjustment measures—have changed over time. While worker dislocations in the 1970s and 1980s were associated with temporary plant shutdowns or the relocation of facilities and therefore were short-term in nature, the significant dislocations that have occurred since 1990 because of shortages of energy and raw materials imports are longer in duration and are not likely to disappear in the near future.

The earlier responses—financial compensation for a limited period of time and reemployment in a similar job—are not viable in the economic context of the 1990s. Instead, the current response to worker dislocations emphasizes mobilization to agricultural activities (for example, the PA) and payment of financial compensation for an unlimited period of time. These measures place a severe financial burden on the economy and pose a major financial challenge to future efforts to restructure the economy to seek higher efficiency.

Chapters 7 and 8 examine two industries that the Cuban economic strategy has targeted as development poles for the 1990s: tourism and biotechnology. In the current development strategy, these industries are counted upon to experience substantial growth, create productive employment, and generate badly needed hard currency.

María Dolores Espino focuses on the tourism industry in chapter 7.

She analyzes the development and performance of Cuba's international tourism industry and its impact on the Cuban economy, including the balance of payments, government receipts, income and employment, and the promotion of growth and development. Espino concludes that, at present, the international tourism industry is small in relation to the national economy, and its overall impact on the economy is rather insignificant. The primary benefit that Cuba currently derives from tourism is the generation of hard currency revenues, with other potential benefits not being maximized.

For international tourism to assume the role of a development pole for the 1990s, Espino contends, it must first become a leading generator of income and employment. This requires, in turn, a significant reduction in imported goods and services used by the international tourism industry and effective linkages with other sectors of the economy, in particular agriculture, services, and retail trade. Cuba's strategy of pursuing tourism development through an enclave mode—keeping the tourism industry separate from the rest of the economy—hinders both the expansionary effect of income generation and the establishment of linkages with other sectors of the economy.

That a developing country would select a high-technology industry such as biotechnology as a pole of development appears, at first glance, to be a chimera, similar to the hopes that the riches of major oil finds would bail out the faltering Cuban economy. However, as Julie M. Feinsilver discusses in chapter 8, this policy might be sound considering Cuba's significant investments and resources in this area and its limited set of options.

The Cuban government justifies its focus on biotechnology as a leading sector for development on the basis of (1) the potential of this industry for generating exportable products, particularly pharmaceuticals, as well as products for domestic use that substitute for imports the country can no longer afford and (2) Cuba's highly advanced medical system and heavy investments in science and technology. Feinsilver finds that Cuba has had some successes in producing a range of biotechnology products for domestic consumption and for export. A current priority is agricultural biotechnology, aiming to produce pesticides, herbicides, fertilizers, and high-yielding seeds that no longer can be imported. Whether Cuba can share in the potentially very large biotechnology market of the future depends on many factors. Critical among them is the ability to compete with other biotechnology companies in the world market; this may require that Cuba form commercial alliances with foreign companies to market its products.

Another strand of Cuba's economic strategy for the 1990s is the promotion of incoming foreign investment, pursuant to legislation first passed in 1982. In chapter 9 I deal with this topic and assess the feasibility of a foreign investment–led economic development strategy within an orthodox socialist economy, drawing on the experience of China.

My research confirms that since about 1989, there has been an upturn in foreign interest in investing in Cuba. Because of the economic crisis, Cuba has broadened the scope of, and liberalized the terms for, foreign investment in the island to the point where there are few limitations on incoming investment, provided the deal is attractive to Cuban authorities. There is evidence that a number of significant deals have been consummated, particularly in the form of joint ventures in tourism, although their magnitude is relatively small when compared with the resource needs of the country and the loss in foreign trade with, and aid from, the former socialist countries. There are also reports of joint ventures in the manufacturing sector, combining foreign raw materials and markets and unutilized Cuban production capacities.

Andrew Zimbalist deals with a fourth strand in Cuba's development strategy for the 1990s: management and organizational reforms aimed at increasing efficiency and supporting the economy's reinsertion into world markets. In chapter 10, Zimbalist argues that during the rectification process, Cuba instituted significant systemic reforms, such as continuing to promote administrative decentralization through the promotion of production brigades in agricultural and industrial enterprises; forming, and transferring planning functions to, industrial associations; reducing the number of commodities and commodity groups subject to central planning; introducing new central planning methods, such as "continuous planning"; and experimenting with pricing policies.

More recently, two reform efforts have been given strong emphasis: enterprise management reform and the decentralization of foreign trade structures. Military enterprises were the focus of early efforts at enterprise management reform, including techniques such as management by consensus, group work, quality control circles, job rotation, and participatory decision making; successes in these enterprises led to the generalization of the techniques throughout the economy. Regarding foreign trade relations, numerous corporations have been set up that operate independently of the central state apparatus, and foreign trade is increasingly being conducted through decentralized trading companies.

In chapter 11 I broach the subject of systemic economic reforms in Cuba. Based on the experiences of three Eastern European reforming countries—Poland, Hungary, and Czechoslovakia—I identify a number of issues that would likely have to be addressed in creating a market economy in Cuba. These issues include stabilizing the economy, transforming government structures, creating an institutional framework for the market, privatizing, and establishing a viable social safety net.

The 1990s promise to be a decade of change in Cuba. The authors of the essays in this collection have endeavored to provide readers with a solid foundation for understanding and evaluating the foundations and implications of those changes.

The editor wishes to acknowledge and express appreciation for the contributions of several individuals and institutions to this collection: first, to each of the contributors for taking on the task of writing the original papers and for revising them for this volume; second, to the Cuban Studies Institute for devoting the agenda of one of its meetings to these topics and providing a forum for their discussion; and third, to the University of Pittsburgh Press for allowing the publication, in revised form, of the essays by del Aguila, Ritter, and Espino, which appeared originally in volume 23 of the journal *Cuban Studies* (1993). To all: heartfelt thanks.

ONE

Leadership Strategies and Mass Support
Cuban Politics before and after the 1991 Communist Party Congress
JORGE I. DOMÍNGUEZ

Cuba's political system has been undergoing a significant transition that began in the mid-1980s and has shaped the contours of the country's politics in the early 1990s. In this chapter I focus on two dimensions of regime transformation in Cuba: the deinstitutionalization at the top and the growing autonomy at the bottom. I concentrate on events and processes that occurred just before and just after the Fourth Congress of the Communist Party of Cuba, held in October 1991.

One major change is that Cuba's political regime has become more personalized. Its institutions, especially the Communist Party and the mass organizations, have lost prestige, authority, and effectiveness. Moreover, many top political cadres who founded the regime and governed it for decades have been dismissed from office or lost much of their power. To a degree unparalleled since the regime's founding, Fidel Castro's personal role is paramount.

Another broad change is that Cuba's society has been resurrected. Ordinary Cubans are now more likely to resist government economic policies, to voice criticism, and to engage in behavior at odds with regime preferences.

Regime Personalization

Since the mid-1980s, a key means to centralize and repersonalize political power in Cuba has been the destruction of the politics of stable oligarchy that was set in place in the mid-1960s.[1]

During the fifteen-year period from 1965 to 1980, Cuba transited out of the revolutionary mass mobilization that had marked the 1960s into more routinized, formal, and bureaucratized politics—what some have called, with exaggeration, the regime's institutionalization. In those years President Fidel Castro delegated substantial powers to other members of the party's Political Bureau and Secretariat to act in various areas of domestic affairs, retaining for himself the right to make key decisions as well as the responsibility for the conduct of foreign policy. Thus the regime became depersonalized. It came to resemble an oligarchy whose members seemed to enjoy indefinite tenure. From 1965 to 1980, through two party congresses, no member of the party's Political Bureau was dismissed, though the bureau's size was expanded gradually to allow for the injection of new blood.

In the mid-1980s, however, Fidel Castro removed from high office many people with whom he had governed Cuba for a long time. By the end of the Third Party Congress (1986), four of the fifteen full members of the Political Bureau who were still alive had lost their posts, including commanders of the revolution Guillermo García and Ramiro Valdés. As interior minister, the latter had successfully built the regime's repressive apparatus in the 1960s; he had been recalled from semiretirement to rescue the regime from the domestic crisis (1979–81) associated with the 1980 Mariel exodus. In addition, five of the eleven Political Bureau alternates lost their posts, including former secretary for ideology Antonio Pérez Herrero, who had been the party's dominant political figure in the early 1980s, and former president of the Central Planning Board Humberto Pérez, who had been the architect of Cuba's economic recovery in the 1970s.

The removal of Valdés and of the two Pérezes broke the back of the stable oligarchy. Valdés had run the security police, Pérez Herrero had run the party, and Humberto Pérez had run the centrally planned economy. Each had designed networks of allies who were accustomed to working with each other. Each had devised procedures to represent and reconcile bureaucratic interests. Each had been a master player within the regime's organizational politics. Each had constructed an organization that marked the regime and enabled it to endure and, for years, to develop. Each had been successful on his own terms, and each had contributed to stabilizing Cuban politics and enabling Cuba to project its influence internationally.

Other events brought about important personnel changes. These were related mainly to the drug-trafficking scandal that became public in 1989. Division general Arnaldo Ochoa, decorated hero of the Republic of Cuba and architect of Cuban military victories in the Horn of Africa war in 1977–78 and the Angolan war in 1987–88, was arrested and executed. The De la Guardia brothers (a general and a colonel), who had run the Ministry of the Interior's unit in charge of breaking the U.S. trade embargo, were also arrested; one would be executed, the other jailed.[2] In turn, the interior minister was arrested for negligence of duty; he subsequently died in prison. Also in 1989, Vice-President Diocles Torralba was arrested and imprisoned for corruption. Earlier scandals included brigade general Rafael del Pino's defection to the United States and Luis Orlando Domínguez's arrest and imprisonment for corruption. Domínguez, former general secretary of the Communist Youth Union and a one-time member of Fidel Castro's personal staff, headed Cuba's civil aviation sector at the time of his arrest. These events weakened the Ministry of the Interior's role in Cuban society; in receivership, in effect, it had to be staffed anew at the top with personnel from the armed forces. More important, a regime that had claimed the right to rule in part on the basis of the probity of its personnel found too many of its top leaders guilty of corruption.

The destruction of the bureaucratic oligarchy continued thereafter. By the end of the Fourth Party Congress (October 1991), six of the fourteen Political Bureau members had lost their posts, including president of the Women's Federation Vilma Espín (Fidel Castro's sister-in-law), former general secretary of the Cuban Workers' Confederation Roberto Veiga, longtime party secretary Jorge Risquet, minister of culture Armando Hart, and government vice-president Pedro Miret.

Considering that no Political Bureau member was dropped in the fifteen years between 1965 and 1980, the changes from 1986 to 1991 are impressive. By the end of the Fourth Party Congress, only five of the 1975 Political Bureau members were still members of that body: Fidel Castro, Raúl Castro, Juan Almeida, Carlos Rafael Rodríguez, and José Ramón Machado.

This pattern continued even within the year following the Fourth

Party Congress. As is discussed in more detail in the following chapter by del Aguila, in early fall 1992 Carlos Aldana was dropped from the Political Bureau, and subsequently from the Central Committee and from the party itself, under vague accusations of corruption. In the 1980s, Aldana had built up impressive political influence and authority. Beginning as late as the mid-1980s, he had become party secretary for ideology, culture, the mass media, and international relations and, by the early 1990s, had positioned himself as one of Cuba's top leaders just below the Castro brothers. His successful construction of an organizational network came to a crashing end, just as similar endeavors had failed in preceding years.

Managing Relations between State and Society

The erosion of the regime's capacity to govern in the manner to which it had become accustomed under the politics of stable oligarchy is also evident in the political decline of officials in the positions most responsible for the management of relations between state and society: party secretaries for each of the provinces and heads of mass organizations.

Including alternates, the Political Bureau chosen at the Third Party Congress had five party provincial secretaries. By the end of the Fourth Congress, only Esteban Lazo, party secretary for Santiago province, remained in the Political Bureau. Such a wholesale removal from the Political Bureau suggests that the key link in the chain between national and local authorities was deemed to have performed ineffectively during the late 1980s. The importance of the role of provincial secretary was highlighted, nonetheless, by the inclusion of four new provincial secretaries (plus the chief party secretary at Cuba's second largest city, Santiago) in the twenty-five-member Political Bureau chosen in October 1991. That linking role must still be performed and, Cuban leaders hope, will be better performed.

Again counting alternates, the Political Bureau chosen at the Third Congress included the top leaders of Cuba's key mass organizations for workers, women, and peasants, which have served to mobilize and organize the population to comply with policies and also to communicate suggestions from the population for policy changes. By the end of the Fourth Congress, all three mass organization leaders had lost their posts on the Political Bureau; two had even been dropped from the Central Committee. The Fourth Congress's Political Bureau included only the new general secretary of the Cuban Workers' Confederation; it did not include any top leader from either the women's or the peasants' associations.

This choice raises the question of how the political leadership chosen in October 1991 might respond to society and the economy. It could do so both in continuing ways and in new ways.

Fidel Castro's personal role would be one factor. With the possible exception of vice-presidents Almeida and Rodríguez, no member of the Political Bureau had the standing and experience to attempt to block a Fidel Castro initiative. Moreover, the near doubling of the size of the Political Bureau and the abolition of the small-group party Secretariat at the Fourth Congress might have a perhaps unintended effect: Fidel Castro would not have to chair a meeting with fewer than twenty-five people. When he had met with a group a third that size (the old Secretariat), the interpersonal dynamics might have made it easier for someone to challenge him to change his mind. As he shifted to chair a much larger group, his role as presiding officer would be enhanced even if that was not the intention of the change.

Second, economics seemed to matter less, even though the economy was in shock and would remain so. Only the seventy-nine-year-old vice-president Rodríguez had been trained as an economist. Carlos Lage, who assumed overall operational command of nationwide economic coordination, was trained as a physician (although he seems to have a good grasp of economic issues). They were the only two Political Bureau members whose designated tasks included involvement with economic policy making. All other members specialized in political or military tasks, and none had training in economics.

Mass organizations mattered the least. The heads of the committees for the Defense of the Revolution, the Women's Federation, and the Peasants' Association were absent from the Political Bureau; nor was there anyone from the top leadership of such organizations in the Political Bureau.

Women and blacks, as such, were not seen as a political problem. Their numbers in the 1991 Political Bureau remained basically unchanged from what they had been in the 1986 Political Bureau (including alternates); these groups remained woefully underrepresented. In addition, the women in the 1991 Political Bureau (a hospital director, a provincial party official, and a staffer to Fidel Castro) had much less independent political standing than had the three women they replaced (the president and general secretary of the Women's Federation and the president of the Academy of Sciences).

There was a political concern about young people. Eleven of the twenty-five members of the Political Bureau were new members, and at the time of their election, the oldest of them was forty-nine. They included the three women and one man who had not had a high political rank before they were chosen Political Bureau members in 1991. The young age of the party secretary in Cienfuegos province (in office only since January 1991) might also explain why he was chosen for Political Bureau membership over other, more senior, provincial secretaries. Three of the youngest new members, however, were politically significant: Communist Youth Union general secretary Roberto Robaina, who had revitalized his organization; Cuban Writers and Artists Union president Abel Prieto, who had skillfully held most intellectuals allegiant enough to the regime; and Carlos Lage, the Political Bureau's only new member who focused on economics. By the end of 1992, Lage would emerge as the government's chief decision maker for economic policy after Fidel Castro.

The military was honored but not dominant, suggesting that the top civilian leadership did not fear a military coup and thus did not believe that it needed to take special steps to secure the allegiance of military officers. The number of Political Bureau members in uniform remained virtually unchanged. It included the ministers of the armed forces and the interior and three key division generals.

There was, in brief, a striking shift in the basis for the relationship between state and society. Instead of the previous efforts to build support by means of good economic performance (in the 1970s), mass organizations, and other means of gaining societal allegiance (from blacks or women, for example), in late 1991 the regime came to emphasize Fidel Castro's personal role and the need to build a bridge across the generations. The suggested strategy implied few hopes for a revival of the Cuban economy as well as little inclination to democratize rule, if that is understood to imply responsiveness to societal organizations and demands beyond an appeal to the younger leaders. More than at any time since the early 1960s, the exercise of power had come to rest with Fidel Castro himself.

In addition, this evidence suggests that, in late 1991, Cuba's top leaders did not fear the political consequences of the likely continued deterioration of the economy. They believed they could recompose their political ability to govern even if the economic decline were to continue (as it would). Their faith in politics extended to their expectation that the armed forces, too, would remain loyal.

The "Blessings" from International Debacles

As the Reagans and the Gorbachevs danced in the White House in December 1987 to celebrate the end of the Cold War in Europe, the last hot war of the Cold War was being fought. At that very moment, thousands of Cuban troops were crossing the Atlantic Ocean, eventually to lift the South African military siege of Cuito Cuanavale in southern Angola and then to push the South African armed forces out of Angola. These military victories and the subsequent negotiated settlement led to the independence of Namibia and accelerated the unraveling of the apartheid regime in South Africa itself; subsequently, they would lead also to the full withdrawal of Cuban troops from Angola.

After the 1980s, tens of thousands of Cubans returned home from all the corners of the globe. They returned from the battlefields of Ethiopia and Angola; from advisory missions in Nicaragua and in the People's Republic of the Congo; from serving as guest workers in East German, Czech, and Hungarian factories; from their studies in the Soviet Union.[3] Repatriation was, of course, a joyous reunion with loved ones, but it was also a symbol and result of the political, military, and economic collapse of the communist world. Cuba's political regime was now alone.

Cuban leaders have had to adjust in myriad ways to their regime's new vulnerabilities. Paradoxically, the change freed them to focus more on problems at home. Fidel Castro no longer needed to spend his time micromanaging battles in southern Angola; he came to have more time to think about the supply of domestic foodstuffs. Cuban enterprises no longer needed to ship their most skilled mechanics to repair tanks in the Ogaden; they could work on Cuba's own aging stock of machines.

Cuban leaders did not choose to concentrate on the boring tasks of peace at home; they had no other option. But an unexpected benefit of the collapse of Cuban foreign policy as it had been traditionally designed and executed was that the entire top echelon of the party and the government acquired the time to focus on the nation's own problems. Whether their attention will lead in fact to improved social, economic, and political performance remains to be seen. In the past, political involvement in the management of the economy was often very counterproductive; Cuba's economic performance in the early 1990s was terrible. Moreover, the international setbacks may have shaken the self-confidence of some Cuban leaders. Nonetheless, in terms of their can-do self-image, their freedom to work to "save the homeland, save the revolution, and save socialism" must be seen as an unexpected asset even though its economic results in the early 1990s were the worst since 1959.

The Resurrection of Civil Society

By the mid and late 1980s, Cuban citizens became less willing to comply with regime policies and more likely to voice their disagreement with such policies by word or behavior. Because of the noted weakening of intermediary institutions between state and society, the capacity of the regime to respond effectively to this growing discontent was limited.

In April 1986, President Fidel Castro announced a policy of "rectification" addressed to what he considered capitalist distortions in Cuba's economy. He sharply criticized the use of material incentives to motivate people to work. "Vile money," as he told the Ministry of the Interior in June 1986, was undermining the construction of socialism in Cuba. Socialism could not be built with the means of capitalism (*Granma: Resumen Semanal*, June 15, 1986, 3). Though Castro emphasized that certain material incentives would continue to be used, he sought to move more toward nonmaterial incentives and toward collective rather than individual incentives.

Cuban workers demonstrated their disapproval of these policies in the only way in which they were capable: they worked less. According to one of Cuba's top academic economists, José Luis Rodríguez, the country's labor productivity fell 1.5 percent in 1986, 1.1 percent in 1987, and 1.7 percent in 1988. Rodríguez believes that Cuba's labor productivity had been growing in prior years; he also believes that global social product (GSP) grew, on an annual basis, by 3.5 percent from 1975 to 1980 and by 7.2 percent from 1981 to 1985. Though in my judgment these GSP growth estimates are too high, they show that Rodríguez has not been a habitual naysayer about Cuba's economic performance; his GSP estimates for the 1975–85 period are worth citing to bolster the credibility of his finding that Cuba's GSP, on an annual basis, fell 0.6 percent from 1985 to 1988 (Rodríguez 1990, 35). In my view, GSP may well have dropped even more in the late 1980s, but in any case there should be no doubt that rectification was associated with economic decline and lower labor productivity that began even before the serious negative impacts on Cuba's economy from the collapse of communist regimes, which came to be felt mainly in 1989 and thereafter. Cuban economist Julio Carranza has estimated that Cuba's GSP fell 3.6 percent in 1990, 24 percent in 1991, and about 15 percent in 1992 (Carranza 1992, 142).

Cuba's peasants have been among the regime's main supporters over time. In the late 1970s, the government decided to promote the cooperativization of the remaining private sector in agriculture. The notion was to move away from individual landholdings toward cooperative though still private farm ownership and production. This shift was viewed as more consistent with the construction of socialism.

At first, Cuban peasants trusted the leadership and responded enthusiastically. The number of peasants in cooperatives, for example, grew from 29,535 in 1980 to 82,611 in 1983. As it became clear that the cooperatives were not solving the problems of the peasantry and that they were far too bureaucratized, however, membership in them began to drop. By 1989 there were 63,838 cooperative members—a drop of nearly 23 percent. In the strategic sugar sector, where government control was strongest, the decline in cooperative membership was more modest—just below 15 percent from 1983 to 1989. But where the government's controls were weaker and thus peasants could more readily act on their preferences, defections from cooperatives were higher. From 1983 to 1989, nearly 35 percent of the members of tobacco cooperatives and more than 36 percent of the members of coffee cooperatives abandoned the cooperatives.[4] This drop in cooperative membership occurred well in advance of the severe negative external economic conditions from which Cuba felt the shock in 1989 and thereafter. The problems of Cuba's political regime were, above all, of its own making.

Some of the regime's strengths and weaknesses were expressed in public opinion surveys conducted in Cuba. In spring 1990, Cuba's leading national news magazine, *Bohemia*, conducted a nationwide public opinion poll (n = 957). Asked about Cuba's municipal government, more than 40 percent of respondents failed to express trust in the delegate elected from their district; more than 48 percent expressed doubts about the delegate's authority to resolve problems for the district; nearly 60 percent believed that improvements needed to be made in Cuba's local government structures and procedures; and nearly 40 percent failed to say that they felt they participated in governing the country (*Bohemia* 1990, 4–9).

These findings suggest serious weaknesses in Cuba's local government, the only level of government in which any direct elections have been held regularly since the mid-1970s. It is likely that the actual percentage of critical views was higher than reported (an undetermined number of respondents may have been afraid to express their true views), but it is striking that the reported percentage of criticism was as high as it was.

The counterpart of the observation that even the regime's most participatory institutions were in trouble is that so many people felt free enough to criticize their government. They did not believe that a totalitarian monster lurked over them. The regime had carefully maintained enough political freedom to permit such criticism. At the same time, the very expression of substantial criticism seemed to signal weak social support for the regime's institutions. The two realities are somewhat contradictory.

In 1989, Cuban scholars carried out a study of the local elections in Santa Cruz del Norte, a municipality in Havana province (Dilla Alfonso et al., 1992). They interviewed nearly 200 voters on the reasons they voted for candidates. Fewer than 10 percent indicated that membership in the Communist Party or the Communist Youth Union was a factor they would take into consideration in determining whether or not to vote for a candidate. The main reasons for voter support of particular candidates seemed to be related not to political affiliation but to personal qualities: whether or not the candidate was a good neighbor, a good worker, a good parent, or sensitive to the feelings of others. These results suggest that the prestige of the party as an institution was quite low at the local level; it was unable to elicit positive support. This finding is consistent with the earlier information on the erosion of the regime's bases of support, but this is the only published survey that bears directly on the party.

On the other hand, it is pertinent once again to note that people felt free enough to give these responses. Moreover, 90 percent of the local candidates elected in the Santa Cruz del Norte districts surveyed were members of the Communist Party or the Communist Youth

Union. Unlike the Communist parties in Eastern Europe and the Soviet Union, Cuba's party had not yet lost those members who were highly regarded by their fellow citizens and neighbors. Ordinary Cubans voted for these people not because of their party affiliation but for other reasons. This underlines the party's weakness as well as its strength in the society. The party as an institution garnered little support, but its members were highly respected. The regime will not fall until and unless those citizens who are highly regarded by others and who have leadership qualities choose to break with the party.

In spring 1990, Cuba's party sponsored a nationwide survey (n = 600) at a time when the negative economic effects from the collapse of European communism were being felt in Cuba (Machado 1990, 2–12). The poll's credibility is high. Only 20 percent of respondents said that the food supply was good, and only 10 percent said that the quality of transportation was good. Respondents were subtle: while 65 percent said that opportunities to play sports were good, only 33 percent said that other opportunities for recreation were good.

Having thus elicited criticism on certain matters, the poll was believable when it reported that 77 percent of respondents thought that health services were good and 83 percent believed in the efficacy of the country's schooling. Despite negative indications—the Cuban public no longer responded as in the past to government moral exhortations to work; Cuban peasants fled from cooperative membership at a much faster rate than they joined; the Communist Party and the Communist Youth Union as institutions lacked the appeal to elicit voter support at the local level; local government institutions were seen as in need of significant change; and the public had serious complaints about certain goods and services—continued and sustained effective performance in health and education still drew support for the political regime.

This last poll raises another issue. Asked whether U.S. military aggression against Cuba was possible, 58 percent of respondents said no. The government's wish to wrap itself with the Cuban flag, asking for support because the homeland might be in danger from U.S. military attack, was no longer credible, even when the public was asked in a Communist Party–sponsored poll.

Public Debate

Consistent with the greater willingness of ordinary Cubans to express views at odds with those of the regime or to engage in behavior that undermined regime policies with regard to productivity or cooperative membership, in the early 1990s there was also growing evidence of significant public debate. I base the comments reported in the following paragraphs on my observations and discussions mainly during a trip to Cuba in September 1991. The occasion was a seminar held just outside Havana under the sponsorship of the United States-based Institute of Cuban Studies and the University of Havana's Center for the Study of Political Alternatives. (I gathered additional information during my trips to Cuba in May 1991, January 1992, and July 1992.) I quote the following from my field notes written at the time of the seminar:

> She stood up to disagree with what the panelist had just stated, she said courteously and in a tremulous but firm voice. There followed a debate between the editor of Cuba's second most important national newspaper, *Juventud Rebelde,* and a leading Cuban television anchorwoman concerning the strengths and weaknesses of Cuba's mass media. In an equally critical though also courteous tone, one of the leading columnists for the newspaper took on her editor over various matters. In most countries, this might have been interesting but not newsworthy. In seven prior trips to Cuba since 1979, I had never witnessed such a substantive debate among Cubans in the presence of foreigners. Gone were the excuses, the apologies, the hiding of problems.

Cuba had begun to change, and the change included a modest political opening provided there was no direct challenge to the regime's legitimacy or continuity. The range of Cuba's public debate remained narrow and tentative; its tone was cautious; and the speed of political change remained measured—especially because many in Cuba's national leadership had learned sobering lessons from Eastern Europe and the Soviet Union about the perils of political reform for communist rulers: for example, they should not reform themselves out of jobs they like.

During the course of my visit to Cuba for the September 1991 seminar, the following topics arose in private and public conversations with Cubans, all of whom had an official role—that is, they were members of the party, government institutions, research think tanks, universities, mass media institutions. This list reflects proposals that, my interlocutors said, had been debated in one way or another at meetings called in the months preceding the October 1991 Fourth Party Congress to discuss recommendations for the congress. They had participated in these meetings; they said that these proposals had received varying degrees of support but that in every case the support was very substantial.

1. Cuba's Communist Party should abolish the atheism clause in the party statutes and officially launch a process of changes to eliminate religious discrimination from the legal code.

2. The party should abandon its past habits of direct administration and limit itself to generally overseeing the actions of the government.

3. The party should drop its self-conception as a "vanguard party" and a "proletarian party" to seek to become a mass party to which all who identify with "the Cuban nation" can belong to "defend sovereignty" regardless of their social class and religious beliefs.

4. The party congress should ratify the policy that welcomed direct foreign investment in various sectors of Cuba's economy (not just in tourism, to which foreign investment had so far been dedicated for the most part), and it should ease the terms that allowed such investors to operate in Cuba.

5. The party congress should rule to permit the free contracting of services to allow individuals who need a plumber to hire one without having to wait for months for the state's plumbing agency to send one.

6. The party congress should rule to permit agricultural cooperatives to sell their products in free markets at prices governed by supply and demand and in locales subject only to sanitary regulations, and to earn profits subject to nonconfiscatory rates of taxation.[5]

7. The party should recommend the amendment of the Constitution and the electoral law to permit and require the direct election of delegates to provincial assemblies and deputies to the National Assembly, with the additional requirement that there be two candidates per post.

8. Candidates for public office should have the right to express their policy preferences prior to the election but not to campaign beyond such expression and the right to write their own campaign materials (campaigning had been prohibited; the Communist Party wrote up all biographies of candidates, even those of whom it disapproved).

9. The party should allow the expression of opposition views over radio, television, or in print, in its own media (even if it were to continue to ban the legal formation of opposition parties); the press should publish critical letters to the editor as had been done briefly in the 1970s.

No one who believes in democracy could be satisfied even if the

Fourth Congress had made all of these changes. Indeed, the list indicates the very narrowness of Cuba's lawful debate over reform. Cuba's human rights and other opposition activists had called for more far-reaching reforms. And yet the utility of the list is to highlight the changes that were being proposed by cadres within the regime itself. It could be considered a statement of softliner views within the regime. Moreover, most of these proposals would have been unthinkable in Cuba only a few years earlier. The fact that they were openly discussed and supported was a measure of modest but real political change.

The Fourth Party Congress adopted proposals 1, 2, 4, 5, and 7. It moved somewhat in the direction of proposal 3. In part because of Fidel Castro's adamant opposition, it made no change on proposal 6. No action was taken with regard to proposals 8 and 9, but neither was any action taken to make their adoption less possible in the future than it had been in the past.

The Fourth Party Congress, in short, was not responsive to the wishes of those who wanted to liberalize and democratize Cuba substantially, but it was responsive to some of the wishes of its core constituency, the middle-level cadres who staffed the regime and on whose personal prestige, the polls showed, the allegiance of ordinary citizens rested.

The Headaches of the Market

The resurrection of Cuba's society was also in evidence in those areas of economic activity that had been most affected by the Cuban government's new openness to private foreign investment and to market mechanisms.

In May 1990, President Fidel Castro inaugurated two new hotels at Varadero Beach: "the first time during the Revolution that we have opened a project with . . . foreign capitalists. It's quite an experience" (*Granma Weekly Review* 1990, 2). That was the inauguration of Cuba's cautious transition to engagement not just with increased international tourism but also, and more important, with private foreign investment in various sectors of the economy (though at first focused mainly on tourism).

Although the Cuban government had high hopes that these new investments would help to rescue Cuba's economy from its near free fall of the early 1990s, some social and political problems associated with such new ventures had already arisen even as they were getting under way. The government sought to bottle up tourists in enclaves, but enterprising Cubans broke through the barriers. In May 1992, the

Sixth Congress of the Communist Youth Union chastised many of Cuba's youth for "inappropriate behavior" toward foreign tourists, ranging from illegal foreign exchange transactions and other participation in "black markets" to prostitution. More worrisome was that some Communist Party and Communist Youth members engaged in such behavior. Also troubling to the regime's leaders was the public unhappiness with arrangements that discriminated against Cubans within the tourist sector: some facilities and services were not available to Cubans unless they were invited by a foreigner (*Juventud Rebelde* 1992, 5).

Even more difficult to manage politically was the fact that some activities necessary for the promotion of tourism are sharply at odds with the social norms that the regime had sought to promote in the past. For example, in early 1991 the government permitted *Playboy*'s staff to enter Cuba, and a government agency procured Cuban women to pose topless (Cohen 1991, 69–74, 157–58).

The cultural components of the tourist industry, in short, would make it more difficult for the regime to manage its political difficulties. The greater the tourist sector's economic success, the greater these social and political problems were likely to become. More young Cubans would be likely to engage in inappropriate behavior; more government and party officials might be tempted. It would be more difficult to contain unhappiness over discriminatory exclusion from tourist facilities. And it would be more likely that some Cuban government agencies would engage in behavior far at variance with norms the regime had believed important.

More speculative, but no less possible, were the prospects of autonomous labor behavior in the labor markets that would serve foreign firms operating in Cuba. In search of foreign investment, Cuba advertised its labor discipline, but there is a question as to whether that discipline would remain unimpaired as foreign firms became more significant.

Cuba's market-based strategies, limited though they still were, had begun to weaken the moral fabric of the kind of socialism the country's leaders had sought to build. Only time will tell whether the cultural consequences of the spread of market forces will seriously weaken the regime.

Increased Repression

The Cuban government had, of course, observed some of the trends discussed above, and it sought to draw a sharp distinction between criticism that was permissible within the regime and behavior that would remain politically impermissible. This repressive strategy was designed to set clear and narrower boundaries for the lawful public debate and also to contain what the regime viewed as the negative consequences of the needed market opening. Above all, it was intended to prevent the spread to Cuba of international trends toward political opening.

Beginning especially in fall 1991, the Cuban government pursued a vigorous repressive campaign against the small human rights and opposition groups that had operated in the penumbra of legality. Several important leaders of the largest coalition of opposition forces, the Cuban Democratic Convergence, were arrested. In late 1991, the government arrested María Elena Cruz, a poet who had years earlier won the national poetry prize awarded by the official National Union of Artists and Writers. In early 1992, Sebastián Arcos was jailed, and his brother Gustavo Arcos was arrested. In late 1992, Elizardo Sánchez was also arrested briefly. These opposition political leaders spanned the democratic political spectrum from center-right to democratic socialism. Their arrests, and countless others, helped to cripple opposition politics and served as added warnings to regime opponents.

Prior to their arrests, these leaders and many others had been subjected to physical assault by regime-sponsored though formally unofficial "rapid response brigades," which were allegedly the spontaneous grassroots organizations that had emerged to enforce political loyalty at the local level by personal force. The brigades made their appearance in mid-1991 and would come to be used repeatedly to intimidate opponents. This innovation was a marked departure from regime practices in the 1970s and 1980s, going back to the earliest days of revolutionary rule.

Government authorities also voiced public warnings, most notably at the December 1991 meeting of Cuba's National Assembly. These warnings followed Cruz's arrest and set the stage for other arrests. The possibility of opposing the regime narrowed greatly in 1992, and forms of criticism that came from people on the periphery of the regime became officially suspect—even the Roman Catholic bishops were put on notice that their sermons were overstepping the line of lawful public discourse (*Granma* 1992, 3–5).

Conclusion

If Cuban leaders continue to maintain their control by means of offering modest political openings, delivering health and education services, building a bridge across the generations to attract younger Cubans, and relying on Fidel Castro's personal appeal, they may defer a more substantial regime transition for an indefinite time despite the country's economic hardships. Cuba was the only country in Europe or the Americas where a communist regime survived years past the fall of communism in eastern Europe and the dissolution of the Soviet Union. Cuba's top civilian leaders did not fear a military coup, nor did they believe that economic hardship alone would bring the regime down.

On the other hand, for various reasons, the regime had lost popular support. Its own institutions were weaker. The performance of provincial party secretaries has been poor. The mass organizations and the party itself no longer connected state and society effectively enough. The frequency of opposition protest rose, as did repression. The political oligarchs who had stabilized Cuban politics and made the regime's organizations more capable in the 1970s and early 1980s were removed from office. The newly important leaders just below the Castro brothers were consolidating their power but did not yet have autonomous enough positions and strategies. The economic hardship was wide, severe, and deepening. Communism in Europe had collapsed. Cuban communists knew that the march of history was no longer on their side; their task was to survive politically against all odds.

Notes

1. This section is based on my biographical files.
2. For the Cuban government's account, *Case 1/1989: End of the Cuban Connection* (1989); for an account supplemented by fine journalistic work, Oppenheimer (1992), pp. 15–129.
3. A few hundred Cubans posted in various countries asked for and received political asylum and did not return home. Most Cubans did return, however.
4. Computed from Comité Estatal de Estadísticas (1989), p. 184.
5. No doubt there must also have been considerable support for allowing individual peasants to sell their products once again in lawful free markets. Because the persons with whom I was speaking were typically party cadres who knew of Fidel Castro's strong opposition to allowing individual peasants to participate in free markets, they emphasized a proposed policy alternative focused on the market rights of agricultural cooperatives, not on those of individual peasants.

References

Bohemia. 1990. July 6, 4–9.
Carranza, Julio. 1992. "Cuba: los retos de la economía." *Cuadernos de Nuestra América* 9, no. 19 (July-December).
Case 1/1989: End of the Cuban Connection. 1989. Havana: José Martí Publishing House.
Cohen, Jeff. 1991. "Cuba Libre." *Playboy* (March): 69–74, 157–58.
Comité Estatal de Estadísticas. 1989. *Anuario estadístico de Cuba, 1989.* Havana.
Dilla Alfonso, Haroldo, Gerardo González, and Ana T. Vicentelli. 1992. "Cuba's Local Governments: An Experience Beyond the Paradigms." *Cuban Studies* 22.
Granma. 1992. January 1.
Granma: Resumen Semanal. 1986. June 15.
Granma Weekly Review. 1990. May 27.
Juventud Rebelde. 1992. March 22.
Machado, Darío L. 1990. "¿Cuál es nuestro clima socio-político?" *El Militante comunista* 9 (September): 2–12.
Oppenheimer, Andrés. 1992. *Castro's Final Hour.* New York: Simon and Schuster.
Rodríguez, José Luis. 1990. "La economía cubana en 1986–1989." *Economía y desarrollo* 20, no. 116 (May-June).

TWO

The Party, the Fourth Congress, and the Process of Counterreform
JUAN M. DEL AGUILA

Before communism collapsed in the former Soviet Union and Eastern Europe, ruling communist parties held congresses at some five-year intervals to evaluate what had taken place in all areas of the state, the party, and society. In principle, congresses mapped out broad economic and social programs conceived by ruling communist parties and set general goals for the society. Usually, ruling parties reaffirmed their ideological commitment to Marxism-Leninism and restated their belief in democratic centralism as the fundamental norm guiding internal party decisions. Parties renewed bonds of solidarity and friendship with each other and often called on revolutionary and liberation movements in the developing world to struggle against Western imperialism. Capitalism and imperialism were routinely denounced at the same time that the Soviet Union was praised as the motherland of all communists. Soviet society was usually cited as one in which advanced socialism was being reached, but other "socialist experiments" were given recognition as well.

Generally speaking, congresses of the Cuban Communist Party (Partido Comunista de Cuba, PCC) held in 1975, 1980, and 1986 followed the pattern established by ruling communist parties elsewhere. At the time, the PCC was part of the worldwide communist movement and did in fact hold something of a privileged position as a ruling party in a developing country. It had extensive political ties with other "fraternal parties," so PCC congresses always featured prominent communists from throughout the world. Finally, as a party born from the Cuban Revolution, the PCC claimed a type of authenticity that eluded some of its more "sovietized" counterparts. For instance, PCC leaders often asserted that Cuban communism embodied indigenous cultural and historical traditions and was shaped more by *fidelismo* and nationalism than by association with Soviet-style communism (Rabkin 1991, chapter 3).

On the other hand, by the time of the 1991 PCC Congress, the Soviet Union was rapidly disintegrating (it would be dissolved as a nation in December 1991); ruling communist parties in Eastern Europe had been thrown out of power either by popular, democratic revolutions or through armed conflict; "liberation" movements were being defeated throughout the Third World; the idea of a communist vanguard spearheading a successful struggle against capitalism had vanished; and Lenin's teachings on revolution were obsolete. As summarized by Brzezinski (1989, 1), "the progressive decay and the deepening agony" of the communist system and its dogma made it "irrelevant to the human condition," thus ending its dominion.

As a result, the PCC had lost most of its international support and could no longer credibly claim to be an instrument of world revolution, much less a party with a promising view of the future. Indeed, the party recognized "the political disaster of communism's collapse," seeing it as "the most severe setback for communists, revolutionaries, and all the people of the earth in this century."[1] Oft-stated predictions regarding the inevitable doom of Western capitalism or the certain victory of progressive forces over those of imperialism and reaction were no longer on the horizon, so the shopworn dialectics articulated by past PCC congresses were now irrelevant as well.

On the domestic front, the PCC ruled over an economy facing irreversible difficulties and a society slipping further and further away from any possibility of economic prosperity. Politically, the regime and the party were severely shaken by the Ochoa/La Guardia scandals of 1989 and the subsequent purges of high Ministry of Interior officials—including minister and division general José Abrantes, sentenced to twenty years for negligence of duty—in some units of the armed forces (Fuerzas Armadas Revolucionarias, FAR) and among key elements of the intelligence services.[2]

General Ochoa, Colonel La Guardia, and their top aides were charged with corruption and involvement in drug trafficking and were subsequently convicted and summarily executed. Much evidence suggests that the top political leaders were generally aware of their underlings' activities, but the government's role was never discussed either in the media or during the trial itself. Subsequently, a *Granma* editorial ("Saquemos las lecciones" 1989) denounced "the repugnant and dangerous corruption and decay in the leadership of the Ministry of the Interior," because it "inflicts greater damage than that from any counterrevolutionary." Given the close relationship between organs of state and the party itself, it could not escape from its responsibilities as the guardian of revolutionary morality.

There is reason to believe that in the subsequent management of these scandals, the process of counterreform dating from the strategic counteroffensive of 1986 (the rectification process) was widened and took on a more distinct political character. In other words, technocrats and corrupt administrators would no longer be the principal targets; rather, party cadres and officials who either openly or privately expressed sympathies with the reforms sweeping the communist world would be affected. In addition, the process included explicit criticisms of the party's work, particularly of its failure to monitor what was happening in the Ministry of the Interior and other state agencies, and probably in the armed forces as well. As has been the case with other shake-ups, the means of "cleansing" party organs involved removing officials, some consolidation of functions to streamline its work and make it more responsive to the objectives of its top leaders, and a massive bureaucratic downsizing.

Further, overhauling internal party work and removing substantial numbers of cadres from its departments and top organs, discussed later, strongly suggested that the rectification process was not going well. The process of counterreform builds on the dissatisfaction with rectification and is as well the means through which the leadership reimposed discipline and orthodoxy in the party. The difference between the counterreform process and rectification is more than a semantic one, because counterreform aims most directly at the party apparatus, while rectification seeks to reinvigorate an exhausted polity and society. In sum, counterreform is a tactical process with a strategic aim; rectification is an effort at systemic renewal through exhortation and moralism.

A second but never stated goal of the leadership was to remove potential reformers from the party, reaching all the way up to the Central Committee itself. The scandals created a climate in which the leadership could use corruption rather than politics as the rationale for purges and reshuffles, because to admit that political disagreements were the real reason for the shake-ups would have indicated that the party was increasingly divided against itself.

Consequently, the argument here is not that everyone removed from either the ranks or the higher party organs was in fact a reformer. Rather, the contention is that the leadership preempted the consolidation of an antiregime faction through a massive bureaucratic restructuring and substantial changes in the composition of top party organs. From this perspective, the process of counterreform is defensive insofar as it circles the wagons around the top, but is also aggressive in its effort to root out contrarians.

Improving party discipline and urging party members to take their responsibilities seriously were part of the rectification process itself, and the "proper conduct of communists" was also prominently discussed during the Third Party Congress in 1986. The reversal of "negative tendencies" that had been expected following that congress was not evident, and the situation was compounded by the party's inept performance before, during, and following the scandals of 1989. In that context, it appears that the top leadership had lost some confidence in the party's ability to revitalize and remoralize a crisis-ridden polity, and thus it decided to deepen the shake-up and justify it as continuing rectification ("Continúa la purga" 1989; "Drug Scandal" 1989; "Purga cubana" 1989).

The party itself was caught up in instances of corruption and negligence. Not only were many of those involved in the scandals party members, but the party had failed to monitor the situation and keep the political leadership informed. It had not fulfilled its mission of being ever vigilant and had failed to detect precisely the kind of misconduct and dereliction of duty that it was charged with monitoring. In effect, instances of individual corruption had clear institutional overtones, and the political leaders feared that the party could be completely discredited if the damage were not contained, the guilty not punished, and the party's overall performance not reevaluated in stricter terms.

Leaders recognized, for instance, that the scandals "involve in one way or another all of the institutions of the Revolution," including the party itself. Second, the party was admonished for not knowing what was going on within the Ministry of the Interior "because the bitter truth is that it acted generally outside of the party's control" ("Saquemos las lecciones" 1989). Activities that should have been detected were overlooked, in some cases because of "tolerance, chumminess (*amiguismo*) and complicity." Practices that constituted the essence of "negative tendencies" were common in the party's relationship with state agencies and were patently harmful to the larger aims of rectification.

Such practices extended to the provinces, where "deficiencies were found in the party's leadership" and in its evaluation "of any organism and its vigilance of any phenomenon that has political connotations." And so "a serious reflection leads to the idea that perfecting society means perfecting the party, and that it is not a subject but also an object of rectification." The inescapable contradiction was that the rectifier needed to be rectified, because the party had forgotten that its role "in direction, orientation, and control does not permit fissures and must establish norms that govern the conduct of leaders and cadres" ("Saquemos las lecciones" 1989).

The need to correct errors and negative tendencies in the party indicated that the gap between the rhetoric of exemplary conduct and the facts of privilege and bureaucratic corruption was growing. Old practices—such as negligence, complacency, and trafficking in personal privileges—were reappearing in spades, and party discipline itself was questionable. In addition, resolutions passed at the Third Congress to the effect that the party must set an example for society and that its members would be incorruptible were being violated in letter and spirit, so that the party's authority suffered. In short, there were enough signs of internal decay, corruption, and organizational weakness for the leadership to act upon and do so in a manner that would restore discipline and efficiency as well as impose political orthodoxy.

In summary, in the wake of the scandals, and increasingly aware of reformist currents that may have been gaining influence in the party, its leaders decided to launch a counterreform process aimed at streamlining it and bringing it under closer management by the top. In doing so, rooting out known and potential *perestroikos* in the ranks became a major goal, particularly individuals who were dissatisfied with the growing orthodoxy and rigidity, or perhaps with the top leadership itself. In the management of intraparty affairs, politics and performance often overlap, so personnel changes in particular could be due to either factor. Paradoxically, the scandals served as the catalyst for this counterreformation, because in all likelihood the process of internal party decay would not have been detected were it not for the far-reaching investigations ordered up and down the line in 1989 and 1990.

The Means and Goals of Counterreform

A crucial phase in the process unfolded in early 1990; the reason given was that the system of one-party rule would remain intact but that some administrative and political reforms would be enacted during a period of severe economic difficulties and political uncertainty. Shifts in personnel would come, but the single-party model would remain. Following an extraordinary plenum, the PCC Central Committee made it clear that as "part of the deepening rectification process," the party would review its policy on cadres "not by making changes to suit public opinion" but in order to "affirm methods and conceptions that permit the permanent perfecting of society, a process that would have the party at the center" ("Pleno extraordinario" 1990). Perfecting the party, of course, meant getting rid of "contaminated" members, potential dissidents, and lazy *apparatchicki*.

In addition, the plenum made it plain that the process was aimed at "perfecting the single Leninist party, based on the norms of democratic centralism," because "concepts regarding the content, methods and structure of party organs were analyzed, so that they may be prepared to give a more efficient response to its two great missions: strengthening the economy and solving social problems; and directing political and ideological work with the kind of effort that it requires" ("Pleno extraordinario" 1990).

Once the leadership framed the need for renewal in the party—which I contend deepens the process of counterreform—and restated the commitment to a single party, the *llamamiento* (calling) to the Fourth Party Congress became essentially a means of legitimating the changes. For instance, the llamamiento contended that "our single party, *martiano* and Marxist-Leninist, assumes great responsibilities before the society" and that party members must strive "to separate ourselves definitively from formalisms, liturgies and other manifestations that undermine political and ideological work." Three themes that would reappear at the Congress were articulated in the llamamiento as well: the rejection of multiparty, "bourgeois" democracy; the insistence that socialism would be preserved at all costs; and the notion that

Cuba has "special historical responsibilities" with the oppressed and progressive peoples of the Third World ("Llamamiento del Partido" 1990).

In addition, the counterreforms sought to perfect the notion of democratic centralism, make intraparty affairs more "democratic," and refuel the process of ideological invigoration. Presumably, the party was "mature" and had learned from the mistakes of others. The climate was deemed favorable for internal debate and creative thinking, but no dramatic changes along the lines of "Cuban-style perestroika" were contemplated. The party pledged to "go to the roots and remain vigilant against opportunism and demagoguery, in order to eliminate symptoms of immobilism or paralysis that may appear in our revolutionary institutions." In short, the llamamiento was a call for resistance and greater unity, but it was also part of the process through which the party would reassert its primacy and cast out any and all internal demons. Democratic centralism, after all, means that what the top decides is accepted by the rank and file.

Subsequently, the party restated the need for a broad debate, yet at the same time one in which clear limits would be set on what would and would not be tolerated. In other words, the process through which the masses would be consulted would be neither democratic nor open-ended, because fundamental issues were off-limits and would simply not be subject to discussion. For instance, in July 1990, the party felt "an unprecedented ideological and psychological turmoil (*asedio*)" spurred by the very consultations it had encouraged. Fearing that the process would get out of control, it categorically announced that socialism itself as a historical determination of the Cuban people, or the idea of a single party, martiano and Marxist-Leninist, would not be "subject to questioning" ("Partido Comunista" 1990). It rejected the argument that socialist renovation would invariably mean multiparty democracy on the grounds that such was little more than reactionary dogma.

Simply put, the masses could expect changes, but no fundamental economic or political reforms. Capitalism would not return, and neither would there be any encouragement for liberal notions of opposition, much less the actual sanctioning of more political parties. What had happened in other socialist countries only served as an object lesson for Cuba on *what not to do* if basic structures were to be preserved. At almost any cost, the prospect of unbridled criticism of the system, the party, and the "historic generation" (the generation that played key roles in the early years of the Revolution) needed to be contained, because to allow it would be suicidal.

The llamamiento explicitly delegitimated raising issues that the leadership and party had not sanctioned and thus focused debate not on systemic matters but on largely inconsequential ones. Rather than an authentic consultation, it was a narrowly conceived set of instructions to be followed after they were articulated by official spokesmen. If some expected a dramatic opening, they were sorely disappointed. Others, committed to the status quo despite the consequences, were probably vindicated. Once the rigid boundaries were set, the congress would take up only secondary matters. As earlier congresses had done, it could thus preserve the unity and harmony of the whole and ratify what the political leadership demanded.

The Fourth Congress was initially scheduled for February 1991 but was postponed until October 1991. The explanation was that the regime was in no hurry and that what was important were the discussions in advance of the congress, not the specific date of its celebration. In all probability, the postponement was caused by unresolved internal debates regarding what subjects would come out at the congress, or it indicated that the leadership and the organizers were not entirely in tune.

The Organizing Commission was established in May 1990, and its seventy-two members were selected by the party's Political Bureau, controlled by the Castro brothers. All members and alternates of the Political Bureau joined the commission, as did fourteen members of the Central Committee and some thirty other individuals from several organizations. It is thus clear that the top political leadership was in charge of the Congress preparations from the start and in all probability approved its selections. One way to control the agenda and set the terms of the debate is to decide who will participate in its discussion, so it is most unlikely that either contrarians or outspoken advocates of fundamental economic and political reforms were asked to serve on the commission.

Three subcommissions were established and ordered to study many of the issues to be debated at the congress. Raúl Castro presided over the one charged with perfecting the structure, content, methods, and operational style of the party; Juan Escalona headed the group that would analyze People's Power; and José Machado's subcommission would study the Communist Youth Union and the mass organizations.

In effect, the party, the electoral system at the local level, and the political base were to be analyzed prior to the congress itself.

More important than the creation of these commissions were the measures taken in October 1990 that pared down the party's bureaucracy and led to a significant restructuring of the Central Committee's work. The political leadership decided to implement these changes before the congress on the grounds that "consensus had been reached," the measures "had been sufficiently studied," and there was no time to waste. Aimed at the party itself, the changes looked to correct *frentismo*, *homologuismo*, and other deficiencies ("Aprobado grupo" 1990). Frentismo means the practice among some sectors of the party of simulating work rather than carrying out assigned tasks; homologuismo, in contrast, refers to waste and the duplication of effort that occur when party units do the same thing. Both practices weaken the party's organizational capabilities and often lead to internal conflicts of interest among departments and sectors.

In addition, the party was instructed to pay more attention to its traditional role of orientation and control and to reduce its intervention in state affairs. The fundamental idea would be "that the party from now on exercise its role of orientation and control in a broader and multilateral sense, adjusting its organization in a flexible manner to the characteristics of the territory in which it acts, and to the concrete priorities of its work, rather than to the nominal attention given to organisms, institutions, branches or sectors in which the state is structured" ("Aprobado grupo" 1990).

It appears that the party's presence would be less intrusive relative to the functions of state entities, suggesting that overlap and duplication of effort between party and state had gotten out of control. This is often given as a reason that communist systems are inherently inefficient and is a source of bureaucratic intrigue and political tension. The party would concentrate on political, ideological work and deemphasize its governing role. Practically speaking, it meant a considerable reduction in the number of party functionaries at various levels: the size of provincial committees was reduced by 50 percent, and the party itself was ordered "not to use one more cadre than is strictly necessary at every level" ("Aprobado grupo" 1990). The position of second secretary was abolished at the municipal and provincial level, facilitating greater control by the first secretaries at these levels and of first secretaries by the higher-ups.

The Central Committee's bureaucracy was also substantially reorganized. Its nineteen departments were consolidated into nine, and its Military Department replaced with a Military Commission supervised directly by the Political Bureau. All told, so many functionaries were either reassigned or temporarily laid off that the committee lost 50 percent of its work force. The abolition of the Military Department, then headed by Brigadier General Sergio Pérez Lezcano, may have been inevitable in the larger bureaucratic consolidation. On the other hand, it suggested continuing dissatisfaction with the top leadership of the armed forces, no doubt because of the Ochoa scandal. General Pérez Lezcano had been appointed only a few months earlier and was not a member of the top military hierarchy.

The party's secretariat was also restructured, and its functions were consolidated. Where there had been seven, only five secretaries remained, including the Castro brothers. José R. Machado took control of the Department of Organization and the newly created Department on Cadre Policy, in addition to several departments involved in industry and consumption. Julián Rizo would supervise departments dealing with construction, transportation, communications, and foodstuffs. Quite significant was Carlos Aldana's appointment to head the Ideological Department as well as those dealing with education, science and sports, and international relations. Subsequently, Aldana would play a leading role in preparing the congress and would remain a visible participant in internal party and domestic policy debates. At the time, he was neither a full member nor an alternate member of the Political Bureau, to which he was elected following the Fourth Party Congress.

As a result of this consolidation, Jorge Risquet, prominent and influential as a top party leader and policy maker for many years, lost his position, as did Brigadier General Sixto Pérez Lezcano. Risquet's complete fall from grace came during the subsequent congress, when he was dropped from the Political Bureau. Some speculate that he and Aldana were bitter rivals and that once President Castro opted for Aldana as the new wunderkind, Risquet was out. But it could also be due to Risquet's alleged chronic drinking problem or to his age (sixty-four). General Pérez Lezcano was also dropped from the Central Committee during the Fourth Congress.

Finally, measures such as eliminating all alternate members and seeking ways to bring about greater flexibility and efficiency in the party were taken. In particular, stricter criteria in the selection of leaders were introduced, and the quality of leaders' work came under greater scrutiny. In fact, this strengthened the filtering process through which leaders are selected, making it easier to detect and weed out genuine reformers.

Wherever possible, party members and leaders would be assigned concrete responsibilities so that their performance could be better judged and avoidance of responsibilities reduced. All in all, these changes would be studied at the congress, with a view toward "deepening the ideas that inspire the perfecting of the political and revolutionary vanguard of our society." In sum, changes in the criteria facilitated rooting out reformers or contrarians and made it much more difficult for such individuals to enter the party. At the same time, because Machado was placed in charge of both the commission and the department supervising the mass organizations, cadres would have to pass the litmus test of political orthodoxy. Since Machado is neither sympathetic to reform nor likely to allow contrarians into the party, his role is clearly designed to minimize the rise of a disastrous intraparty opposition movement. It may not be a foolproof way of reimposing party unity, but it does partly explain why leaders were so concerned.

The ideological tone for the congress was shaped by speeches and "orientations" from top leaders. For instance, President Castro left no doubt regarding what path Cuba should take, asserting that "no one should have any illusions regarding concessions from Cuban socialism, or that the Cuban Revolution will make concessions, because we will have a party, a single party, that corresponds with the long revolutionary phase! A single party, like the one founded by José Martí to carry on the War of Independence! And there will not be a market economy, by whatever name; it has nothing to do with socialism. Our economy will be programmed and planned" (Castro 1991). Subsequently, Vice-President Carlos Rafael Rodríguez weighed in with a rejection of multiple parties on the grounds that "as long as opposition parties created in the United States are instruments of U.S. policy, all notions of multiple parties are little more than weapons against our country, where we have the kind of democracy that Abraham Lincoln defined at Gettysburg: a government of the people, by the people, and for the people" (Rodríguez 1991).

Finally, in summarizing the llamamiento, the party itself argued that "political power in our country, as an expression of the will and interests of the great majority, could be perfected through continued institutionalization of real and broad popular participation, without nourishing pseudo-democratic illusions or granting space for intellectual speculation" ("Todas las preguntas" 1991). In sum, the parameters of the discussions were set well in advance of the congress, reducing it in most instances to an assembly for ratification rather than a forum for genuine political contestation.

Personnel and Other Changes Approved by the Fourth Congress

With the fundamental issues out of the way, the congress did in fact approve changes in the composition of top party organs and in the electoral system. It also ended discrimination against Catholics and other "believers" by making them eligible for membership as long as "there is no contradiction with the party plan and the party's earthly doctrine." In other words, if prospective members can somehow reconcile their private beliefs in a God and a spiritual life with dialectical materialism, then they may be considered good communists and become eligible for party membership. This is a calculated change designed to deepen the "dialogue between Christians and Marxists" and curry favor with radical Christians and liberation theologians rather than an effort to "christianize" the party.

The composition of top party organs underwent considerable turnover. As seen in table 2-1, the Political Bureau includes twenty-five members, twelve of whom are new. Lage, Robaina, and Ross were promoted to candidate membership in a February 1990 shake-up and are now full members. The position of candidate member was abolished for all levels of the party, reducing the period of "apprenticeship" and in theory making all members equal. Only eight members remain from those elected to full membership at the Third Party Congress. Influential "historical" figures like minister of culture Armando Hart, Pedro Miret, Julio Camacho, Jorge Risquet, and Women's Federation president Vilma Espín were dropped from the Political Bureau. All remain members of the Central Committee. Politically, they have been eclipsed.

It appears that a rotational process among provincial party secretaries determines who will reach the top. For example, Esteban Lazo and Jorge Lezcano retained their positions, but party secretaries from Guan-

Table 2-1. Members Elected to the Political Bureau of the Cuban Communist Party during the Fourth Congress

Member(s)	Office(s) Held
Fidel Castro Ruz	President, Council of State
	President, Council of Ministers
	Commander in Chief, Armed Forces
	First Secretary, PCC
Raúl Castro Ruz	First Vice-President, Council of State
	First Vice-President, Council of Ministers
	Minister, Armed Forces
	Second Secretary, PCC
Juan Almeida Bosque	Vice-President, Council of State
Carlos Aldana Escalante[a]	
Concepción Campa Huergo[b]	Director, Finlay General Institute
Julio Casas Regueiro[b]	Division General
	Vice-Minister, Armed Forces
Osmany Cienfuegos Gorriarán	Member, Council of State
	Member, Council of Ministers
Carlos Rafael Rodríguez	
José Ramón Machado	Vice-President, Council of State
Abelardo Colomé Ibarra	General
	Minister of the Interior
	Vice-President, Council of State
Carlos Lage Dávila[c]	Vice-President, Council of State
	Vice-Director, President Castro's staff
Roberto Robaina[c]	Member, Council of State
	General Secretary, Communist Youth Union
Esteban Lazo	PCC First Secretary, Santiago de Cuba
	Vice-President, Council of State
Jorge Lezcano Pérez[b]	PCC First Secretary, City of Havana
	Member, Council of State
Julián Rizo Alvarez[c]	
Alfredo Hondal González[b]	PCC First Secretary, Ciego de Avila
Alfredo Jordán Morales[b]	PCC First Secretary, Las Tunas
Pedro Ross Leal[c]	General Secretary, Cuban Workers' Confederation
	Member, Council of State
Ulises Rosales del Toro[c]	Division General
	First Vice-Minister, Ministry of the Armed Forces
	Chief of Staff of the Armed Forces
	Member, Council of State
Yadira García Vera[b]	Member, President Castro's staff
María de los Angeles García[b]	Member, PCC Executive Bureau, Santiago de Cuba

Table 2-1. (Continued)

Member(s)	Office(s) Held
Cándido Palmero Hernández[b]	Chief, Blas Roca Workers' Contingent
Abel Prieto Jiménez[b]	President, National Union of Writers and Artists
	Member, Council of State
Leopoldo Cintra Frías[b]	Division General
	Chief, Western Army
Nelson Torres Pérez[b]	PCC First Secretary, Cienfuegos
	Member, Council of State

Sources: Alfonso (1991); "PCC Elimina" (1991); "Aldana cree" (1992); "Aldana es expulsado" (1992).

[a] Carlos Aldana was removed from the Political Bureau in a major shakeup in September 1992 and was subsequently expelled from the PCC itself. María de los Angeles García assumed some of Aldana's responsibilities in the areas of education, science, and culture. José R. Balaguer, a former ambassador to the Soviet Union, was promoted to the Political Bureau and took over Aldana's responsibilities in foreign affairs and ideology. Ricardo Alarcón was also promoted to the Political Bureau while serving as minister of foreign relations. Subsequently, Alarcón was removed from this post and "elected" to the presidency of the National Assembly of People's Power.

[b] New members following the Fourth Party Congress.

[c] Former alternate members of the Political Bureau. Roberto Robaina was appointed minister of foreign relations in 1993, replacing Alarcón.

tánamo (Raúl Michel), Matanzas (Luis Alvarez), and Camagüey (Lázaro Vázquez) were replaced by those from Ciego de Avila, Las Tunas, and Cienfuegos. Those replaced remain members of the Central Committee. Alfredo Hondal and Nelson Torres worked in the party bureaucracy, and Alfredo Jordán came up through the Communist Youth Union.

Three women were named to the Political Bureau for the first time. Two of them (Yadira García and Concepción Campa) appear to be President Castro's protégées: García is an engineer who serves on his staff, while Campa, a scientist, worked on the research and development of the vaccine against meningitis B, one of the president's pet projects. María de los Angeles García comes from the party bureaucracy in Santiago. There was no increase in the number of women at the highest level, though the elimination of candidate membership means that the three newly appointed women are full members, compared to only one (Vilma Espín) following the 1986 congress. In all likelihood, these new members will play a marginal role in the Political Bureau's decisions, given their lack of political experience and the idiosyncratic nature of their appointments.

Four of the twenty-five members of the Political Bureau are division generals, a slightly greater representation than at the Third Party Congress. General Colomé is second only to Raúl Castro in the military hierarchy and was named minister of the interior following the arrest of General Abrantes in 1989. General Rosales del Toro presided at the tribunal that sentenced General Ochoa. Ochoa's replacement as commander of the Western Army, who was also sent to Angola in 1988 to replace him, is General Cintra Frías. In all probability, Cintra Frías's promotion comes as a political reward for a job well done. Curiously enough, General Julio Casas was promoted ahead of his brother Senén, who was dropped from the Political Bureau altogether. Julio Casas is a professional air force officer who has held important administrative positions as well. His promotion could be due to increasing concern by the Castro brothers about the dependability of the Cuban Air Force following the 1987 defection of General Rafael del Pino and some reports that it is the least loyal of the military services.

Finally, two surprising appointments were made: Abel Prieto and Cándido Palmero. Prieto, president of the National Union of Writers and Artists, may have been rewarded for maintaining cultural orthodoxy in the union and pushing the official view on culture, literature, and the arts or for keeping troublesome intellectuals in line. Palmero, chief of one of President Castro's most favored worker contingents, has absolutely no political background, nor has he held any state office. He has reportedly distinguished himself as a labor leader and has done well in tasks assigned to him. Still, the fact that he was chosen over senior political figures or military officers suggests that he too is one of President Castro's current favorites. It is hard to imagine Prieto and Palmero as influential policy makers, nor can one be certain in this instance that their promotion means that they have finally achieved permanent favored status.

In summary, the new Political Bureau includes a hard-line group of Castroites, rising influentials like Carlos Lage and Carlos Aldana,[3] neither of whom is identified with reform, loyal military officers committed to the system, provincial party secretaries whose turn came up, and lesser figures who are either President Castro's favorites or control a key sector such as labor. There is a clear hierarchy in the Political Bureau, and it is inconceivable that the newcomers will have an impact on major policy decisions. In one way or another, all but the core Castroites owe their inclusion in the Political Bureau to the top leaders, so it is difficult to expect them to challenge the status quo.

On the other hand, there is some speculation to the effect that this is not a monolithic group and that some of them are closet reformers convinced of the need for change. Holding proreform views privately does not necessarily mean that policy makers at this level are going to promote a genuinely reformist agenda that would repudiate President Castro's known views or challenge what the congress explicitly sanctioned. Second, there is no credible evidence of substantive divisions in the leadership, in the sense that none has even hinted that the political system or the economic model needs to be thoroughly reshaped. Mr. Aldana, for instance, had stated that "a lot can be expected, except that we would cease being socialists, and that we would be transformed, after thirty years, into a U.S.-style democracy." Technocrats like Carlos Lage and others may be convinced that centralized socialism has failed and may be working at the margins for modest economic changes, such as expanding opportunities for foreign investment in the tourism industry, but such views are consistent with President Castro's own. Finally, it really is impossible to determine whether some of them harbor suspicions, sympathize with perestroika and glasnost, or are secretly plotting to reverse what President Castro blessed and the congress approved. In my judgment, Cuba's Gorbachev or Yeltsin is not among its top party elite. What you see is what you get.

It appears unlikely that the Castro brothers are going to surround themselves with advocates of what in the end would be their own demise. If anything, their launching a process of counterreform is precisely to forestall that unpleasant surprise. Indeed, counterreform is another of the Castros' preventive strikes and is therefore entirely in character and consistent with past practices. For these reasons above all, to define oneself as either an authentic reformer or a contrarian, particularly at the highest levels of the party, is still politically fatal and likely to remain so as long as the Castro brothers control it.

The Central Committee itself underwent considerable turnover, reflecting the need to take the process of counterreform to the second-highest party organ. According to PCC Second Secretary Raúl Castro, the committee's "composition reflects a number of factors that would represent not only our party, but the entire society" ("Raúl Castro" 1991). At the same time, including so many new members (discussed below) allowed the leadership to get rid of people who may have been identified with reformist currents and thus reduce the potential for the consolidation of an antiregime coalition. In short, the continuity and stability of the committee are affected by the very high turnover, but its potential as a source of antiregime sentiment is reduced.

The Central Committee is composed of 126 new members (56 percent) and 99 old members. The average age of the 225 members is forty-seven, and their educational level compared with that of the previous body is higher. It has slightly greater representation from the interior provinces than the previous committee, and there is a 20 percent increase among those who have been party members for fifteen years or fewer. The number of "founding" members (dating back to 1965) is now twenty-three, so that members who were not there when the party was reorganized now constitute an overwhelming majority in the Central Committee. Age is a factor in this change, as are various political circumstances, merit, or idiosyncratic and peculiar criteria that at times determine membership.

In his study of the Fourth Congress, *Los fieles de Castro*, Alfonso (1991) finds that among the 225 members there are 189 men and 36 women, some 84 and 16 percent, respectively. In this, there is practically no change compared to the male/female ratio following the 1986 congress. Women continue to be severely underrepresented at the party's highest levels relative to their numbers in the general population. On the other hand, their proportion in high party organs generally corresponds to their proportion as party members.

In an unprecedented step, the Central Committee was given extraordinary powers to cope with the current crisis, on the grounds that "the nation requires as never before the ability to adopt quick decisions and do whatever the moment demands" (Alfonso 1991). The committee can either make decisions that affect the economy, society, or polity on its own, or it can order legislative or state action that may be necessary. It is now able to intervene at all levels of state and society, circumventing local, provincial, and national state and party organs. Rather than increasing the autonomy of lower state and party organs, the Congress authorized the Central Committee to override these bodies' prerogatives.

This change is designed to expedite the leadership's control in times of crisis, because it can assert itself quickly within the committee. The assumption is that such extraordinary steps would be taken only under truly dire circumstances; but in reality, once the machinery is in place, the leadership can summon the committee at any point and demand action. To put it bluntly, while the committee's actions carry the force of law, it is thoroughly subordinated to the Political Bureau and recast in the leadership's preferred mold.

The party's Secretariat, its nerve center and administrative bureaucracy, was abolished. Its responsibilities now fall to a core group within the Political Bureau charged with "attending to the daily activities of the party's direction, and with informing the Bureau of their work." This change may not have any practical functional consequences, especially if the core group includes the five members left over from the 1990 reorganization. On the other hand, it is likely to produce either more layoffs or staff reassignments, paring down the bureaucracy even more.

The most significant change in the electoral system was in the election of deputies to provincial assemblies as well as to the National Assembly of People's Power (Asamblea Nacional del Poder Popular). The Congress resolved that "given the people's maturity," deputies to those assemblies should be elected directly, thus abolishing the method of indirect election in force since 1976. The National Assembly subsequently approved the changes that needed to be formalized before they went into effect.

Candidates are to be nominated from the mass organizations but cannot use the published press or electronic media to campaign. A special committee designated by the party will make the final decision on who the candidates will be, ensuring that the PCC will play a major role in determining who runs or does not. On the surface, this appears to be a significant departure from past practices, in the sense that "voters" will choose their representatives directly. Theoretically, this democratizes the relationship between rulers and subjects, strengthens accountability, and limits the pervasive influence of the party over legislatures. It is seen as an improvement of a political system that is, according to President Castro, "the most complete democracy that exists" ("Castro Calls Cuba" 1991, 39).

And yet, though the process changes, the context hardly does. This arrangement does not provide for genuine competition, nor is it designed to promote outsiders, antisystem or antiparty candidates. Those who support socialism and the party but favor modest market-oriented reforms would not consider these to be favorable changes because the process does not legitimate nonparty or nongovernmental challengers.

Democratic competition is impossible as long as President Castro ("Defiant Castro" 1991) maintains that "the principle of one party is important because we do not want to divide our society into a thousand pieces" or calls a multiparty system "multigarbage." In sum, a modern understanding of democracy holds the idea of a single party democracy to be no more than a profound intellectual abomination, and there is no reason to accept Castro's definition of it.

Second, without access to the mass media and unable to criticize socialism, the party, or the leadership or to comment on fundamental issues of domestic and foreign policy, candidates are not independent political actors. Debate becomes stultified and surrealistic in this context, because the root of the crisis—the manner in which power is exercised—is off-limits. Instead, candidates mechanically articulate secondary and trivial grievances because they cannot offer a coherent alternative to the party's program. Direct elections to provincial legislatures or to the National Assembly mean little when the content of political articulation is severely limited and candidates are subjected to political litmus tests.

Third, without their own political organizations—parties and the like—that reflect an authentic opposition, candidates have no leverage on the system. As long as the political culture fostered by the regime is obsessed with unity and defines opposition as treason, candidacies are ritualistic and tantamount to affirmation. In fact, even a partial opening would not constitute a first step in a process of genuine liberalization, but rather a means of legitimating an inherently exclusionary system. Under present rules, this is a dilemma that anyone considering a challenge to the regime must consider very seriously.

Finally and most important, because the single-party model is unaffected by these changes, the hegemony of the PCC remains unchallenged. Noncommunist political organizations are illegal, and the party in fact monopolizes all the resources that guarantee its domination. Through its stranglehold over the nominating process, the party will ensure that only candidates whom it can trust are nominated, even if in some cases they are not communists as such.

In summary, the changes in the composition of top party organs strongly indicate that new members are politically correct and will not lead a proreform movement from within. Neither will the marginal reforms of the electoral system create a significant political opening. Control over the party itself was further centralized, and greater scrutiny was given to the selection of its top elites. The direct election of deputies to provincial and national assemblies means little in the absence of competition and is in fact partly designed for foreign consumption. It retards liberalization and freezes out opponents, so the system remains exclusionary.

Conclusions

A process of counterreform aimed at downsizing the Communist Party bureaucracy through removal of cadres and centralization of administrative and ideological controls at the top culminated at the Fourth PCC Congress. As the spinal cord of the system of one-party rule, the party could not be allowed to drift and decay—as had its counterparts in the former communist world—because that would undermine its authority and bring on its demise. Cleansing the party would be painful and perhaps risky, but for the leadership that was the only choice.

There is no reason to doubt the fidelity of the newly elected Central Committee to either President Castro or to the model of political domination defined in the one-party state. Simply put, the leadership reasserted itself in the face of potentially destructive contrary currents, suggesting that its stranglehold on the system is fundamentally unaffected by internal difficulties and external crisis. No significant changes in governance can be expected as long as that is the case. Who holds power and why is not subject to revision.

On the other hand, the triumph of orthodoxy means that the polity will stagnate even more, because the solutions ratified by the Congress neither address the real sources of the crisis—the system itself—nor are likely to energize a listless populace. The Congress became the forum through which the leadership restated its unflinching commitment to a grim future, and the fact that no challenge emerged from the Congress indicates just how shortsighted its delegates were. If it were truly the case that a significant proportion of the delegates believes that the path outlined by President Castro, namely "the zero option" and "Socialism or Death," will save the nation, then at some point they too must be held accountable for their complicity.

The party retains its central role, and its affairs are open to much closer scrutiny from above than appears to have been the case formerly. The formation of a viable internal resistance front is very unlikely because the party has been shaken up and detoxified. It cannot be expected to become a vessel of change until there is a critical mass in its top organs convinced of the need for radically new departures. The mix of old and new mediocrities joined in its Political Bureau indicates that its gestalt points in exactly the opposite direction.

Notes

1. Resolution on foreign policy passed at the Fourth Congress, as reproduced in Alfonso (1991, 201).
2. General Abrantes died in mysterious circumstances while in detention. The official explanation that he suffered a fatal heart attack is not entirely credible, given the general's good health and fitness. Little publicity has been given to his death, and if any official investigation was conducted, its findings remain secret. Skeptical observers, myself included, believe that because Abrantes was truly "the man who kept the secrets," he needed to be eliminated quietly. Until evidence to the contrary surfaces, the presumption of guilt falls upon the regime.
3. Aldana's fall from grace in September 1992 does not refute my argument, which is that he was a bureaucratic opportunist who spoke as a reformer to the foreign press or while traveling through Western countries but of whom there is no evidence that he believed in fundamental reforms or challenged the Castro brothers on that issue. It is inconceivable that he would have risen so fast and so far if he were an authentic reformer, and I know of no instance in which Aldana deviated from the official line on politics or economics. For example, many dissidents saw him as a loyal and quite ambitious functionary, not as someone biding his time to "spring a surprise" on the Castro brothers. Finally, the reasons given for his removal did not mention policy differences with other leaders and in fact alluded to corruption and bureaucratic turf wars. See "Most significant shuffle" (1992) and "Cuban official confirms fall" (1992).

References

"Aldana cree justa su destitución." 1992. *El Nuevo Herald*, October 6, 1A.
"Aldana es expulsado del Partido Comunista Cubano." 1992. *El Nuevo Herald*, October 15, 1A.
Alfonso, Pablo. 1991. *Los fieles de Castro*. Miami: Ediciones Cambio.
"Aprobado grupo de medidas sobre estructura y funcionamiento del Partido." 1990. *Granma: Resumen Semanal*, October 14, 9.
Brzezinski, Zbigniew. 1989. *The Grand Failure*. New York: Scribners.

Castro, Fidel. 1991. "Texto del discurso en el 30 aniversario de la Victoria de Girón." *Granma Internacional*, July 16.
"Castro Calls Cuba 'Most Democratic.'" 1991. Havana Radio Rebelde Network, October 13. In *FBIS-LAT-91-199S*, October 15, 38–40.
"Continúa la purga de altos cargos en Cuba." 1989. *El País Internacional*, July 7, 7.
"Cuban official confirms fall of senior leader Carlos Aldana." 1992. *Miami Herald*, September 26, 6A.
"Defiant Castro Calls Western Democracy 'Complete Garbage.'" 1991. *New York Times*, October 14, A4.
"Drug Scandal Gives Castro Excuse for Purge of Dissidents and 'Plotters.'" 1989. *Caribbean Report*, August 24, 1.
"Llamamiento del Partido." 1990. *Granma: Resumen Semanal*, March 25, 1.
"Most Significant Shuffle in Years." 1992. *Miami Herald*, September 24, 1A.
"PCC elimina a figuras históricas." 1991. *El Nuevo Herald*, October 15, 1A.
"Partido Comunista promueve amplio debate nacional." 1990. *Granma: Resumen Semanal*, July 19, 1.
"Pleno extraordinario del Comité Central." 1990. *Granma: Resumen Semanal*, February 25, 9.
"Purga cubana llega a cultura y economía." 1989. *El Nuevo Herald*, August 25, 1.
Rabkin, Rhoda. 1991. *Cuban Politics: The Revolutionary Experiment*. New York: Praeger.
"Raúl Castro on Central Committee Turnover." 1991. Havana Radio Rebelde Network, October 13. In *FBIS-LAT-91-199S*, October 15, 40.
Rodríguez, Carlos Rafael. 1991. "Discurso del Vice Presidente Carlos Rafael Rodríguez ante el Congreso Latinoamericano de Sociología." *Granma Internacional*, June 16.
"Saquemos las lecciones y sigamos adelante." 1989. *Granma: Resumen Semanal*, September 10, 1.
"Todas las preguntas tienen respuesta." 1991. *Granma Internacional*, May 16, 10.

THREE

Continuity and Change in Cuba's International Relations in the 1990s

DAMIÁN J. FERNÁNDEZ

The overarching challenge for Cuban foreign policy in the 1990s is to redefine the island's position in the world. The process of redefinition has begun, but change takes time and presents risks. Elites need to filter information, choose courses of action, and react to internal and international developments. For the Cuban leadership, the greatest problem is that the process of rearticulating Cuban foreign policy cannot be divorced from domestic politics. Change in Cuba's international politics will lead to domestic transformation in ways that are unexpected and are unpalatable to the top leadership.

Changes in the Communist bloc resulted in the breakdown of Soviet aid to the island, accelerating an economic and ideological crisis. As a consequence, Cuba's foreign policy and the island's position in global politics have been altered. For the first time since its independence, the island is not in a special relationship with a superpower. The price of independence has been steep, much higher than that of dependence. Autonomy, the elusive quest of Cuban nationalism, has proved the maxim "Be careful what you wish for, for you might get it."

Elites and masses have felt the consequences of political and economic transformations under way in countries as different as Mexico, Vietnam, and Poland. The Cuban state cannot shield itself from the effects of current happenings in the world or from the global economy. In the 1990s Cuba will have to adapt its foreign policy and its domestic system to the prevailing international context. The process of adaptation and redefinition of the state is not unprecedented in the history of the island, which recast itself in 1902 through the Platt Amendment and in 1961 through the adoption of Marxism-Leninism. Like all nation-states, Cuba has adapted to its environment in the past; it is in the process of doing so once again.

The 1990s are the twilight of Cuba's revolutionary foreign policy. That the island had lost its minipower status was evident in the late 1970s, when Cuba sent thousands of troops to Africa. From the vantage point of the 1990s, the island's power seems but a mirage. By the end of the decade Cuba's international relations will be indistinguishable from those of other small, weak states. Trying since 1959 to shed its subordinate position in world politics, Cuba has found it impossible to escape its limitations. Thirdworldliness has caught up with the island. Even in such fields as medicine, Cuba's prowess is diminished. Moreover, the island's moral capital abroad is at risk.

In this chapter I will focus on the relationship between change, both international and national, and continuity from several perspectives. First, I will analyze how international changes elicited modifications in Cuba's relations with other countries and regions. Second, I will show how international transformations are associated with the dynamics of domestic political change and continuity on the island. Third, I will suggest a connection between the external environment and the operational code (both intellectual and strategic) under which Cuban foreign policy has been formulated since the advent of the revolution. I will analyze how decision makers interpret new international conditions and fit them into their operational code without radically altering the strategic foundation of their thinking. In short, in this chapter I will try to connect the international with the national in multiple ways.

To accomplish these goals, I will review the factors of change and continuity in Cuba's foreign relations, focusing on the post-1980s period, then show how new and old foreign policy elements have been expressed in specific regional and bilateral contexts as well as in the economic and political issues of the foreign policy agenda. Finally, I will examine how the external environment affects the politics of domestic elites and how decisions on foreign policy are made in Cuba.

There are two theoretical bases for my examination. The first is that interdependence and pluralism are concepts that stress the linkages, the fluidity, and the mutual effects between domestic and international politics. The state is perceived as one among many actors on the global stage. The nation-state is permeable by outside forces, and internal groups form linkages with counterparts across borders. In the economic arena, interdependence undergirds the global economy. The second concept is that leaders and their worldview matter in foreign policy making. Leaders make decisions based on a reality filtered and reconstructed through their operational code. The central question in this case is how one accounts for change in Cuban foreign policy while the leadership has remained constant. One possibility is that the leaders' worldview has changed. A more sophisticated analysis would indicate that the operational code is multilayered, and only the less firmly fixed elements of it have been recast to accommodate lessons recently learned.

The New and Not-So-New Look of Cuba's Foreign Policy in the 1990s

The resolution on international relations adopted by the Fourth Congress of the Cuban Communist Party (Partido Comunista de Cuba, PCC) in 1991 is striking on three counts: 1) its brevity as compared to resolutions of preceding congresses, 2) the emphasis on foreign economic policy encapsulated in the document, and 3) the coexistence of elements of the old foreign policy discourse with the new. That the resolution is brief (one full page in *Granma*, as compared to several pages in previous congress documents) is an indication that Cuba's commitments and role in world affairs are not so large as they once loomed.

The regime's foreign policy in the 1990s has a bicameral heart: its elements are economics and politics. Since the late 1980s Havana's emphasis has been on securing trade partners and attracting investment and tourism to the island. The political side of the foreign policy agenda, though less dramatic than the economic side, is as important. The politics of Cuba's international relations cannot be divorced from the turn toward a foreign economic policy.

Ricardo Alarcón, the former minister of foreign relations, stated that "the country's foreign policy . . . is a continuation of domestic policy. . . . This means doing abroad what our people are doing every day at home to save the nation, the revolution, and to overcome material difficulties" (Foreign Broadcast Information Service [FBIS] 1993, 1).[1] In a similar vein, current minister of foreign relations Roberto Robaina has said that he will create a national Ministry of Foreign Relations (MINREX), pointing to the importance of foreign policy issues (such as human rights and Cuba's overtures to international businessmen) for domestic society. The idea of creating a national MINREX also suggests that the international work of the ministry might take a back seat, particularly with a minister who commands little international expertise. This is another indication of the island's diminished global projection.

Although the context and the tactics of Cuban foreign policy have changed, the main goal of Cuban foreign policy has not. The priority has been and will continue to be to safeguard the regime in power. The international and the national, the political and the economic, are inextricably intertwined. Nevertheless, one can discern a political agenda and an economic one.

The new look of Cuba's international relations features economic pragmatism. The intensified search for trading partners has been the driving force behind the diplomatic offensive since the demise of the Soviet-Cuban aid and trade regime in the early 1990s. The strategy is to attract foreign investment and tourism, locate markets, promote new exports (for example, in biotechnology), and deepen economic cooperation with old and newfound friends. To achieve these aims, Cuba must have smooth political relations and must expand those relations to include as many countries as possible. The Caribbean has become the primary target of diplomatic opportunity, followed by the rest of Latin America, China, and Europe. The approach was firmly entrenched by 1991. Its roots, however, are to be found in the moderation of the island's foreign relations since the early 1980s, which was due to factors largely outside Havana's control.

Undergirding Cuba's foreign economic policy is the idea that collaboration with a variety of governments is possible. According to Fidel Castro, in spite of prevailing global problems, inequities, unipolarity, and dislocation, the international context is conducive not only to functionalism among states but also to negotiated solutions and pluralism. Economic pragmatism precludes an ideological litmus text for potential trading partners. Cuba has previously accommodated political differences in its foreign policy; throughout the past thirty years the country has maintained healthy economic bonds with countries whose political systems were not ideologically palatable to Cuban leaders (for example, Mexico, Spain under Franco, and China during some periods). What is new in the present foreign policy is that economics is its mind, if not its heart. In the past, the goal of financial gain did not command Havana's actions worldwide. Economics took a backseat to ideological and political considerations. This was possible because of the financial lifeline flowing from Moscow, in which the USSR supplied oil to Cuba at a cost below world market price while buying Cuban sugar at a price above that on the world market.

Remnants of the old Cuban policy persist in the new. Revolutionary nationalism at home and anti-Americanism continue to imply solidarity with Third World causes abroad. While support for guerrilla movements is on the wane, Cuba continues to advocate global economic reforms and promote such long-standing issues on its agenda as resolution of the Latin American debt crisis, an end to apartheid in South Africa, settlement of the Palestinian question, and opposition to U.S. intervention in Latin America, among others. In Fidel Castro's official discourse in instances as different as the Gulf War (1991) and the Iberoamerican summit conferences (1991 and 1992), continuity, rather than change, predominates. The rhetoric continues to highlight U.S. imperialism, confrontation between rich and poor, and the image of Cuba as a beacon of morality in a world exploited by capitalism.

The old and the new are interwoven in the fabric of Cuban foreign policy. The tone of the island's rhetoric continues to manifest moral outrage not only against the developed countries, particularly the United States, but against those groups who allowed or engineered the dismantling of socialism in the Soviet bloc. The revolutionary solidarity Cuba once reserved for the Soviet Union has been replaced by solidarity with China and the remaining communist countries. Marxism-Leninism is still enshrined as the ideological guiding light for Cuba's foreign policy, but nationalistic and anti-U.S. dimensions of Cuban political culture have been reemphasized. Proletarian internationalism, however, is absent from the resolution of the Fourth Congress, and this is a telling omission. In fact, the conduct of Cuban foreign policy since the late 1980s and in the early 1990s shared points in common with Gorbachev's policy of new thinking, specifically in terms of international capitalism, improved relations with Europe, and peaceful settlement of disputes. The principal point of divergence revolved around the issue of relations with the United States.

Meeting the Challenge of Global Change (Part 1): The Economics of Cuba's Foreign Policy

The stage on which Cuba must conduct its foreign affairs in the 1990s presents contextual changes of significance. In addition to the end of Soviet aid to Cuba, other transformations are relevant. Among these are the discrediting of Marxist-Leninist models of government, the end of bipolarity, the internationalization of human rights, the decline of the Third World movement, the globalization of the world economy, and the worldwide trend toward privatization and integration. Cuba is not immune to repercussions from these factors and has reacted to them. Havana's strategy for weathering the storm has been twofold, including domestic economic adjustment (the rectification process begun in 1986 and the "special period in time of peace" begun in 1991) and international readjustment without significant political change at home.

Cuba's international readjustment has had several dimensions: 1) recognition of the newly independent states of the former Soviet empire and establishment of economic relations with them to the extent possible; 2) partial reinsertion in the global economy through attraction of foreign investment, tourism, and the export of traditional and nontraditional items; 3) a turn to the Caribbean and Latin America, not only economically but also politically; and, 4) a search for new trading partners.

One of the ways Cuba has adapted to global transformation is through changes in its trade patterns and its policy toward foreign investment and tourism. While seeking to promote economic relations, Cuba has also encountered political tensions with most of its trading partners. Furthermore, Cuba's program to seek new trading partners to replace the former socialist countries (on whom Cuba relied for over 80 percent of its commerce) is undermined by financial and structural weaknesses in the Cuban economy and by the U.S. embargo. The economic crisis since the mid-1980s has had a negative impact on Cuba's capability to import from key trading countries. For example, imports from Canada, one of Cuba's top Western economic associates, fell around 70 percent between 1986 and 1991; the total volume of trade between the two countries also fell, although Cuban exports to Canada have increased from $71 million in 1986 to $152.8 million in 1991 (Cuba Report 1992, 4).

Relations with the Former Socialist Bloc

The volume of key items (oil and foodstuffs, for example) in Soviet-Cuban trade decreased sharply after the late 1980s. In 1990 Cuba received 3.4 million fewer tons of fuel than in 1989; in 1991 the island received less than 50 percent of the agreed-upon volume of foodstuffs (FBIS 1991b, 1). Moreover, as of 1991, bilateral trade was to be conducted on the basis of market prices and hard currency. Because of Cuba's dependence on Soviet subsidies for sugar exports (also cut, although the Soviets continued to pay prices above those on the world market) and oil imports (including the earnings from resale of Soviet oil at world prices), the country's economy went into a tailspin. The austerity program implemented in 1986 under the banner of the rectification process gave way to the special period in time of peace, which consisted of additional belt-tightening measures. Trade between Cuba and the former Soviet Union dropped dramatically between 1990 and 1992. Exports fell by 73 percent; imports also decreased sharply—54.8 percent for raw and processed foods and 65 percent for oil and oil products (Economist Intelligence Unit [EIU], 1992, 18). The loss of trade with the former socialist partners has not been offset by gains from trade with the West. In 1991, trade in hard currency, one of Havana's strategies for survival, increased a mere 8.9 percent (EIU 1992, 18).

The Cuban government reacted quickly and pragmatically to the disintegration of the Soviet Union. In December 1991, Fidel Castro announced that Cuba would recognize the former Soviet republics and seek to establish good relations based on mutual benefits. Since then, Cuba has extended recognition to at least eleven of the independent republics. Trade accords have been signed with Russia and other members of the Commonwealth of Independent States (CIS). Although such actions lay the foundation for the future, the amount and terms of the trade pale in comparison to those before 1990.

Russia is the chief economic partner among the new constellation, buying primarily sugar, nickel, and citrus. In the first six months of 1992, Cuban sugar was bartered for Russian oil. But the future of Russian-Cuban relations is clouded by Cuban debt to Moscow and the national and international lobby against the island's regime and communism. Production shortfalls in the former socialist states and pressure from Washington (which at times has said it would make aid to the former Soviet Union conditional on its ending concessionary treatment of Cuba) have also limited trade between Havana and Moscow. Cuba's ability to deal with private enterprises, different republics, and a host of foreign economic agencies will be a determining factor in the development of Cuban relations with Russia and the CIS republics. This means that Cuba must adapt its own economic structure toward decentralization to negotiate with foreign firms. The creation of *sociedades anónimas* (quasi-private firms) is one of the first steps in this direction.

The collapse of the Soviet Union and of communism in Eastern Europe presented not only economic but also political challenges. Two are of particular interest. First, the former socialist allies who voted loyally with Cuba in international forums no longer do so. The UN debate over human rights in the island is a case in point. Bulgaria, Russia, the former Czechoslovakia, Hungary, and the former Yugoslavia, among other states, have recently voted against Cuba, showing that Havana has fewer friends than it used to and, as a result, will be more vulnerable to outside pressure. (Only Angola, China, Ghana, Iran, Iraq, Libya, and Syria have continued to side with Cuba.) Second, the repatriation of Cuban *internacionalistas* (civilian or military workers overseas) and students in the former Soviet Union and Eastern Europe became a cause of concern for the regime. Many internacionalistas and exchange students did not want to return to their homeland. Those who returned might have been infected with the virus of reform and therefore ideologically suspect to the leadership.

Another thorn in Cuba's flesh with regard to its former benefactors was the withdrawal of the Soviet brigade from the island. Havana reacted strongly against the decision to remove the brigade because it was taken unilaterally by Moscow and because it put the island in a vulnerable position vis-à-vis the United States, according to Havana. Havana proposed unsuccessfully that the withdrawal, which was expected to be completed in 1993, should be simultaneous with a U.S. pullout from Guantánamo. The Soviet withdrawal decision signaled the end of the Soviet-Cuban security regime, although negotiations for arms sales have taken place since then. One of the results of the termination of the security regime has been the downsizing of the Cuban Revolutionary Armed Forces (FAR) announced in 1993.

Cuba's foreign policy agenda has changed in other ways in response to the transformation in the Soviet bloc. Since the late 1980s Cuba has given other regions of the world priority in its foreign policy agenda and has sought foreign investment through joint ventures on the island, international tourism, and new markets. Although the roots of this course of action are to be found in the 1980s (for instance, international tourism was already a priority sector in the late 1980s, and the joint venture law was passed in 1982), its priority has risen in the 1990s. More details are provided on tourism in chapter 7 and on joint ventures in chapter 9.

Relations with Latin America and the Caribbean

Although Spain seems to have the lead in foreign investment in Cuba, Latin America is the most represented region among Cuba's foreign investors. Of the twenty-four countries attending the 1991 Havana Foreign Trade Fair, ten were Latin American (*Nuevo Herald* 1991, 3). Among Latin American countries, Mexico is at the forefront in investments. Cuba's efforts to court its Latin American neighbors have produced tangible results in the case of Brazil, with bilateral trade increasing fivefold between 1988 to 1989. The two countries also negotiated tariff reductions in 1989 and are planning joint ventures; Brazil is expected to invest up to $800 million in the island.

Cuba has also orchestrated a campaign to expand its trade with other Latin American and Caribbean nations. Argentina, like Brazil, has purchased biotechnology from Cuba and has expressed interest in nuclear cooperation. Several Argentinean firms have expressed interest in taking over grain exports formerly made by two subsidiaries of U.S. multinationals (Cargill and Continental) that stopped grain sales to Cuba after the passage in 1992 of the Cuban Democracy Act. Economic cooperation, however, has occurred at a time of political tension between the two countries. Buenos Aires's alignment with Washington has been expressed in a series of anti-Cuban government positions. For example, Argentina voted against the Cuban government at the UN human rights debates in Geneva, and Guido de Tella, the Argentinean foreign minister, criticized Castro's regime at the General Assembly. The president of Argentina, Carlos Menem, met with Jorge Mas Canosa and other top executives of the Cuban-American National Foundation, the largest organization of Cuban exiles, and expressed his support for a "free" Cuba. Nevertheless, Argentina expressed its opposition to the Cuban Democracy Act and has announced new trade agreements with Cuba.

Cuba's overtures to South America have included discussions with Brazilians and Venezuelans regarding offshore oil exploration; reestablishment of a Colombian consulate in Havana (1991); trips by Chilean businessmen to the island; and reestablishment of relations with

Paraguay. Air links with Latin American and Caribbean countries have been inaugurated, evidence that functional integration with the region is under way.

Cuba's latest reinsertion into the Latin American community has been in part a result of the foreign policies of the democratic governments in the region. Since the early 1990s, the guiding principles behind the foreign relations of the regional democracies were ideological pluralism and reduction of regional tensions. Both principles served the domestic goals of these countries and ushered in better relations with Havana. Moreover, with the collapse of Soviet communism Cuba no longer represented a security threat. On the contrary, cordial relations with Havana helped consolidate democracy in several Latin American countries by satisfying the Left and demonstrating their autonomy from Washington.

During the 1980s and early 1990s, Cuba established, normalized, or repaired relations with Brazil, Uruguay, Bolivia, Peru, Venezuela, Ecuador, Chile, and Colombia. During this period Cuba became a full member of the Sistema Económico Latinoamericano (SELA) and the Latin American Parliament and participated in the Asociación Latinoamericana de Integración (ALADI). In 1990 Cuba was elected Latin American representative to the UN Security Council and continued to be active in the Latin American group of the Nonaligned Movement.

Although Cuba is not a member of the Organization of American States (OAS), that organization's 1985 statement regarding ideological pluralism in the region and the inclusiveness of the inter-American system indicated an opening for the island. Since then several Latin American presidents have expressed interest in the reincorporation of Cuba into the organization, but the Declaration of Santiago in 1991 casts doubt on this possibility because it stipulates that democracy is a prerequisite for OAS membership. Signals from the OAS are mixed; democracy has been on and off as a priority for the inter-American community. The same leaders who call Cuba to the regional fold ask for reforms on the island. In turn, the Cuban government has declared that it will not accept conditions to join the OAS. While putting additional pressure on Cuba to open its system, most Latin American countries beckon Havana to the inter-American family and, with few exceptions (such as Argentina under President Menem), are not keen on toeing the tough U.S. line.

The frequent travels of Cuban officials, Fidel Castro among them, to neighboring countries and the amendment of the Cuban constitution to eliminate solidarity with the former Soviet Union are additional indications of the new regional priority. Havana's expressed willingness to sign the nuclear nonproliferation treaty for Latin America and the Caribbean underscores this regional priority and the regime's efforts to court the Latin Americans.

Cuba's courtship of Latin America has produced modest and mixed results. The island's trade with the region has hovered around 5 percent of the total value of Cuban trade, although it has experienced growth with specific countries (such as Brazil) (Valdés Paz 1992, 108). The principal oil-exporting countries of the region have not been willing to provide Cuba with preferential prices. Mexico and Venezuela did not extend the San José Accord (which subsidizes oil sales) to Cuba, though Mexico did give Cuba a $300 million credit line. The island has renegotiated its debt with that country as well as with Colombia and Argentina.

Constraints persist, however. The prospects for significant increase in trade between the island and other regional countries are not bright. One reason is that Cuba's traditional exports compete with those of other smaller economies (for example, the Dominican Republic). Another is that to expand commerce with the larger economies, Cuba needs to find hard currency to pay for imports. Argentina, Brazil, and Mexico, among others, are willing to sell to Cuba but less willing to engage in barter arrangements, principally because they do not need Cuban products. Where investments are concerned, Latin Americans are cautious partly as a result of Washington's (especially the U.S. Congress's) pressure against economic relations with Cuba after the passage of the Cuban Democracy Act and partly because of the structural limitations of the island's economy.

The turn of events in Haiti, Peru, and Venezuela brought into question the singularity of Castro's refusal to embrace democracy. The Cuban Democracy Act has also served to shield the island from international pressure. The law, signed by President Bush in late 1992, attempts to tighten the U.S. embargo of Cuba by, among other measures, penalizing subsidiaries of U.S. firms that do business with that country. Cuba has orchestrated an offensive to muster solidarity in the face of the tightening U.S. embargo. In this regard, Cuba and its trading partners (particularly Canada, Spain, and Mexico) share a common interest in opposing Washington.

Perhaps the most remarkable economic and political overtures are those between the island and its Caribbean neighbors. In the recent past, Cuba has reestablished relations with Jamaica, normalized relations with Grenada, and has opened relations with Saint Lucia and Saint Vincent. The Cuban–Dominican Republic Enterprise Group has been established to promote bilateral economic ties; Dominican investors have visited the island on several occasions.

These developments must be understood as an expression of Cuba's interest in joining the Caribbean Common Market (CARICOM). A Cuban delegation observed the CARICOM summit in the summer of 1991, and CARICOM teams have visited the island to discuss a host of political and economic issues ranging from sugar and biotechnology to integration (FBIS 1991a). Several stumbling blocks to Cuba's insertion into CARICOM have been removed. One of them was the normalization of relations with Grenada. Other obstacles remain, however. Competition for tourists is an area of concern. This issue is being addressed by promoting multidestination tourism within the Caribbean. Cuba's image as a subversive state, another issue of concern for the island's neighbors, might be erased because of Havana's efforts to dispel fears in the new international context.

CARICOM is especially attractive for Cuba on political and economic grounds. Unlike other subregional groups, the organization does not require potential members to uphold democracy. Thus it opens the door to Cuba, who otherwise would be left out of integration associations. Being the largest island economy gives Cuba a potential for bigger benefits as the most advanced economies stand to profit more from integration. For these reasons, as well as for other external constraints, Havana has decided that CARICOM is a priority.

Relations with Western Europe

Relations between Cuba and Western Europe are also of increasing interest to Havana. In spite of political differences on particular issues, the Cuban government has been successful in strengthening bilateral relations with several countries and is orchestrating a campaign to cement economic and political ties. But debt problems, foreign exchange constraints for imports, and the quality and availability of Cuban exports, not to mention competition with other Third World countries for European attention, limit the possibilities. While Cuban trade with some European countries has fallen, it has increased moderately with others (for example, France).

Spain is Cuba's chief partner in Europe and a potential bridge to the European Community (EC). Bilateral relations between Havana and Madrid mirror the possibilities as well as the dilemmas of Cuban foreign policy in the 1990s. Spain has been a steadfast friend of Cuba since the 1960s. Commercial relations between the two countries have been dynamic, particularly in joint ventures. In the late 1980s and early 1990s, however, several issues have strained these relations.

Spanish-Cuban economic relations are mutually beneficial, asymmetrical, and hamstrung by certain problems. Spain is the island's top capitalist trading partner, followed by Canada and Japan. Yet the balance of trade between the two countries has been negative for Cuba since the mid-1970s. In 1990, Spain's exports to Cuba reached the $302.4 million mark, while imports from the island totaled $80.4 million (EIU 1991). Trade deficits (totaling over $566 million between 1987 and 1990) are not the only obstacles to the expansion of economic relations between the two countries; Cuba's cumulative debt to Spain is probably the major economic obstacle. By 1991, Cuba was Spain's third-largest debtor country ($1.7 billion). Repayment is unlikely, as is the prospect of continued Spanish credit lines for Cuban purchases. The lack of competitiveness of Cuban products, weak marketing mechanisms, and a narrow range of exportable goods are additional constraints. Yet Spain has always manifested a special interest in the island and has extended it privileges, such as more development aid than it has given any other Latin American country. In addition to tourism, Spanish businessmen have minor investments in Cuba in cigar production and have established marketing agencies for Cuban products (coffee and seafood, for example). By 1990, total Spanish investment in the island was a mere .001 percent of Spain's total investment abroad (García-Gonzalvo 1993).

Since 1980, when Madrid incorporated the promotion of democracy as one of its foreign policy goals, political differences between Spain and Cuba have become a source of friction. The issue of human rights has taken on prominence for Spain, with the result that the country has become increasingly willing to cooperate with other European nations on behalf of Cuban dissidents in particular and in support of a political opening in general.

Two examples reveal the political tensions inherent in Cuban-Spanish relations in the 1990s. The first was the crisis that ensued after several Cubans sought asylum in the Spanish embassy in Havana in August 1991. The stand-off led to the withdrawal of the Spanish envoy, the cancellation of a modest but symbolically significant development grant of $25 million, and biting criticism of Spain from Fidel Castro. Although the crisis was settled after negotiation, the incident temporarily threatened an otherwise healthy relationship and could have undermined the investments of Spanish businessmen in Cuba.

The second occurred during the Iberoamerican summit conferences in 1991 and 1992. Spanish prime minister Felipe González, a socialist, was the leading critic of Cuba's political system and indirectly of Fidel Castro. In 1991, González met with the Cuban leader to try to convince him to initiate a process of democratization. Spain's posture contrasted with the quiet diplomacy and moderation pursued by Mexico and Venezuela. These two countries, among others, welcomed Cuba back to the Iberoamerican fold but with reservations. The Spanish effort failed and contributed to cooling relations between the two heads of state. But Spanish-Cuban relations are characterized by a pragmatic adaptability. Spanish leaders and businessmen who find Cuba's system unpalatable manage to negotiate with the Cubans.

Relations with the People's Republic of China

One of the salient features of Cuba's international relations in the 1990s, its political and economic closeness with China dates to a rapprochement in the early to mid-1980s (Fernández 1993).[2] After a slight decline in 1985, two-way trade dipped to 180 million pesos in 1986 and slightly over 186 million in 1987. Trade increased 100 percent in 1988, and by 1989 total trade between the two countries surpassed the 1984 level (*Anuario estadístico de Cuba* [AEC] 1989). Cuban-Chinese trade was important for both countries. According to one authority, "Bilateral trade for 1990 was almost $500 million, representing an 11 percent increase from 1989. In the first quarter of 1989 Cuba sold China 67 percent more than what it purchased, signalling a positive trade balance for the Cubans. By the beginning of the 1990s, China was Cuba's third largest supplier of consumer goods" (Gunn 1990). Yet by the late 1980s the island's trade with China accounted for less than 5 percent of the total value of Cuba's merchandise trade (Pérez-López 1991).

Although the trade basket has diversified, sugar has continued to be Cuba's principal export to China. (China is Cuba's second-largest sugar buyer.) Sugar exports increased after the mid-1980s, reaching their highest level in 1988 at 1.3 million tons; they fell to 892,000 tons in 1990. Cuba's sugar sales to China, unlike those to the former Soviet Union until the late 1980s, have not been at subsidized prices. In 1988, China paid Cuba 7.7 cents per pound for sugar while the world market price was about 10.2 cents per pound (Pérez-López 1991, 113). With the decline in the sugar harvest in 1993, sugar sales to China are in question.

Cuba is studying the experience of China's free-trade zones and joint ventures, especially in Shanghai. Sino-Cuban joint ventures in light industries on the island are a possibility. China and Cuba have built a bicycle factory and a fan factory jointly in Cuba. Other joint ventures in the sugar industry and in the production of processed foodstuffs have been discussed (Zuikov et al. 1992).

The rapprochement has not only been in economic terms; it has been associated with Cuba's endorsement of China's political model as well. Although Cuba did not justify the massacre of the students in Tiananmen Square in June 1989, the government failed to criticize the action. Cuba's position on the June events was a defensive one: it defended China's rights to act according to its national interest and, at the same time, defended Cuba's own human rights policy. The official Cuban position was that the Tiananmen situation was a domestic affair and that China had the sovereign right to address it in any way it saw necessary, without international meddling. Based on this experience, Cuba and China have claimed that they share similar positions on human rights. The policy has had costs, though. Havana's support of Beijing drew criticism from old friends, especially Latin American leftists (Monsivais 1989, 36).

In spite of the broad spectrum of Sino-Cuban cooperation in place since the mid-1980s, the relationship has encountered constraints that will limit its possibilities in the future. The geographic, lingual, and cultural distance that separates both countries, although not insurmountable, presents obstacles. More serious constraints, however, are of an economic and political nature.

Economic possibilities are limited. China is not the Soviet Union and will not adopt Cuba at an annual cost of billions of dollars. The Chinese have no intention of replacing the Soviets as the benefactor of the Cuban economy. Economic prospects are handicapped by both nations' structural deficiencies as well as by lack of foreign reserves. In the short term, trade will continue to expand slowly. As Cuban foreign reserves dwindle and sugar harvests shrink, imports will be cut and the reserves available will be used for top priority items (oil and food). This will affect trade with China, which was on the upsurge at least though 1990.

An additional constraint will be the United States. Washington might pressure Beijing to curtail favorable, and sensitive, trade with Havana. This could affect not only Chinese loans and subsidies but also any assistance China might extend Cuba in its nuclear projects (which are of particular concern to Washington). Therefore Chinese-Cuban relations might become once again, to some extent, triangular: Sino-U.S.-Cuban relations instead of Sino-Soviet-Cuban. The result would be that bilateral relations would tend to become more difficult to manage.

Relations with Other Countries, Regions, and Organizations

Africa, never a significant economic partner, has lost its political importance to Cuba. The Middle East has experienced a similar decline in Havana's agenda, with the exception of some key countries (Iran and Iraq). Havana is particularly interested in countries that can supply oil or other types of economic assistance (for instance, for the island's nuclear program). Iran has been willing to barter oil for sugar and provide modest assistance to Cuba's nuclear program. Like others, Tehran does not want to jeopardize relations with Washington for the sake of helping Havana. Cuba also successfully courted the Arab countries that participated in the human rights debate in Geneva.

Nowhere is the duality of Cuban foreign policy in the 1990s more evident than in Cuba's posture vis-à-vis Israel. On the one hand, both countries have made overtures to each other in recent months (including signing a tourism agreement), raising the possibility of normalizing relations. On the other, Cuba was one of the few countries that once again voted to uphold a UN resolution equating Zionism with racism.

Several of the organizations in which Cuba displayed its international influence have changed in ways detrimental to the island. The Nonaligned Movement (NAM) is not only divided but searching for its identity in a post-Soviet era. It is a shadow of what it once was, and so is Cuba's role in it. The United Nations, another forum in which Cuba's influence was proportionally larger than what one would expect of a small Third World country, has a new esprit de corps much more conducive to cooperation with the United States (as the Gulf War and the operation in Somalia have evidenced) and therefore less willing to support Cuba's agenda. Cuba, a member of the Security Council at the time of the Gulf War, stood almost alone in opposition to resolutions allowing the United States to orchestrate Operation Desert Storm. In late 1992, however, the General Assembly voted overwhelmingly in favor of Cuba's resolution condemning embargoes.

Meeting the Challenge of Global Change (Part 2): The Politics of Cuban Foreign Policy in the 1990s

The political agenda revolves around three main issues: 1) the U.S. embargo, 2) human rights, and 3) the image of Cuba in the world. Regarding the U.S. embargo, the strategy is to denounce U.S. policy toward the island and garner support for Havana worldwide. According to Minister of Foreign Affairs Alarcón, "For our Foreign Ministry the main thing in 1993 is to continue to fight against the U.S. embargo" (FBIS 1993, 1). Alarcón's replacement, Roberto Robaina, has continued the same course of action. The purpose is to muster international solidarity by condemning the economic pressure of the United States and to avoid the political and economic isolation of Cuba. Another purpose of the campaign is to portray Cuba as the victim of U.S. aggression.

If Cuba is perceived as a victim, other countries will be less likely to side with the United States on issues in which Cuba is under criticism. In this sense, the UN resolution condemning economic aggression represented a victory for the Cuban government. To combat the possibility that international organizations may become arenas in which to judge the island, the Cuban government has spearheaded an effort to democratize institutions such as the United Nations. The underlying principle is that these forums are tools of the big powers and therefore biased, unrepresentative, and illegitimate. The irony underlying Cuba's lobbying effort is that relations with the United States will unleash forces that would destabilize the socialist system. Nevertheless, the end of the embargo would give access to the international credits Cuba needs, if and when the island enters the International Monetary Fund (IMF) and World Bank. Tourism from the United States would also fuel the Cuban economy, as would U.S. investments.

To address the issue of human rights, Cuba has launched a campaign to convince international public opinion that the government does not violate civil liberties and that, on the contrary, it guarantees the economic rights of all Cubans. The effort has been an uphill one, for the island has been severely criticized by the special UN rapporteur assigned to investigate the human rights situation.

The Cuban government, through its foreign affairs ministry (MINREX), has conducted a public relations offensive at home and abroad. The human rights debates in and outside the island have included a discussion of the essence of democracy. Cuban officials have argued that the island's one-party socialist system embodies the most equitable and representative democracy possible. Yet the government has not allowed the UN-appointed human rights rapporteur to visit the country to collect testimony.

The human rights campaign goes hand in hand with the 1992–93 elections on the island. The goal of the human rights offensive is twofold: first, to gain international moral capital by debunking the image of Cuba as a pariah state and, second, to appropriate the language of human rights initially associated with the opponents of the regime in and outside the island. By so doing, the government is attempting to disarm the opposition and the United States.

The new image Cuba wants to create requires not only new (and younger) faces but also a new vocabulary. The regime has appropriated terms in vogue during the early 1990s: democracy, human rights, trade, investment, tourism, common interests. Such language shows that Cuba is in tune with the world and is no longer the revolutionary threat of yesteryear. Nowhere is the new image more graphically portrayed than in tourism publicity, which proclaims that Cuba, an island of sun and fun, can be friend for the traveler and partner for the businessman.

But the image is not all rosy. In practice it has entailed the acceptance that the island is a poor country that needs international capitalism to survive. The portrayal of Cuba as a powerhouse is also a thing of the past. The terms of aid donor-recipient have been reversed: Cuba has become the recipient of aid from other Third World nations since adverse climatic conditions befell the island in 1992 and 1993. Cuba is concentrating its diplomatic energy on international organizations and bilateral relations. The effort is aimed at counteracting the perception that the island is isolated and its political system is anachronistic. Havana's interest in CARICOM is a case in point, as is Cuba's election in 1992 to the UN Economic and Social Council. Proletarian internationalism has been replaced by traditional state-to-state relations and participation in international forums. Fidel Castro's declaration that Cuba would no longer support revolutionary groups abroad is acknowledgment not only of the island's lack of resources but, more significant, of the changes in the world that make the old Cuban policy untenable.

U.S.-Cuban Relations

Redefining U.S.-Cuban relations will be the single most important task for Cuba in the 1990s. It is unlikely to occur in the near future. From the perspective of the White House, the optimum scenario in the short to medium term would be more of the same: deterioration of the political and economic situation on the island without violence and without a direct causal role being played by the United States. Any major development in Cuba could unleash a series of taxing situations for a U.S. president whose agenda is already demanding his full attention.

Transition in Cuba will raise the specter of massive immigration to the United States and the possibility of military intervention in case of a civil war at worst or the prospects of massive foreign aid at best. The incentives to stay the course therefore overpower any interest in altering it. Furthermore, the president's room to maneuver is circumscribed by the lobbying power of the Cuban-American National Foundation (which supports a tough line with regard to Castro's government), the Cuban Democracy Act (which the president supported as a candidate and has implemented through an executive order), and the Democratic Party's attempt to make inroads among Cuban-American voters (who are overwhelmingly Republican). The absence of an alternative constituency demanding a change in U.S.-Cuban relations does not bode well for the prospect of different policy, in spite of international opinion against Washington for pursuing a hard, unilateral line toward Havana.

Cuba is hardly a priority for the Clinton administration. The statutory guidelines to deal with it in the near term have already been set by the Cuban Democracy Act, which the president is executing. He will not alter the course, for a policy of neglect is the wisest option from the president's perspective. The course does not preclude that the State Department and Treasury Department advocate minor changes, especially in terms of allowing humanitarian aid, expanded communication (as postulated in the Cuban Democracy Act), and a regularization of immigration.

The expectations of the Clinton administration regarding Cuba's interest in rapprochement are not high. Juan Escalona, former president of the National Assembly, encapsulated this sentiment: "Cuba does not cherish any hope that Washington's policy toward Cuba will change with the new President. . . . It will not be worse because it is impossible for Clinton to be more aggressive, hardline, and arrogant than former President George Bush" (FBIS 1993, 1). The Cubans acknowledge that the island is not at the top of the Clinton agenda.

Both Washington and Havana have their own reasons for believing the present course should be maintained. As a consequence, one can expect more of the same, in spite of the facts that some U.S. businesses are interested in opportunities in Cuba, that the Cold War ideology has disappeared everywhere else (including in U.S.-Vietnam relations), and that Cuba is no longer a threat to U.S. security interests. The most recent attempt to establish a dialogue between Cuban and U.S. officials, spearheaded by Wayne Smith in December 1992, came to naught, as Havana claimed that it will not accept intermediaries in lieu of direct talks with the U.S. government. Yet negotiations regarding migration have been ongoing, and the Cuban government has continued to pursue a policy of selective engagement with friendly Cuban exile organizations in the United States, opening the door to them in areas such as travel and business.

In the medium to long term, Cuba, regardless of who is in power, must come to terms with the geographical fact that it lives ninety miles from the only superpower in the world. This presents both opportunities and constraints. The key is to maximize the benefits (such as trade and investment) and minimize the costs (in terms of loss of national identity and sovereignty). In turn, Washington should recognize that its policy toward Havana has an impact on elite politics within the Cuban government. The tightening of the embargo seems to strengthen the hard-liners in Cuba by legitimizing, at least superficially, their position that the United States is Cuba's nemesis and that liberalization would result in loss of national sovereignty. The reformists might be given greater space in the Castro government if Washington agreed to reconsider the embargo.

Foreign Policy and Domestic Elites

The new look of Cuban foreign policy fashioned since the late 1980s suggests that the new bureaucracies and individuals with technocratic expertise will become increasingly important in the formulation and conduct of the island's international relations. The Chamber of Commerce is such an institution. Once in the shadows, it has led the effort to attract foreign investors. Several agencies previously influential in foreign policy have lost their old raisons d'être and are searching for new roles within the charted course. Such is the case of the Department of the Americas of the PCC, at one time in charge of coordinating support for anti–status quo groups in the region. The Department is now focusing on strengthening political and economic ties with Caribbean governments. The bureaucracies related to African affairs, military internationalism, and assistance to revolutionary groups are devoid of function.

At the top echelons, old-timers such as Jorge Risquet, at one time in charge of Cuban policy in Africa, have given way to new faces. MINREX has undergone personnel changes, as has the PCC. Since the mid-1980s, MINREX has revamped its China section, increasing the number of people who deal with that country. Career diplomat Ricardo Alarcón, Cuba's long-time ambassador to the United Nations, was named minister of foreign affairs, replacing Isidoro Malmierca, and later appointed to head the National Assembly. The UN post will be filled by Alcibiades Hidalgo, a forty-six-year-old first deputy minister of MINREX and a PCC Central Committee member. The section of MINREX dealing with the United States and the Cuban community in exile also experienced personnel changes in the early 1990s. Outside of MINREX, Carlos Lage has been placed in charge of the foreign investment program. Many of these individuals have proven to be skilled negotiators, perhaps a different brand of diplomat from the old guard. They are also younger than their predecessors and may be more prone to favor reforms.

A new wave of economists and international relations graduates has found niches in different bureaucracies, contributing to the new look in Cuban foreign policy. These changes point to a partial circulation of elites at the secondary and tertiary levels of the bureaucracy and to the new tendency toward pragmatism and technocracy. This is occurring at a time when the reins of the domestic political system remain in the hands of the old guard.

The External Environment and Decision Making

The conflict between pragmatism and ideology in Cuban foreign policy seems to have been overstated. Pragmatism and ideology have meshed since the 1960s. The latest expression of this duet emphasizes economic pragmatism without abandoning fundamental ideological and strategic underpinnings. How do we express change and continuity in Cuban foreign policy under Fidel Castro? The strategic goals of the island's foreign policy have remained basically unchanged since 1959. Since 1989, perpetuating the revolution and its leadership has been the chief objective of the regime's foreign relations. Whenever sustaining the regime has entailed ideological shifts such as aligning with Moscow in the 1960s or attracting foreign capital in the late 1980s, the government has done whatever was necessary.

At first glance this would seem to indicate that the ideological operational code of the leaders is malleable and unfixed.[3] A good way to conceptualize the shift in the ideological tenets of Cuban foreign policy is to picture the operational code as a three-tier pyramid:

While the basis of the pyramid is fixed, the top is more likely to change. The ideological foundations of Cuba's international behavior are Cuban nationalism, history, and culture (including anti–North Americanism). Cuban culture and history establish a tradition, a style, and a polity that influence the form and substance of politics in general and foreign policy specifically. The second tier is Castroism (Fernández 1992). The top tier includes the general principles of Marxism-Leninism, which constitute the official ideology of the state and the "lessons" learned by the leadership during the past thirty-eight years. These lessons are not fixed. They are reevaluated and relearned, and this process results in policy shifts or reversal. In this way, fixed beliefs coexist with pragmatic concerns that change through time. In the late 1980s there was a process of reevaluation that led to the new look of Cuban foreign policy while sustaining the foundations of Cuban tradition and Castroism.

The external environment places constraints on, limits options for, and presents lessons to the decision makers. The change in the "objective conditions" in the international context must be filtered through the policy makers. The adverse international context of the late 1980s and early 1990s and the concomitant domestic crisis convinced many among the primary and secondary circles of policy makers that new policies should be adopted to address the situation. As the economic crisis worsened in 1991 and 1992, economists on the island (among them Pedro Monreal and Julio Carranza) articulated a consensus that a mixed economy was the best option. Even leaders at the top (Aldana, Lage, and Meléndez, among others) supported in words and deeds the notion of an economic opening.

At the same time that these ideas were being articulated around and outside the inner circles of power, the discourse of Fidel Castro gave no indication of support for such a course. On the contrary, the language of *socialismo o muerte* (socialism or death) suggested an orthodoxy that precluded policy flexibility and alternatives. By 1993, however, faced with a continuing economic downturn, increasing social dissatisfaction, and no international lifeline, Fidel Castro indicated that pragmatic policy options that might undermine socialist principles should not be discarded if they could be harnessed to help the regime survive.

Consideration of new policies does not imply the abandonment of the foundation of the regime's foreign policy but an emphasis on the nationalistic, rather than Marxist-Leninist, dimensions that have been the pillars of the operational code of the Cuban leaders. The changes, however, present challenges to the socialist system and give rise to contradictions (which will be discussed below). These challenges and contradictions will slowly whittle away the ideology and praxis of socialism, contributing to the crisis of legitimacy and governability on the island.

Conclusions: International Challenges, Domestic Dynamics

At present, the emphasis on foreign economic policy to solve the island's crisis contributes to the problem the regime faces. The new foreign policy approach will breed additional domestic difficulties for the regime. The dilemma stems from the conception of foreign policy as both shield and opening to the outside world.

Cuba's new foreign policy sets forth contradictions that will continue to produce periodic strain in bilateral and multilateral relations on the one hand and domestic repercussions at the level of the state and the society on the other. The changes within the elite and the state discussed above might result in tension between the old guard and the new and between the ideologues and the technocrats.

Among the other effects of the new foreign policy, its impact on the fabric of society is the most significant. First, tourism and foreign investment will bring to Cuba ideas and goods that do not mesh with rectification or the special period. Governmental control will be increasingly eroded if it is exercised through repression. These byproducts will test the government's legitimacy and its ability to govern.

Second, domestic groups, dissident and nondissident, will continue to establish international and increasingly autonomous or semiautonomous connections. Domestic politics will in this way become internationalized, and the government will be increasingly vulnerable to external pressures. The international lobbying campaign of exile political organizations will contribute to the pressure on Havana.

Third, a process of bureaucratic decentralization of authority will tend to follow the new foreign policy. To respond to dozens of multinational firms, Cuba is decentralizing its foreign policy bureaucracy and setting up private enterprises. This in turn will contribute to the formation of interest groups within the state that will probably have constituencies outside the bureaucratic agencies. This process of decentralization is another way in which pluralism will continue to emerge in the island, although centralization of authority in Fidel Castro will continue (allegedly he oversees each foreign investment proposal). Centralized and decentralized decision making will coexist.

Fourth, the regime will confront bottlenecks in its foreign economic policy because of limits imposed by the domestic economy, including a decline in sugar production and the high import content of the tourist sector.

Fifth, periodic tensions will surface with partners over political issues at a time when the Cuban government is trying to expand economic relations.

The 1990s will be a period of redefinition for Cuba's nation-state. The process has domestic and international dimensions, inextricably tied and mutually influential. The decade will also witness the continued downsizing of Cuba's role and commitments throughout the world. Cuba's thirdworldliness dictates that the island's foreign policy will in the long run look like that of many other small, poor nations. No deus ex machina exists for these nations in the international political and economic system. The heart of the matter is not Cuba's supposed isolation; to perceive Cuba as isolated is misleading. Rather, the central issue is that Cuba is not incorporated into the major political and financial international regimes, which offer some limited opportunities. Isolation is not possible in a world of fax, phones, satellites, radios, videos, televisions, tourism, literacy, and economic interdependence. Ideas continuously penetrate the national territory, challenging the domestic society and pushing elites to synchronize their watches to world time.

Notes

1. All Foreign Broadcast Information Service references are from the *Latin America* serial and will be referred to throughout the text as FBIS only.
2. Most of the following discussion is based on Fernández (1993).
3. The model of decision making is presented in full in Fernández (1992).

References

Anuario estadístico de Cuba (AEC). 1989.
Casanova Montero, Alfonso, and Pedro Monreal. 1989. "Cuba and the United States: The Potential of their Economic Relations." In *U.S.-Cuban Relations in the 1990s*, edited by Jorge I. Domínguez and Rafael Hernández. Boulder, Colo.: Westview Press.
Cuba Report. 1992. 1, no. 3.
Economist Intelligence Unit (EIU). 1991. *Cuba, Dominican Republic, Haiti, Puerto Rico: Country Reports*. London.
———. 1992. *Cuba, Dominican Republic, Haiti, Puerto Rico: Country Reports*. London.
El Nuevo Herald. 1991. October 30, 3.
Fernández, Damián J. 1992. "Opening the Blackest of Black Boxes: Theory and Practice of Decisionmaking in Cuba's Foreign Policy." *Cuban Studies* 22, 53–78.

———. 1993. "Cuba's Relations with China: Economic Pragmatism and Political Fluctuation." In *Cuba's Ties to a Changing World*, edited by Donna Rich Kaplowitz. Boulder, Colo.: Lynne Rienner.
Foreign Broadcast Information Service (FBIS). 1991a. *Latin America*. May 6.
———. 1991b. December 30, 1.
———. 1993. January 22, 1.
García-Gonzalvo, Vicente. 1993. "The Economic Relations between Spain and Cuba in the 1980s." Master's thesis, Graduate Program in International Studies, Florida International University.
Gunn, Gillian. 1990. "Will Castro Fall?" *Foreign Policy*, no. 79: 132–50.
Monsivais, Carlos. 1989. "Cuba: Todos somos ortodoxos." *Proceso* (Mexico), July 24, 36.
Pérez-López, Jorge. 1991. "Swimming against the Tide." *Journal of Interamerican Studies and World Affairs* 33, no. 2: 81–139.
Valdés Paz, Juan. 1992. "Política de Cuba hacia América Latina y el Caribe." *Cuadernos de Nuestra América* 9, no. 18: 96–109.
Zuikov, G., et al. 1992. *Informe sobre la economía de Cuba*. Madrid: Fundación Liberal José Martí.

FOUR

Cuba's Economic Strategy and Alternative Futures

ARCHIBALD R. M. RITTER

Cuba's world has fallen apart. It has become an international orphan, economically and politically, having lost its mentor and supporter, the Soviet Union, as well as most of the family of nations of the Council for Mutual Economic Assistance (CMEA). Adjustment to its new reality will require deep-cutting changes in Cuba's economic institutions, strategies, policies, and structures. Blocking such reforms and modifications in the short term will likely generate even more severe, disruptive, and perhaps traumatic change in the future.

In economic terms, Cuba is facing its worst crisis since Independence. The generous subsidization from the former Soviet Union, which created an illusion of economic prosperity and growth, is gone. Its cessation has led to major declines in the availability of foreign exchange, in the capacity to import, in levels of economic activity and investment, and in real living standards. Maintaining nutritional levels, the quality of social services, and productive employment are among the central economic challenges that Cuba currently faces.

The Fourth Congress of the Cuban Communist Party was notable for its hesitation to reanalyze and reorient the economic system in any significant way. Indeed, the objective of the congress with respect to the economic crisis seemed to be adjustment without change in the basic character of the economic and political systems.

My central objectives in this essay are to describe briefly Cuba's economic strategy in the 1990s and to explore Cuba's alternative economic futures. There is at this time a variety of economic destinations and paths leading toward specific futures. What is the range of possibilities? What are some of the central factors that will influence Cuba's future economic evolution, notably the objectives toward which it aspires and the possible reform policies and strategies it employs? What are the more desirable destinations and appropriate transitional policies and strategies available to Cuba?

Cuba is in a unique historical moment when it must choose among a variety of economic futures—the current approach being unsustainable for any lengthy period of time, as argued below and elsewhere (Ritter 1992). The transitional process will be economically and politically difficult. The interaction of economic reform moves and political changes will undoubtedly be extremely complex. Once the processes of change begin, they may generate their own dynamic and proceed with uncontrollable and unforeseeable velocity and direction.

It is probably impossible to predict where Cuba and its economy are going and how the transition will evolve. This task is especially difficult and doubly speculative because there are no independent political movements, parties, or think tanks in Cuba able to analyze and articulate alternative scenarios, blueprints, or designs for socioeconomic change. Yet avoiding such discourse at present may make the process of transition even more incoherent and chaotic in the future.

The Unsustainability of Cuba's Development Strategy and Economic Organization

So far in the 1990s, Cuba has been traveling along a dead-end street. Its essential economic organization and development strategy cannot be sustained for long, despite major efforts by significant proportions of the Cuban people and small-scale successes in some economic endeavors. In the absence of the old levels of hidden subsidization by the former Soviet Union, the basic deformations in Cuba's institutional architecture will ultimately require major structural transformation. So far, it appears that Cuba's political system and Castro's position are highly resilient in the face of economic adversity. However, as the crisis in the short and medium term deepens and the unsustainability of the current path becomes clear, support for the current economic approach may become fragile and brittle and at some point may change quickly.

The Constellation of Current Crises

The 1990–93 macroeconomic crisis in Cuba has arisen essentially as a result of the elimination of the subsidization of the Cuban economy that was obscured—hidden from many Cubans themselves, including President Castro—in the inflated or above-world prices of Cuba's exports of sugar and nickel, in the subsidized or below-world prices of some of Cuba's imports (most notably petroleum), and in middleman profits accruing to Cuba through the reexport of petroleum to other countries and of sugar to the USSR (Ritter 1990). These hidden aid elements made the value of imports lower and the value of exports higher than they would otherwise have been. Thus the 2-billion-peso trade deficit of 1988, for example, understated Cuba's foreign trade problem. More than this, the USSR provided significant overt development assistance prior to 1989 (see table 4-1). The changes in the Soviet bloc that ended its special trade and aid relationship with Cuba also eliminated both the implicit subsidization and development assistance. Thus, from 1989 to 1991, the value of Cuba's imports from the Soviet Union fell by about 70 percent (Rodríguez 1992), while total imports declined by around 50 percent in the same period (JUCEPLAN 1992, 12). The value of exports has fallen in a similar manner.

Another way of viewing the foreign exchange crisis is to consider Cuba's effective terms of trade. Sufficient information is not yet available to calibrate accurately the commodity terms of trade over the disrupted 1989–92 period. However, the terms of trade between sugar exports and oil imports, often referred to by President Castro (1991, 9), are instructive. From 1984 to 1987, 1 metric ton (MT) of sugar purchased 3.2 MTs of crude petroleum (Comité Estatal de Estadísticas [CEE] 1988, 431, 447). In mid-1992, however, at world prices, 1 MT of sugar would purchase about 1.2 MT of oil; that is, the commodity terms of trade between sugar and oil, or the purchasing power of each ton of sugar, had fallen by 62 percent from the mid-1980s to mid-1992.

It is difficult to know what Cuba's foreign exchange earnings may be after all the changes in trading patterns and prices have worked themselves through. A lack of information since 1989 hinders the attempt to clarify these changes. Some estimates of possible foreign exchange earnings are presented in table 4-2, which sketches a range of possible earnings by commodity groupings on the basis of pessimistic and optimistic assumptions. According to these estimates, total foreign

Table 4-1. Major Cuban Macroeconomic Indicators, 1987–92

	1987	1988	1989	1990	1991	1992
Real GSP Growth (%)	−3.5	2.1	2.0	−1.5	−15 to −24[a]	−6 to −11[a]
Real GSP Growth, per capita (%)	−4.6	1.0	0.9	−2.6	−16 to −25[a]	−7 to −12[a]
Total Exports (million pesos)	5,401	5,671	5,592	5,185	3,910	2,240–2,970
Total Imports (million pesos)	7,612	7,579	8,124	6,745	n.a.	2,270–3,000
Sugar Harvest (million metric tons)	7.47	7.23	8.12	8.43	7.62	6.5[a]
Sugar Exports (million metric tons)	6.70	6.48	6.98	7.17	6.77	5.6[a]
Oil Imports (million metric tons)	13.7	13.0	n.a.	10.1	8.6	4–6
Domestic Oil Production (million metric tons)	.9	.7	.7			
External Debt						
Soviet Debt ($US millions)	n.a.	n.a.	24,500[b]	n.a.	n.a.	120[b]
Hard Currency Debt ($US millions)	5,657	6,450	6,201	7,000	7,000[a]	7,000[a]
Development Assistance						
Non-CMEA ($US millions)	86.6	38.1	30.7	29.0	n.a.	30.[a]
CMEA, Overt	841.0	884.3	1.9	n.a.	0.	0.
CMEA, Hidden	3,187.5	n.a.	n.a.	n.a.	n.a.	0.
Total	4,115.1	n.a.	n.a.	n.a.	n.a.	30.

Sources: EIU, no. 2 (June 8, 1992); Country Report, no. 1 (1991); JUCEPLAN (1992); CIEM 1 (February 1, 1992), 20-31; CIEM 1 (March 3, 1992), 20-22; Toronto Globe and Mail (July 9, 1992), B8; Pichs (1992), 13; and author's estimates.

[a] Estimate.

[b] Russia's estimation of Cuba's debt is $US28 billion. If one uses the ruble-dollar exchange rate of September 1992, however, the real debt would have largely evaporated, leaving about $120 million. The debt for 1989 is converted to dollars using the exchange rate of November 1989.

exchange earnings in 1992 may be in the area of $2.2–3.0 billion, compared to $5.7 billion in 1988.

In the near future, the value of Cuba's imports cannot exceed the value of its exports by any significant amount for the following reasons:

- Cuba's development assistance and credits from the former Soviet Union have disappeared, and credits from other countries have been relatively low, around $27–30 million per annum.

Table 4-2. Cuban Foreign Exchange Earnings by Commodity or Service, 1988—92 ($US millions)

Commodity Group	1988	1989	1990	1991	1992 Pessimistic	1992 Optimistic
Sugar	(7.3m MTs) 4,087	3,914	3,645	2,575	(5.5 MTs; .085$/lb.) 937	(6m MTs; .095$/lb.) 1,257
Minerals and Concentrates	440	485	400	280	250	320
Tobacco and Products	98	85	110	95	95	120
Fishery Products	146	127	125	130	130	150
Fruits and Vegetables	213	179	185	155	150	175
Biotechnological	55	58	100	50	50	150
Other	479	544	345	300	275	350
Tourism [Gross]	153	200	275	325	350	450
[Net (.5 * Gross)]	(77)	(100)	(138)	(163)	(175)	(225)
Total	5,671	5,592	5,185	3,910	2,237	2,972
Total (allowing for imported inputs in Tourism)	(5,594)	(5,492)	(5,048)	(3,748)	(2,062)	(2,747)

Sources: Rodriguez (1992), 8; CEE (1989); U.S. Central Intelligence Agency (1992), 9, for 1990–91 estimates based on trade partners' data; author's estimates for 1992 data and adjustments for tourist earnings, 1988–91.

Note: 1 MT = 2,204.6 lbs.; 1 MT = 7.3 bbl.

- Cuba can no longer run bilateral deficits with the republics of the former Soviet Union, deficits that previously were rolled into the bilateral debt between Cuba and the former Soviet Union.
- Credits from commercial banks, official bilateral sources, and even suppliers may be difficult if not impossible to obtain because of the unilateral moratorium declared by Cuba on its debts with many of the same creditors.
- Cuba is not a member of most of the relevant international institutions that could provide credits or assistance.

As a result, the estimated value of Cuba's imports in 1992 was about 28 to 30 percent of their value in 1988 (see table 4-1).

It will be hard for Cuba to increase the value of its foreign exchange earnings in the near future. Indeed, Cuba will be fortunate if it can maintain the levels estimated for 1992 in table 4-2. The sugar harvest will be difficult to sustain at a level of 7–8 million metric tons per year, with sugar exports of 6.5–7.5 million tons, in the face of fuel shortages; disruptions caused by the switch from tractors to oxen; replacement parts shortages; and the diversion of resources, attention, and energy to food production. It will also be hard to maintain levels of citrus fruit exports in the future in the absence of the guaranteed and protected East European markets and in view of quality problems.

Expected levels of biotechnological exports ($560 million for 1992) are unlikely to be achieved in 1992 or soon afterward. Although biotechnology products are officially considered to be a "miracle export" (see chapter 8), Cuba will likely have continuing difficulties in expanding these exports because of patent problems, because of doubts concerning the thoroughness of testing processes for new drugs, and because of difficulties in establishing a viable international marketing system for only a few product lines. Moreover, Cuba's biotechnology products have high proportions of imported components, so net exports are low vis-à-vis gross exports.

Tourism has been considered as another future miracle sector that could generate large volumes of foreign exchange. In fact, gross earnings from tourism have increased considerably in the last few years. While tourism undoubtedly has major long-term potential in Cuba, it also is problematic for a number of reasons discussed more fully in chapter 7. First, the net earnings from tourism fall short of gross earnings because of a substantial import component (for example, imports of duty-free consumer goods for tourists and capital equipment for the new hotels) and the high leakages to foreign factors of production in joint ventures in tourism (profits expatriated without tax for a ten-year tax holiday period and expatriated managerial salaries). Second, tourism is politically volatile. Even a hint of political instability can lead tour operators and tourists to avoid a given destination, so tourist earnings may dry up overnight, leaving a whole sector of the economy idle and consuming resources rather than generating them. Foreign investors, who are expected to provide the convertible currency inputs and management for the new hotels, are also highly sensitive to political risk and uncertainty. In view of the fundamental uncertainty regarding Cuba's political future, foreign investors require a high degree of audacity—and a very favorable return—to invest in Cuba at this time.

Exports of nickel concentrate may be reasonably strong in the distant future given the magnitude and quality of Cuba's nickel reserves. But nickel prices in 1992 were low and may not increase until a few years of strong demand have reduced inventories. Nickel extraction and concentration are also energy-intensive, and the metal's commercial viability is not clear in a situation of unsubsidized oil import prices. Demand for exports of cigar tobacco and cigars should continue in the near and longer term, but Cuba has lost its protected East European markets for cigarette exports.

Finally, it will continue to be difficult to expand other nontraditional exports because of (1) the uncompetitive and undiversified character of Cuban industry and agriculture, (2) the problems Cuba will face in trying to upgrade its capital stock and quality of entrepreneurship, and (3) the inappropriate exchange rate and structure of prices. In sum, the export picture for Cuba in the near future is not encouraging under most foreseeable circumstances.

The foreign exchange crisis and resulting contraction of imports have generated other crises. First, levels of output have declined sharply (see table 4-1, rows 1–2). From 1989 to 1992, real Global Social Product (GSP) in per capita terms will likely have declined by a total of 24–36 percent, with even larger reductions for the whole of the 1986–93 period. There are numerous reasons for this contraction, many involving the shortage of foreign exchange and trade disruptions. Among these are

- inadequate imported inputs, replacement parts, and fuel to maintain production volumes;

- production disruptions caused by attempts to substitute for imports that can no longer be afforded (notably foodstuffs and fuel); and
- disruptions in trade with Eastern Europe and consequent difficulties in marketing exports and obtaining appropriate imported replacement parts, capital equipment, raw materials, and intermediate goods.

A second impact of the foreign exchange crisis, closely linked to the first, is an energy crisis. With net imports of petroleum accounting for about 93 percent of total petroleum supplies and 67 percent of total primary energy supply in 1990 (Economist Intelligence Unit [EIU] 1991–92, 23), shortfalls in petroleum imports have quickly resulted in severe domestic fuel shortages. Oil imports have been reduced from the customary 13 million MTs in 1989 to about 5.8 million MTs in 1992 (EIU 1992, 19). Imports in 1992 include some 4 million MTs from Russia together with as yet unknown amounts from Iran and perhaps from Mexico and Venezuela, among other countries. The petroleum import deficit has forced cuts in public transportation and the private use of gasoline; reductions in electricity generation; cutbacks in manufacturing output, especially in energy-intensive industries such as cement production; and the well-known substitution of oxen for tractors in the sugar agroindustrial system. Unless petroleum imports can be increased significantly in the next few years and off-oil substitution can proceed as well, the ramifications of a continuing oil deficit will likely worsen.

A third consequence of the foreign exchange crisis is a food and nutrition crisis. Estimates by the Junta Central de Planificación (JUCEPLAN 1992, 9) indicated that imports accounted for 57 percent of the total human consumption of protein in Cuba and 50 percent of the total consumption of calories. The reduction in foreign exchange has thus created a danger that food supplies may be insufficient and/or nutritionally inappropriate for domestic needs. In response, an emergency program to increase the production of fruit and vegetables was undertaken in mid-1990 (see chapter 5). A mobilization of urban dwellers has taken place that is reminiscent of the labor mobilizations of the late 1960s trying to achieve the 10-million-ton sugar harvest target of 1970. So far, some of the reported results of the program appear to be positive, but a clear and complete evaluation of the program cannot yet be made because of the lack of data.

A further result of the foreign exchange crisis is a reduction in new and replacement investment. With imports accounting for 75–80 percent of total machinery and equipment for investment (JUCEPLAN 1992, 9), and with the urgent priority of fuel and food imports in contrast to the postponability of investment, the volume of investment has probably fallen dramatically—although there is yet no statistical corroboration of this.

The reduction of foreign exchange earnings also means that some of the megaprojects that have absorbed huge amounts of foreign exchange and investable resources have been, or will soon be, delayed or even abandoned. Thus the resources sunk into such projects are now temporarily without any economic payoff and in some cases may never have a payoff—that is, the investment may be totally wasted. Completion of the large two-reactor nuclear installation near Cienfuegos has been delayed for lack of hard-currency foreign exchange with which to pay Russia. Other megaprojects of dubious viability would include new nickel processing capacity, a new oil terminal and pipeline to a new oil refinery, and recently completed oil-based electric generating capacity.

Some of the central features of Cuba's policy response to these interrelated crises that either emerged during or were ratified by the Fourth Congress of the Cuban Communist Party have already been noted. The main features of the response so far have been the following.

- A program of import substitution, including the *programa alimentario* (PA), to replace some food imports.
- Energy substitution, replacing petroleum with animal power and human power (bicycles), as well as the reduced output in oil-intensive lines of production.
- A major effort at export promotion, including the development of markets for traditional exports (especially sugar) and the development of new exports. In particular, high hopes have been placed on biotechnology exports and tourism, but expectations for these sectors may be excessive, as noted.
- A greater welcome for direct foreign investment. Indeed, President Castro presented a strong rationale for renewed foreign investment at the Fourth Congress of the Cuban Communist Party (Castro 1991). In view of the extreme political and economic uncertainties gripping Cuba at present, however, any major increase in foreign investment is not likely.
- Some management reforms to increase efficiency and productivity.

- Toleration of a high degree of decentralization, autonomy, and improvisation in the actual functioning of enterprises.

So far there has been virtually no response involving an enhanced role for small private businesses or for the market mechanism. Chapters 5 through 10 in this book discuss the above-mentioned policy initiatives in more detail.

The Medium- and Long-Term Crises

In the longer term, Cuba faces a variety of difficulties, some partly rooted in the foreign exchange problem but most arising mainly from weaknesses in the institutional structure of the economy and from changes in the international system. These difficulties make Cuba's long-range economic development strategy unsustainable, except at a very high cost to the people.

Spare Parts and Capital Stock. Unfortunately, Cuba will confront an intensifying problem in obtaining spare parts and compatible machinery and equipment for replacement of the capital stock. This is because much of the machinery and equipment is of Soviet and East European origin and many of the enterprises that produced such equipment have shut down or are switching to updated product lines.

More serious is the nature of the existing capital stock. Much of the Soviet and East European machinery and equipment is obsolete. It is highly energy intensive, especially oil intensive. Although this was not a problem when oil imports from the former Soviet Union were relatively abundant and cheap, it is obviously problematic now, when the real cost of imported oil is much higher. Soviet capital equipment is also relatively wasteful in its use of other raw materials, and this is another cause for concern.

The existing capital stock from the former Soviet Union and Eastern Europe is also generally environmentally unfriendly, if not patently destructive, in comparison with more contemporary machinery and equipment from the developed market economies that have been designed and redesigned to meet ever tighter environmental specifications. Cuba's stock of buses and trucks is an obvious case in point.

Finally, the capital equipment acquired from the former members of the CMEA is generally uncompetitive in terms of producing goods that are marketable in the international economy relative to the products from the developed market economies and the "newly industrializing countries."

In consequence, Cuba is going to have to replace much of its capital stock in order to make it cost effective, environmentally friendly, energy efficient, and internationally competitive.

Regression to the "Campaign Technique of Plan Implementation." In the 1960s, Cuba's economic managers mobilized human energies through large militaristic campaigns of conscripted, voluntary, and semivoluntary-semiconscripted workers in youth brigades, redeployed urban labor brigades, and the like rather than the regular routinized mobilization through "material incentive" structures. These quasi-military mobilizations, used intensively from 1966 to 1970, were largely dropped after 1970 because they had proven to be wasteful of labor. They also incurred very high opportunity costs, as the other sectors were sacrificed when workers were taken from their normal activities to work in agriculture. Related to this type of labor mobilization is the high degree of centralization of economic decision making that it facilitates.

Resource mobilization through quasi-military campaigns has certain advantages, notably when large-scale and rapid shifts in the use of resources are required. This may have been the case in 1990–92, when food production had to be increased for domestic consumption because of the foreign exchange crisis. While this approach may be useful for a short while, there are some risks and longer-term problems. First, the normal processes of trial and error through small scale and gradualism are leapfrogged, so that massive errors may be made. Second, resource use may be relatively ineffective. Third, the approach has not proved to be sustainable elsewhere or previously in Cuba. The most serious drawback to using the campaign approach at this time is that it enables the Cuban government to postpone "thinking the unthinkable" and implementing market-oriented and private entrepreneur-oriented solutions to economic problems. Further postponing the search for enduring solutions may increase the eventual costs of transition.

Cognitive Dissonance and Economic Architecture. Cubans live in a multitier and multiple ideology economic system. At one level is the tourist economy, which is large and slated to grow rapidly. It is tied closely to the international economy in terms of imports, foreign exchange earnings, and lifestyle or consumption patterns. It is also considerably "capitalistic" in orientation, with a role for private foreign ownership, management, labor legislation, and management style. With the exception of those employed in the sector or providing ancillary public or private, licit or illicit, services, Cubans do not participate in this part of the economy, although most are well aware of its functioning.

The second level of the economy, and the one in which most Cubans live for much of the time, is the "socialist" economy with work norms and salary scales, rationing, controls, public ownership, and bureaucratic control over resource allocation.

The third level of the economy is the private sector, some of which is recognized officially and is legal, some of which appears to be only tolerated, and some of which is quite illegal. The officially recognized private sector in 1988 included in that year some 102,000 private farmers and 41,400 nonfarm entrepreneurs and employees (CEE 1988, 192). In addition there were large numbers of unregistered informal sector microenterprises in such areas as shoemaking and shoe repair; house construction, renovation, and repair; tradesmen's services (carpentry, plumbing, masonry, electrical work); electric and electronic repair; gardening; secretarial services; and auto mechanics. Although hard information on the unofficial economy is sketchy, it appears that large numbers of Cubans—probably the vast majority—participate in it most by purchasing goods or services unavailable in the state sector or the legal private sector, many by buying and selling at a retail level and many by providing goods and services full-time, part-time, or occasionally. It appears that virtually all Cubans find it necessary or desirable to participate in the black market as well.

The coexistence of these three economic tiers generates a problem. The first internationalized and quasi-capitalist tier is rather exclusively for tourists; the second, socialist, level is the legal economy for Cubans; and much of the third tier is in the gray areas of the legal, semilegal, or illegal private market–oriented economy. The main contradiction is that the Cuban people are officially required to remain in the socialist economy while participating surreptitiously in the local, capitalist, small-scale enterprise sector and the black market and while knowing that the legal international market-oriented economy is reserved for foreign tourists. With an expansion of the tourist sector planned, and with greater reliance on the unofficial economy made necessary by the general economic deterioration, the difficulty of containing the capitalistic "contamination" emanating from the marketized sectors will intensify with consequent increase in "cognitive dissonance" experienced by Cubans regarding the nature of their economy. How long and how much further can this continue?

Institutional Architecture in the Longer Term. The institutional structure of the Cuban economy embodies a number of weaknesses that will make it as unsustainable in the longer term in Cuba as it proved to be in Eastern Europe. These weaknesses make the economic system inflexible, resistant to change, and increasingly "sclerotic," unable to adjust to its changed circumstances, to innovate, and to diversify exports in the competitive international system.

One such weakness is the absence of a formalized and legal small- and medium-sized enterprise sector. The bureaucratized allocation of resources and the near absence of markets in the socialist core of the economy are also problematic. There is also a continuous tendency for the bureaucracy to expand. Various types of changes that would occur spontaneously under a market system become difficult bureaucratic issues, if not crises. The command economy structure invites and makes possible a high degree of centralization, if not overcentralization, in economic decision making. President Castro has willingly utilized this potential for centralized control.

Generally speaking, the centrally planned, demarketized system worked well in permitting basic human material needs (nutrition, health care, education, and housing) to be fulfilled quite quickly so that extreme poverty was eliminated and an egalitarian income distribution was achieved early in the 1960s. The problem is that over time, the system has blocked the economic improvement and diversification necessary to maintain and enhance these welfare gains—gains made possible to a large extent by the massive subsidization from the Soviet Union.

General Factors Shaping the Process of Change

A number of factors may combine and interact in various complex ways over time, producing a variety of possible processes and patterns of change for the Cuban economy. The more relevant factors are listed on the vertical axis of table 4-3, below. The factors include some uncontrollable external forces (weather and geological factors), relations with the United States, the nature of the transitions in Eastern Europe, the role of Fidel Castro, the depth of Cuba's economic problems,

Table 4-3. Some Alternative Scenarios for Cuba's Economic Future, 1993–95

	Optimistic		Realistic		Pessimistic
Scenario	Max. Good Luck	Reasonably Fortunate	Probable	Relatively Negative	Max. Bad Luck
Probability	0.1%	21.9%	56%	20%	2%
Determining Factors					
1. Relations with U.S.	U.S.-initiated normalization	Rational reconciliation	Status quo	Worsening	Blockade or hostilities
	U.S pays embargo reparations	Zero net financial transfers			
	Reasonable exile role in economy	Modest exile role in economy	No exile role		
2. Meteorology and Geology					
a. Weather	Excellent	Above average	Average	Below average	Drought and hurricane
b. Petroleum Discoveries	Net oil exports	Greater oil production	Modest success	No discoveries	Exhaustion
3. Global Economy					
a. Int'l. Macroeconomy	Strong recovery	Moderate growth	Limping recovery	Continued slump	Global depression
b. Sugar Prices	> $20/lb.	$13–19/lb.	$9–12/lb.	$7–8/lb.	$5–6/lb.
c. Petroleum Prices	> $30/bbl.	$10–18/bbl.	$18–23/bbl.	$23–30/bbl.	>$30/bbl.
4. East European Transition					
a. Ease of Transition	Quick and smooth	Steady improvement	Gradual recovery	Steady worsening	Reform reversed
b. Market Recovery for Cuban Exports	Good market recovery	Some improvement	Maintenance of mkt. shares	Zero	Zero
5. Institutional Architecture					
a. Role of Market Mechanism	Expansion	Gradual phase-in	Minimal role	Reduced further	"War economy"
b. Private Sector Legalization	To reasonable limits	Gradual expansion	Minimal role	Reduced further	Elimination
c. Castroite Centralization	Immediate and complete phaseout	Gradual phasedown	Status quo	Enhanced role for Castro	Economic commander in chief
6. Internal Economic Policy					
a. Macroeconomic Policy	Money supply control	Improved monetary policy	Suppressed inflation	Worsening	Bad

b. Incentive Structure	Rational material incentives	Improved structure	Material, some immaterial	Disregarded, decomposed	Militarization, conscription
c. Investment Allocation	Economically rational	Improved rationality	Some centralization	Further centralization	Through centralized enthusiasm
7. External Economic Policy					
a. Exchange Rate Policy	Realistic exchange rate	More realistic	Unrealistic overvaluation	Unrealistic	Unrealistic
b. Bureaucratic Organization	Major reform	Some opening	Complete	Complete	Complete
c. Export Promotion	Market-oriented effort	Improving effort	Major bureaucratic effort	Reduced effort	Further reduction
d. Direct Investment Policy	Stronger *apertura*	More *apertura*	Some *apertura*	Some tightening	Closed
e. Debt Renegotiations	Successful	Partial	Moratorium continues	Moratorium	Moratorium
8. Political Dimension	Smooth democratization	Liberalization	One-party system	Official paranoia	Severe repression
Results					
1. Foreign Exchange Balance	Export boom	Easing of constraints	Continuing crisis	Worsened crisis	Meltdown, *opción cero*
2. Macroeconomic Balance	Maintained	Improving	Deterioration	Worsening	Sharp decay
3. Economic Growth	Rapid reactivation	Recovering	Negative	Major declines	Severe contraction, low productivity
4. Equity					
a. Employment	More jobs; productive	Transitional problems	Problematic		
b. Safety Net	Maintained	Maintained	Maintained so far	Threatened	Deteriorating
c. Income Distribution	Problematic	Problematic	Equitable	Equitable poverty	Shared poverty, problematic
5. Economic Sustainability					
a. Firmness of Foundation	Strong, sustainable	Approaching viability	Unsustainable	Unsustainable	Unsustainable
b. Policy Realism	Appropriate	Better	Unsustainable	Unsustainable	Inappropriate, unsustainable
6. Transitional Costs	Minimal	Manageable	Postponed, worsened	Postponed, worsened	Postponed, worsened

and the character of the economic policies that could be adopted and implemented.

The policy of the United States toward Cuba has been and will continue to be influential in shaping the course of events within Cuba. In the past, U.S. hostility toward Cuba leading to the diplomatic break, the embargo, and the Bay of Pigs invasion likely contributed to the radicalization of the regime and to the consolidation of support for Castro. Continued U.S. hostility could sustain support for Castro as the champion of Cuban nationalism and independence and could help maintain the political and economic status quo. The current U.S. policy toward Cuba may also lead to steadily rising costs for the Cuban people as a direct result of the embargo, the opportunities it blocks, and the policy paralysis in Cuba that it helps to perpetuate. A less hostile U.S. approach to Cuba, including terminating the embargo (generally an approach similar to that vis-à-vis the countries of Eastern Europe), would likely stimulate more pragmatic economic policies and, in time, a more liberal political system.

Normalizing political and economic relations would eliminate the anti-U.S. underpinnings of Castro's leadership and invalidate the excuse that the need for war preparedness requires a militarized political system. Economic normalization would stimulate Cuban exports, tourism, and direct foreign investment from the United States; encourage the transfer of technology from the United States; and create a significant role for entrepreneurs in the Cuban community abroad in Cuba's import and export trade and a variety of business ventures. All of these would benefit the Cuban economy and the material well-being of the people. It is very likely that the process of marketization and economic liberalization would be strengthened and accelerated by the imperatives, opportunities, and challenges of renewed economic interaction with the United States.

Will the United States open a door, in political jargon, and let Cuba find a way out, or will it continue to apply a big stick? The latter appears to be the probable U.S. approach for some time to come.

The role of President Castro is obviously central in shaping the course of events in Cuba. Castro has dominated the political scene since 1959. Not only did he lead the guerrilla forces in the 1950s, but also he has been the paramount decision maker ever since. His persona is of historic dimension. He has been successful in defending his vision of revolutionary social change, in maintaining what may be a revolutionary consensus, and in spearheading efforts to make Cuban society more egalitarian. On the other hand, Castro's overpowering central role has resulted in massive and costly mistakes. By the 1990s, it appeared that his role had become intensely conservative. He now seems to be intent on preserving the political and economic status quo. He appears willing to impose what is, in effect, a retreat to the mountains for the Cuban people as a means of dealing with the foreign exchange crisis, while maintaining the political system and economic institutions intact.

Will Castro continue to oppose meaningful movement toward political pluralism and economic liberalization? So far, this appears to be probable. If this continues to be case, then Castro would have to retire or be replaced as *máximo líder* before such change could occur.

The nature and success of the reform process in Eastern Europe, the former Soviet Union, and other countries of Latin America may influence events in Cuba. The transitional processes in the political and economic systems of the countries of Eastern Europe are proving to be particularly difficult. If transitional costs are high in terms of economic contraction, persistent unemployment, impoverishment of vulnerable groups, and worsening social inequalities, then one might expect many Cubans to hesitate to embark on similar changes and to support the institutional and strategic status quo. On the other hand, if the reforms in Eastern Europe prove successful over time, and if there are a number of highly successful cases, then the risks of attempting an economic transition will appear to be lower. How will the Eastern European reforms turn out? It appears that some will be reasonably successful in a relatively short period—the Czech Republic, Hungary, and Poland may be cases in point—while others may be more lengthy and painful and may be reversed, temporarily or permanently. Thus Cuba will likely receive mixed messages from the East European experience, at least in the medium term (1993–98).

The experiences of other Latin American countries may also influence Cuba. The great difficulties the region confronted in the 1980s strengthened Cuba's confidence in the wisdom of its own path. The growing success, however, of countries such as Chile (after 1990) and Costa Rica in achieving social justice, improved economic performance, and political democracy—using what is, in effect, a social democrat philosophy—must be of increasing influence. This approach includes strong economic management with an external and market orientation and with social policies targeted at reducing critical poverty and meeting basic human needs. If the economic and social success and improvement in countries such as Chile and now Mexico and Argentina are sustained, it is likely that the social democracy model will be increasingly attractive for Cubans.

Geological and meteorological factors may affect events in Cuba. For example, major oil discoveries could eventually partly or wholly relieve the foreign exchange crisis. This might either facilitate a transitional process or shore up the status quo. The weather will also be of periodic significance, especially in influencing the sugar harvest and agricultural output generally. Occasionally hurricanes or droughts have sharp impacts on Cuban agriculture.

The global economy could be a major influence, especially through world prices for petroleum imports or sugar, nickel, or other exports. Unfavorable world prices for imports and exports would hurt Cuba, but it is not clear whether they would provoke reform or promote the status quo. Nor are the impacts of highly favorable prices particularly clear.

The depth of the problems of the Cuban economy will likely influence the course of any transition that is undertaken. Severe economic difficulties would likely increase the incentives for change while reducing the capability for undertaking reform. If the economic difficulties are transitory and moderate, the effects would be reversed—that is, the incentive for change would be reduced, but the capability for reform would be increased.

Finally, the design of Cuba's economic policy will be all-important in shaping Cuba's economic future. The relevant policies include those affecting institutional structures as well as both internally and externally oriented policies.

Alternative Economic Futures

There are many and varied possible economic futures for Cuba and many paths toward each possible future. These can be outlined only briefly in a short essay. To examine the possibilities with some logic and coherence, I employ two approaches here. In the first I assemble the various factors that could shape the economic future, array them from worst-case to best-case scenarios, and suggest what the results of the various cases might be. In the second, I sketch a number of archetypal models out of the myriad possibilities.

Optimistic and Pessimistic Scenarios

Cuba's possible economic futures, ranging from the most optimistic to the most pessimistic, are illustrated (with a touch of levity) in table 4-3. Factors that will help shape the economic future are listed vertically in the first column, while their possible characteristics are arrayed along the horizontal axis from best-case to worst-case. The probable results of the various combinations are summarized at the bottom of the table. Each of the possible cases is rated with a probability in percentage terms, these being the author's crude estimates.

The range of possibilities for 1993–95 presented in table 4-3 are not described in detail here but are left for the perusal of the reader. To illustrate the use of the chart, however, it may be useful to examine briefly some of the scenarios.

In the "maximum good luck case," the most optimistic scenario, given a probability of only 0.1 percent, everything goes well if not perfectly. The United States initiates normalization and pays embargo reparations. The exile community plays a positive and reasonable role in rebuilding the Cuban economy. Sugar harvests are excellent, and world sugar prices are high. Cuba discovers large amounts of oil and becomes a net oil exporter, and international petroleum prices are high. The former CMEA countries recover and become a good market for Cuba. Marketization and some privatization proceed smoothly. Internal macroeconomic policies and international economic policies are all well designed. Finally, Cuba makes a smooth transition to multiparty pluralism and liberal democracy. In this case, the socioeconomic results are very favorable: the economy would perform well, with sustainable growth and stability at minimum transitional cost. The results also would be good in terms of equity, with the rapid creation of productive jobs and an ability to maintain the social safety net. However, income disparities would likely increase in this case vis-à-vis the present situation, mainly because allowing the market to determine incomes would favor some individuals or groups over others.

In the "maximum bad luck case," with an estimated probability of 2 percent, everything goes wrong: the embargo intensifies, hurricanes strike, sugar prices fall, no oil is discovered and domestic supplies are exhausted, oil import prices rise, and so forth. The results of this scenario are devastatingly negative. The "probable case," given a 56 percent probability, is essentially a continuation of the status quo with no dramatic policy improvement or worsening, no change in relations with the United States, and so on. The results in this case are on the whole negative and worsening, and the approach is likely to be unsustainable.

Probably Cuba's economic future will be shaped by a complex combination of determinants, some of which have a positive and others a negative effect. In other words, none of the specific five scenarios is probable in its entirety; a mix of elements from all five cases is more likely. But who can foretell which combination will occur?

Some Archetypal Possibilities

From the infinite variety of Cuba's conceivable futures, a number of archetypal models might be distilled. But each such model may occur with great variation, and indeed Cuba will likely evolve through a number of these general types of models.

The first archetypal model is that of the status quo, already mentioned. But the status quo is unlikely to be sustained for long: Cuba will either evolve further toward a command economy or else will be subject to a variety of reform measures that would shift it in the direction of a type of mixed-market system. While this model is unsustainable in the long term, the short term through which it might endure would depend on how long President Castro is willing and able to make it survive.

It appears that the current socioeconomic system may be developing further into a war economy or command economy model. This case, typified by the Cuba of the late 1960s, would be characterized by

- an exceedingly high degree of centralization in economic decision making (with heightened economic powers for President Castro);
- direct bureaucratized and physical control over resource allocation, determination of the output mix, and the distribution of goods and services;
- deemphasis on economic calculus in decision making at all levels of the economy;
- deemphasis on material incentive structures in mobilizing human

energies for the tasks of the economy, and greater emphasis on voluntary, semivoluntary, and conscripted labor.

Movement in this direction is necessitated by the current economic crisis, together with an unwillingness to consider marketization. Thus, to shift resources to food production rapidly, and given the government's refusal to consider permitting small farmers to expand production for private sale through the farmers' markets, urban workers must be mobilized directly through labor brigades and work campaigns, late-1960s style. Similarly, with major contractions of output, it is increasingly necessary to further extend the rationing system. This type of socioeconomic organization is not sustainable for a long period of time for a variety of reasons, including those noted above. A further reason, however, is that the war economy model functions in a situation of continuous crisis in which the atmosphere is one of sustained emergency. While this can continue for a while, eventually the population seems to prefer that the prosaic chores of an economy should become institutionalized, routinized, and made somewhat more tranquil.

A conceivable (but most improbable) archetypal model would be an annexation model, similar to the reunification of West and East Germany. In this case, Cuba would not only adopt a U.S. version of a market economy but would also be swallowed up and incorporated into the United States, either as a fifty-first state or with some sort of semiindependent status. This of course would be a nightmare for Cuban nationalists. In my view, there is virtually no possibility that this scenario will occur; it is incompatible with a century or more of Cuban nationalism and political culture. Cuban annexation would also be indigestible for the United States politically. The economic costs of incorporating Cuba into the United States would be exceedingly high—witness the transitional costs and difficulties that West Germany faces in the incorporation of East Germany. (Though the size disparity between the United States and Cuba might make incorporating the latter easier, the cultural, economic, and political differences would make the annexation option unappealing for the United States.) Moreover, even with severe economic disintegration and decomposition in Cuba, this model probably has little that would recommend it to most Cubans.

A fourth possible model is a mixed-market system, U.S.-style, but with political independence. Virtually all countries are characterized by various mixes of: (1) resource allocation by market or by bureaucratic control, (2) public and private ownership, and (3) general public-policy orientations emphasizing distributional equity on the one hand and efficient resource allocation on the other. The U.S. socioeconomic system has leaned further toward reliance on the market mechanism, private ownership, and a public policy preoccupation with efficiency than most other higher-income countries have done.

Is it likely that Cuba might evolve toward this variant of the mixed-market socioeconomic system? Again, this is conceivable but improbable for the near and medium term. Most Cubans will likely continue to be anxious to maintain the achievements of the revolutionary government in education, health, nutrition, and housing. Large proportions of the population have benefited from easily accessible education and health care, both of reasonable quality. Indeed, for much of the last thirty years Cuba has been a leader in these respects, not only in Latin America but among all developing countries. Despite fairly strict rationing of foodstuffs in the past—and stricter limits at present—Cuba has also achieved good average levels of nutrition. Many Cubans have also obtained improved housing in the last three decades, though this perhaps remains a weak area of basic human-need fulfillment in Cuba since 1959. In any case, Cubans would likely want to safeguard these important measures of distributional equity in the future. A mixed-market economy of the current U.S. variety might jeopardize a number of these gains—especially in health and nutrition—for a significant proportion of the population. On the other hand, it is possible that once the process of change is under way, Cubans might strongly reject the inherited Soviet-type economic model, especially if it evolved further toward a war economy variant. In this case, a radical shift toward a Reaganesque U.S. model could conceivably occur, but in my view it would not endure for long.

Finally, an archetypal model that may be attractive to many Cubans is the social economy of the market or a "mixed-market economy with a human face." This model blends the free market with a planned economy, mixes private and public ownership, and balances a concern for efficiency against equity. It does, however, place less emphasis on the market, private-sector ownership, and efficiency in favor of distributional equity and public-sector involvement in the economy.

With this type of model, Cuba could maintain and improve public health and education and could continue to provide a strong social security safety net. A reasonably large public sector could include natural monopolies, infrastructure, large-scale resource extraction, health, education, and possibly even sugar. However, for the myriad small-scale enterprises that would emerge to provide numerous goods and services, private ownership within the market mechanism (as the means for the social control of economic activity) would be appropriate. A significant proportion of the existing state-sector enterprises in industry, transport, services, and so forth can also be subject to competition within relevant markets and thence could be eventually privatized. (Privatization is a difficult process that has to be implemented cautiously in order to avoid inequities in the process of changing forms of ownership.) The emergence of a dynamic private sector would also require the creation of an income tax system and the establishment of a strong regulatory framework covering areas such as health and safety, environmental protection, consumer protection, and policies guarding against combines (or for maintaining competition). Unshackling private initiative under the market mechanism would reconstruct and sharpen the structure of incentives so that the micro-level allocations of resources would be orchestrated in a socially desirable way.

I estimate that over the long term Cuba will likely evolve toward this type of model. There seems, in fact, to be a general trend in this direction in almost all higher-income countries, in some of the newly industrialized countries, and in some middle-income Latin American countries, as noted earlier. Will Cuba move in this direction? How will it get there? What are the likely problems of a transition?

Transitions

Outside Cuba, there is much discussion, analysis, and speculation concerning future economic social and political changes in Cuba (for example, see Association for the Study of the Cuban Economy [ASCE] 1991, Castañeda 1992, Gunn 1992). But within Cuba, open discussion of significant alternatives appears to be blocked. To my knowledge, no Cuban think tank has produced plans of action for change. No political groups or interest groups inside Cuba have been able to analyze or propound alternative visions for Cuba's future.

As I argued in the previous section, Cuba will likely evolve toward a social economy of the market or a "market economy with a human face." Here I will comment only briefly on the central issues involved in a shift in this direction. (Major projects are currently under way that examine comprehensively and in depth the economic and political aspects of a transition to political pluralism and a market economy [Cuban Research Institute 1992, for example].)

First, the transition to a mixed-market economy is immensely difficult, more difficult than almost anyone imagined before the changes that began in Eastern Europe in 1988. Once change begins, there is a significant risk that the old institutions of centralized planning could break down and lose their resource-allocative capability before new market mechanisms are able to function effectively, so the economy may be without a working allocative system. (This seemed to be the case to some extent in the former Soviet Union in 1992.) The economic costs of this type of breakdown are very high. Careful strategic planning is essential to try to minimize the costs of disruption. Without such planning, unforeseen crises could unleash uncontrollable forces that could quickly destroy the central planning system before an alternative market system can begin to function.

Second, shifting toward a mixed-market economy is a complex task. As is discussed in more detail in chapter 11, in Eastern European countries it has involved the following components, among others:

- liberalization of prices;
- allowing enterprises to be established and to function;
- establishing a regulatory framework within which enterprises could function;
- processes of privatization of some state enterprises;
- macroeconomic stabilization policies in circumstances of release of inflationary pressures long suppressed by price controls;
- taxation reform, especially the establishment of personal and corporate income taxes;
- opening the economy to international trade, that is, abolishing the bureaucratic controls on imports, putting competitive pressure on domestic enterprises—which often had national monopoly power—for the first time;
- income policies to contain inflationary wage demands;
- reform of the financial system, and interest rate liberalization; and
- modifying foreign investment policy and policies affecting international financial flows.

All of these policy changes—each entailing large and contentious political issues in most countries—are a major challenge to new, insecure, and fragile governments facing strong internal opposition, economic contraction, rising unemployment, and intense inflationary pressures, all during a severe international recession. This is a good deal more complicated than reestablishing private farmers' markets or legalizing small businesses, useful as these might be as first steps in a Cuban reform process.

Third, what would be the more appropriate sequence of reform measures? Would a Czech-style big-bang approach, in which all of the above types of policy reforms are undertaken simultaneously, be more appropriate than a gradualist, sequential approach? It appears that the former might become necessary if the old system were to collapse quickly, or if extreme inflationary pressures were unleashed in a process of price decontrol (in a situation of huge monetary overhang). Then strong measures, perhaps of big-bang dimensions, might be necessary. Because policy reform will be necessary in so many areas, however, probably a phased-in sequence of reforms would be more appropriate. A variety of possible sequences might be desirable, depending on the particular circumstances of the time. A detailed analysis and sequence of policy changes cannot be presented here because of space limitations. (Castañeda [1992] presents a general reform proposal and a specific reform sequence.)

Conclusions

Cuba's current development strategy and economic organization are essentially unsustainable after the elimination of the high levels of implicit as well as overt subsidization from the former Soviet Union. Ultimately, Cuba has no alternative but to embark on a process of economic reform in the direction of marketization and economic liberalization if it is to maintain and improve the material foundation for the economic and social well-being of the Cuban people.

How Cuba's economic future will eventually unfold depends on a variety of factors. These include U.S. policy, the role of President Castro, the nature of the processes of economic change elsewhere in the world (notably in Latin America, Eastern Europe, and the former Soviet Union), and the severity of the problems faced by Cuba, as well as other factors.

The archetypal model for the future of broadest appeal to Cubans is likely to be a social market economy, that is, a mixed-market economy that emphasizes distributional equity. This model would permit the continuation of social achievements and would also stimulate the efficiency advantages made possible by the orchestration of economic activity by the market mechanism.

It is of fundamental importance that analysts in some of the major think tanks within Cuba should explore and evaluate alternative transitional paths and policy reform sequences and the design of specific policy areas. Without such analyses, the policy changes will undoubtedly be less thoughtful, more chaotic, and more costly to the Cuban people than they need to be.

References

Association for the Study of the Cuban Economy (ASCE). 1991. *Cuba in Transition*. Miami, Florida.
Benjamin, M. 1990. "Things Fall Apart" and "Soul Searching." *NACLA Report on the Americas* 24 (August).
Business International. 1992. *Developing Business Strategies for Cuba*. March.
Castañeda, Rolando H. 1991. "Cuba: Una opción por la libertad, el desarrollo y la paz social." In ASCE, *Cuba in Transition*, 257–308.
———. 1992. "Cuba: Hacia el crecimiento sustentable con libertad y equidad social." Unpublished manuscript.
Castro, Fidel. 1991. "Speech at the Opening Session of the Fourth Congress of the Communist Party of Cuba." In Foreign Broadcast Information Service, *Latin America: Supplement*. Washington, D.C., October 14.
———. 1992. "Discurso pronunciado en el acto por el XXXIX aniversario del asalto al Cuartel Moncada." *Granma*, September 8.
Centro de Investigaciones sobre la Economía Mundial (CIEM). 1992. *Boletín de Información sobre Economía Cubana* 1 (January-April).
Comité Estatal de Estadísticas (CEE). 1988. *Anuario estadístico de Cuba 1988*. Havana.
"Cuban Economy Still Running on Sugar." 1992. *Toronto Globe and Mail*, September 7.
Cuban Research Institute. 1992. *Cuba in Transition: A Proposal*. Miami: Florida International University.
Economist Intelligence Unit (EIU). 1991–1992. *Cuba: Country Reports*. London.
———. 1992. *Cuba: Country Profile, 1991–1992*. London.

Gunn, G. 1992. "Cuba's Search for New Alternatives." *Current History* (February).
Junta Central de Planificación (JUCEPLAN). 1992. *Situación Actual de la Economía Cubana*. Havana: Instituto de Investigaciones Económicas, March.
León, Francisco. 1991. "Cuba: Procesos y dilemas." *Revista Cono Sur* (December).
López Segrera, Francisco. 1991. "Cuba en los 90: Alternativas y escenarios." Unpublished manuscript.
Mesa-Lago, Carmelo. 1992. "Is There Life After the U.S.S.R.?" *Hemisfile* 3, no. 1.
"Ottawa Fights U.S. Ban on Trade with Cuba." 1992. *Toronto Globe and Mail*, September 25.
Pérez-López, J. F. 1991a. "Bringing the Cuban Economy into Focus: Conceptual and Empirical Challenges." *Latin American Research Review* 26, no. 3.
———. 1991b. "Swimming against the Tide: Implications for Cuba of Soviet and East European Reforms in Foreign Economic Relations." *Journal of Interamerican Studies and World Affairs* 33 (Summer): 2.
Pichs, Ramón. 1992. "Problemas y opciones del sector energético en Cuba." In CIEM, *Boletín de Información sobre Economía Cubana* (May).
Ritter, A. R. M. 1990. "The Cuban Economy in the 1990s: External Challenges and Policy Imperatives." *Journal of Interamerican Studies and World Affairs* 32 (Fall).
———. 1992. "Cuba in the 1990s: Economic Reorientation and International Reintegration." In *Cuba in Transition: Crisis and Transformation*, edited by S. Halebsky and J. Kirk. Boulder, Colo.: Westview Press.
Rodríguez, J. L. 1990. "El proceso de rectificación y la economía cubana en 1990." Unpublished manuscript.
———. 1992. "La economía cubana ante la cambiante coyuntura internacional." In CIEM, *Boletín de Información sobre Economía Cubana* (January).
U.S. Central Intelligence Agency. 1992. *Cuba: Handbook of Trade Statistics*. Washington, D.C.

FIVE

Reflections on Economic Policy
Cuba's Food Program

Sergio G. Roca

When the Cuban Communist Party held its Fourth Congress in October 1991, the resolution on economic issues admitted to "the complexity of the challenges that we face and the adverse international conditions in which we are forced to act" (Partido Comunista 1991). Indeed, the document identified the prevailing international economic scenario as "the most unfavorable ever confronted by the Cuban economy in the entire history of the Revolution." Among the policy measures proposed by the Cuban leadership to address such dire conditions, the food program (*programa alimentario* or PA) was at the top of the list. There is widespread agreement about the importance of the PA. Carlos Lage (1992a), a Politburo member, stated in November 1992 that "the food program is the fundamental priority because the basic objective of the Party and the Government during the Special Period is to guarantee food to the population at present levels." At about the same time, Gillian Gunn (1992) concluded, "The food program is the most important element of the short-term strategy [designed] . . . to maintain political stability."

The main objective of the PA is "to secure in the shortest possible time an increase in the output of a group of basic foodstuffs for the benefit of the Cuban population" (Cardet Hernando 1991). Although it would be possible to analyze the policies, targets, and outcomes of the PA in straightforward fashion, such an approach would likely generate a narrow and boring piece. Instead, I will examine the PA in this chapter from the broad perspective of past and future Cuban economic policy: what impact the long trajectory of revolutionary economic policies has had on the PA and what, if any, influence the PA may have upon future policy developments.

The central theme of this chapter is the analysis of the PA as a reflection of the past economic practices of Cuban socialism and as a projection, albeit incipient, of an economic model that the rules of the new world economic order impose on the Cuban regime. The main argument is that the PA contains several policy elements that have remained fairly constant, with greater or lesser emphasis depending upon the different stages of economic policy making, since the start of the Revolution.[1] It is also possible, however, to surmise in the PA several attempts to implement economic policies that could be projected to lead the Cuban economy toward structural adjustment and insertion into the world economy, objectives largely accepted as unavoidable, given the collapse of the socialist community and Cuba's open economy.

After this introductory section, I proceed in the chapter to (1) discuss the origins and outline of the PA; (2) examine the PA as a reflection of the Cuban revolutionary experience, including a brief assessment of production results; (3) present evidence about the isolated use of market-type policies in the PA; and (4) summarize the major points and conclude with some comments about what lies ahead for Cuban economic policy.

Origins and Outline of the PA

The start of the PA is linked with the decision to implement the rectification process and specifically with the elimination of the free peasant markets (*mercado libre campesino*, MLC) in mid-1986. In other words, the PA is part and parcel of the reinstitution of economic centralization and the return to the mobilization model.[2]

My own tentative hypothesis, still untested, is that both the rectification process and the PA were largely a reaction to the Cuban-Soviet long-term trade pact of October 1984. The treaty identified Cuba as the supplier of sugar, nickel, and citrus within the Council for Mutual Economic Assistance (CMEA), limited industrial exports to a single item (agricultural machinery), intensified Cuba's dependency on food imports, and imposed more severe terms and conditions in economic relations with the island. The genesis of the rectification process and the PA may be traced to a meeting of the Politburo in November 1984, which also authorized the formation of the Central State Group that neutralized the Central Planning Board (Junta Central de Planificación, JUCEPLAN) and led to the dismissal of its president, Humberto Pérez, and other technocrats in summer 1985.

Be that as it may, it is clear that the PA is a creature of the mid-1980s. According to Luis A. Cardet (1991), a prominent economic official, some time after 1984 "decisions were quickly made to take prompt action on the most significant sectors which now integrate the Food Program." Until early 1992, Cardet was an economic advisor to the Council of Ministers and president of the National Association of Cuban Economists. Additional evidence on the start of the PA comes from minister of agriculture Adolfo Díaz (1990). Speaking before Cuba's legislative body, he stated that the PA "was conceived four years ago" and that "since the rectification process this program has received maximum priority." To Castro (1992a), the PA was the Cuban state's answer to the challenge to produce more at lower cost than the MLC: "The free peasant markets were suspended. When that happened the food programs also started. If it was a question of producing bananas, tubers, vegetables and fruits, let the state do it since it has all the necessary resources. Thus it can be said that the full-scale food program started that way."

In sum, after some preparatory studies in 1985, the PA planning process shifted into high gear in May 1986, with preliminary output targets announced by Castro in Camagüey in spring 1987. The PA's production plans were implemented in 1988, and the first reports of results were spread over three pages of *Granma* on September 25, 1989. The key point to be stressed here is that the PA was not provoked by and is not connected to the "special period in time of peace," which started in mid-1990. Indeed, Castro (1992a) himself stated that the special period "came to interrupt the momentum displayed by the [food] programs." The PA is a reflection of the shift toward radicalization under the rectification process that began in early 1986.

According to Minister of Agriculture Adolfo Díaz, the main objective of the PA (Asamblea Nacional del Poder Popular [ANPP] 1990, 2–6) is "to sustain and to expand, on firmer bases, a food system which

Table 5-1. Cuban Annual Per Capita Food Consumption, 1982–89 (kilograms)

Items	1982	1983	1984	1985	1986	1987	1988	1989
Cereals	106.5	108.7	112.0	109.9	112.31	109.2	110.0	108.0
Meat	39.3	40.8	41.7	43.1	42.9	41.6	41.5	41.6
Milk & Dairy	152.9	150.7	153.3	151.3	151.1	146.6	149.4	144.7
Eggs	226.3	245.9	250.0	242.0	244.0	236.0	230.0	230.0
Fish	17.9	18.6	18.0	19.5	19.9	19.2	18.7	18.2
Fats	17.9	17.4	17.4	17.8	17.6	17.5	16.9	16.7
Tubers	72.8	76.4	79.6	77.0	79.5	72.6	73.1	66.4
Vegetables	59.2	53.0	55.4	57.5	57.3	58.2	62.2	58.6
Sugar	54.7	54.4	54.8	53.1	52.8	51.6	51.8	51.3
Beans	11.0	11.5	11.9	12.0	11.8	11.0	11.4	12.3
Fruits	62.4	62.7	56.9	62.7	59.5	65.2	71.2	55.8

Source: Pérez Marín and Muñoz Baños (1991).

has made it possible for every Cuban citizen" to achieve in 1989 the consumption levels reflected in table 5-1. In his speech, Díaz cited only the data for 1989. As table 5-1 indicates, consumption levels in 1984–86 were higher except for vegetables and beans. The PA was also designed to achieve (1) a sustained increase in agricultural yields and in the efficiency of material and human resources allocated to the food sector, (2) a reduction of food imports and an increase in domestic food-production capacity, and (3) a significant saving of hard-currency expenditures for food items and related inputs.

In December 1990, output targets for 1993–95 were announced for tubers, vegetables, rice, milk, beef, fish, eggs and fruits (see table 5-2). At other times, production goals have been set for poultry, pork, and other items. At the Fourth Communist Party Congress, the PA segment of the economic resolution concentrated mostly on how to achieve such targets and goals, with "the maximum use of scientific and technological advancements" serving as the warrantor of success. This topic is discussed further below.

The PA as a Reflection of the Past

The PA is an accurate summary of the Cuban socialist economic model in that it compresses into a single economic initiative three decades of blunders in economic strategy and practice. It is a microcosm of the errors committed and the dead-end streets encountered by the Cuban

Table 5-2. Cuban Food Production, 1980–92, and Food Program Targets, 1993–95

Items	1980	1985	1986	1987	1988	1989	1991	1992[h]	Targets[a] 1993–95
Tubers	737	680	675	632	653	681	568	750	1,030
Vegetables	466	594	551	550	675	610	453	536	910
Rice	478	524	570	466	489	536	397	449	610[b]
Milk[c]	899	929	926	940	919	924	—	—	1.98[bd]
Beef[c]	293	299	302	290	292	289	—	—	470
Fish	186	220	245	215	232	192	—	—	222[e]
Eggs[cf]	2.37	2.52	2.52	2.50	2.46	2.52	—	—	3.25
All Fruits	790	1,181	1,130	1,275	1,463	—	—	—	900[g]

Sources: Production: AEC (1988), 316, 333; Ministerio de Agricultura (1992); and same as table 5-1. Targets: *Granma* (1990b), 2.

[a] Total output, in thousands of metric tons, of both state and private sectors, unless otherwise noted.
[b] Total import substitution.
[c] State sector only.
[d] Millions of liters. Roughly equivalent to 2 million tons.
[e] Includes 60,000 tons of freshwater catch.
[f] Million units.
[g] Excludes citrus exports (which amounted to 535,000 tons in 1988).
[h] Official forecast as of May 6, 1992.

revolutionaries. Several examples drawn from the Cuban experience will illustrate the reflective quality of the PA. Alternatively, it is also possible to undertake this analysis from a systemic perspective and with a theoretical focus, as exemplified in the recent work of Janos Kornai (1992). In this case, however, it is the Cuban praxis that will be examined.

Standard Features of CPEs

In many ways, the PA exhibits the usual elements of centrally planned economies. First, production and consumption goals have been set largely in physical terms. For instance, 13,600 *caballerías* (about 183,000 hectares) were to be planted in rice; 2 million liters of milk were to be produced; and 15 million *quintales* (68,000 tons) of vegetables, tubers, and fruits were to be distributed to consumers in the city of Havana.[3] Because of the use of physical targets in Cuba, costs, profitability, and other efficiency indicators were frequently neglected.

Second, the PA has a very high ideological and political quotient. Production successes will demonstrate the superiority of socialist property, and central planning and labor mobilizations will develop *conciencia* among the younger generations. In February 1991, with reference to mobilized workers, Castro (1991a) said, "We are looking not only at the productive aspect but also at the political content, that people participate and internalize this program . . . [so that] it may have a revolutionary outcome." Later that year, Julián Rizo (1991), a Politburo member, stated, "Without taking into account ideological and political factors and moral motivations, our new agricultural-livestock strategy could not advance. At its core, the food program is essentially a political program."

Third, the PA has established ambitious production targets and implemented taut planning with tight deadlines. Despite the clear stagnation since 1985 in the production of all agricultural products (except vegetables), the PA's output targets for 1993–95 tend to be heroic, with fulfillment requiring production increases of 25, 40, and even 100 percent in 3 to 5 years (see table 5-2).

The data on state sales of tubers, vegetables, and rice for 1990 shown in table 5-3, and the 1992 production forecast shown in table 5-2, corroborate the challenge that the posted targets represent. From 1990 levels, milk output was scheduled to double in six or seven years. Cuba's livestock herd, however, was diminished by 30 percent in the period 1967–87, and Castro admitted that the entire sector needed "a colossal shake-up" to improve its efficiency. Among the capital equipment needed by the forty recently created rice production brigades were 880 ground levelers and 300 bulldozers. In its record year, however, Cuba's mechanical industry turned out only 380 graders and 4 bulldozers. Finally, while in September 1990 Castro announced an annual production target of 15 million *quintales* of vegetables and tubers for Havana province in 1992–93, the production record stood at 9.5 million in 1988 with only 6 million harvested in 1989 (*Granma* 1990a). Total production for 1992 was projected to be 11.4 million.

Castro's Meddling

The PA shows quite clearly the marks of the Cuban president in both its strategic design and its operational detail. While involvement at the macropolicy level is appropriate for the top political leadership, micromanagement usually produces detrimental results. In the PA, the Cuban president has involved himself with trivial details and peripheral matters. He has also rendered decisions on complex scientific and technical matters requiring expertise beyond his competence. There is a strong precedent for this modus operandi in the Cuban practice of the 1960s, ranging from Castro's "special plans" and cattle-breeding techniques to the monumental 10-million-ton sugar plan in 1970.

Castro's early and continued involvement with the design of the PA can be easily established. According to Adolfo Díaz, in the official review of the program at the National Assembly of People's Power in December 1990, the PA was "a task undertaken by the Revolution under the direction and personal attention of our *comandante en jefe*" (ANPP 1990, 2–7). Díaz added that "from the start, this project was conceived, directed and executed personally by our *comandante en jefe* in charge of each one of the programs. . . . In September 1988, comrade Fidel assumed personal control of the Executive Committee of the Council of Ministers, supervising and pushing forward the food program, exercising weekly control over its implementation."

In addition, several examples of operational meddling come to mind. The case of the Havana province vegetables and tubers program serves to illustrate the shortcomings of micromanagement. According to Castro's own story, in 1990 he asked agricultural workers to engage in special late plantings of some crops, even though "the workers knew that the harvest would be lost" (Castro 1991b). Throughout the summer, weeds grew "taller than a man," a labor shortage "dramatically ensued," and, in the end, production declined (see table 5-3). The problem of shortages of agricultural workers has confronted Cuban policy makers since the early 1960s, however, and thus should not have surprised PA planners.[4] In September, in the aftermath of the debacle, Castro designed the Havana self-sufficiency program based on labor mobilizations, with the highest governmental body in charge of "the elaboration of plans, planting schedules, and the setting of production goals for state farms, cooperatives and private farmers."

More specifically, and with greater potential for harmful consequences, Castro's penchant for detailed involvement in decisions pertaining to scientific subjects and technological processes appears to extend to the PA. In mid-1991, while visiting a laboratory where work was in progress on an experimental azotobacter-based fertilizer, Castro was informed by the scientists that 100,000 liters of the product would

Table 5-3. Cuba's Food Sector: State Sales, 1980–90, and
Food Program Targets, 1993–95 (thousands of metric tons)

Items	State Sales[a]					Targets
	1980	1985	1988	1989	1990[d]	1993–95
Tubers	606	594	546	557	456	1,030
Vegetables	419	572	651	580	446	910
Rice	434	498	472	510	365	610[b]
All Fruits	770	1,172	1,435	1,201	1,705	900[c]

Sources: Production: AEC (1988), 319; BEC (1990), 81–82. Targets: Granma (1990b), 2.
[a] Sales by state farms, cooperatives and small private farms to state enterprises, acopio and consumers. Excludes rural self-consumption.
[b] Total import substitution.
[c] Excludes citrus exports (535,000 tons in 1988).
[d] Estimated total 1990 state sales based on the ratio of first-half results for 1989.

be produced by year's end, but he found that unacceptable. Within 72 hours the Cuban leader had arranged for 1 million liters of azotobacter to be produced in the same time frame (Granma 1992a). It was reported that azotobacter fertilizer production reached that level in 1991, with an output spurt in June-December. One is left to speculate about opportunity costs, however, since the fertilizer was produced in the fermentation equipment of the Ministries of Sugar and Food Production and in the Santa Cruz rum factory (Granma 1992b).

Among the PA engineering projects and technical innovations sponsored or patronized by Castro are microjet irrigation systems (aerial and drip), a field drainage method for sugarcane plantations, a leveling technique for rice cultivation, Voisin's rational grazing system, sheep raising in special soils with zeolite mixture, a national irrigation system with massive locks and canals, animal feeds based on sugar byproducts, and others. There is little if any evidence that these projects and techniques were adequately evaluated using economic and technical criteria prior to implementation.

Consider, for example, the case of the sugarcane field drainage method (*drenaje parcelario*). While Cuban experts agreed, on the basis of test results reported as early as 1986, that the system impacted positively on sugarcane yields, there was no methodology in place for its economic evaluation even as late as 1991 (Zumaquero Posada et al. 1991). Indeed, it may be argued that the authors were first and foremost recommending that an economic evaluation should be undertaken, as if they feared that none had been completed or would be scheduled. They concluded, "The extensive investment involved in the application of field drainage requires that, as with any other capital-improvement measure, an economic evaluation be conducted." (Zumaquero Posada et al. 1991, 141). The field drainage program was suspended in mid-1992 for lack of fuel.

The basic problem is that too often Castro has emphasized the use of science and the application of technology for their own sake in the economy, with technical proficiency prevailing over economic efficiency. In September 1990, Castro (1990) declared, "The food program is the application of science and technology to agriculture to increase productivity per worker and per hectare." Again, in fall 1991, he insisted that the PA was primarily based "on the maximum introduction of scientific and technical achievements." In early 1992, an anthology of roughly 400 of Castro's "concepts and reflections" about the "decisive role" of science and technology on social and economic development was published, meriting a prize from the Cuban Academy of Sciences (Castro 1992b). According to the review in *Granma* (1992c), "Without any doubt, it will be required reading whenever the subject of scientific development in Cuba is broached." A previous volume covered the years 1959–89.

The correlation between technological improvements and productivity gains in Cuban agriculture has not always been positive, however. Over several decades now, the performance of cooperative and private farms (as measured by crop yields, planting losses, and the like) has exceeded that of state-owned agricultural units, despite the latter's superior resource base (tractors, fertilizers, and other state-supplied inputs). In 1989, a high-powered research group investigating sugar mills in Havana province concluded that high sugarcane costs indicate that technical results (that is, highest agricultural yields in the country) "are achieved at the expense of the profitability of the mills; that is, investments and expenditures on irrigation, fertilization, agricultural equipment and so on, have not generated a commensurate production response" (Morales Pita et al. 1989).

More recently, Oscar Trinchet (1990), a Cuban agricultural economist, undertook a comparative analysis of crop yields and resource use involving several countries from 1970 to 1985. His findings were quite devastating for the socialist island. Trinchet concluded that Cuba showed an excessive use of tractors, fertilizers, and irrigation compared to the other countries but reported significantly lower yields in tomatoes, rice, coffee, and sugarcane, with only potato yields being above average.

Distortions of Socialist Trade

The PA also quite clearly reflects several detrimental aspects of the legacy of economic relations with the former Soviet Union and other socialist countries. For thirty years, socialist markets, subsidies, credits, and technical assistance provided significant benefits to Cuba. These advantages, however, concurrently introduced severe misalignments in the Cuban economy, with distortions affecting strategic production patterns as well as resource allocation and consumption decisions. After the socialist debacle, these dormant distortions have been transformed into major economic bottlenecks threatening the regime's survival.

For one thing, there has been an excessive concentration in sugar and citrus to the detriment of domestic food production. Table 5-2 shows that, except for vegetables, the output of every other basic item in the Cuban diet decreased from 1985 to 1988. Indeed, for those products for which data are available, 1989 output is barely above 1980 levels. Table 5-3, which records state sales rather than total production, shows a more mixed but still negative picture. As already indicated, annual per capita food consumption in Cuba remained basically stagnant in the decade of the 1980s (see table 5-1) Nevertheless, in May 1988 Castro was still proclaiming the need to produce 10 million tons of sugar, and a large increment in the output of citrus fruits is a key target of the PA (ANPP 1990, 89–90).

There is some evidence that Cuban officials are aware of the opportunity costs involved in the sugar-citrus strategy. In December 1990, Castro himself admitted that the livestock sector "suffered a great deal" when the best lands were converted to sugar, rice, and citrus production, while the "worst lands in Havana province were assigned to dairy farms" (ANPP 1990, 82). In partial redress, since 1987 about 5,000 *caballerías* (67,000 hectares) of sugarcane lands have been allocated to the cultivation of tubers and vegetables, representing an increase of over 30 percent in their total area.

In an interesting essay on Cuban agriculture and diet, Pérez Marín and Muñoz Baños (1991, 13) conclude, "If within the so-called socialist international division of labor Cuba was assigned the role of sugar producer . . . today this situation must be re-evaluated; the same is

Table 5-4. Selected Cuban Imports, 1958–89 (millions of pesos)

Items	1958	1970	1980	1985	1989
Poultry	a	n.a.	20.7	27.7	44.5
Canned Meat	a	n.a.	40.0	78.3	69.0
Milk and Dairy	2.7	37.5	67.8	84.7	83.9
Cereals[b]	64.9	103.2	378.6	445.5	384.1
Fish	7.3	13.3	27.0	53.8	42.8
Animal Feeds	3.1	13.7	67.2	48.8	122.0
Edible Oils/Fats	5.7	20.6	57.4	81.6	78.3
Fertilizers	6.1	44.5	81.4	136.0	157.7
Herbicides/Pesticides	2.1	23.9	60.4	64.5	80.8

Source: AEC (1989), table 11-10.
[a] Under 1 million pesos.
[b] Mostly corn, rice, and wheat.

true of citrus production. This fact, together with domestic factors, created a certain dependency upon the international market for the food consumption of the population of a basically agricultural country." More recently, Gerardo González (1992), a researcher at the Centro de Estudios sobre América, presented a conference paper in which he attempted to explain some of the factors "which have perturbed the efficient course of the economy." His list included "the undesirable results of the relations with the countries of Eastern Europe which fostered an attitude of excessive trust and accommodation based on the conviction that such a market satisfied most of our needs and, in turn, was not too demanding of the quality and volume of our production and exports."

From the perspective of resource allocation, another dormant distortion affecting the PA is related to price subsidies formerly extended to key imported commodities. The availability of cheap foreign oil gave rise to an overmechanized and overfertilized agriculture, while extensive imported supplies of low-priced cereals and grains resulted in excessive consumption of such by humans and animals (see table 5-4). That is, irrational Soviet prices (below world market levels) produced misallocations in both factor and product markets in the island.

For instance, Pérez Marín and Muñoz Baños (1991, 8) concluded that "the dependency on external sources of energy and modern techniques/technologies (either domestic or imported), based on fertilizers, chemicals, cereals, herbicides . . . constitute an impediment to agricultural development under the current conditions of the oil crisis and the effects of the foreign debt." Oscar Trinchet's findings about the large number of tractors in Cuban agriculture were reported above. In November 1991, about 12 percent of the operational stock of agricultural tractors was idle because of a lack of fuel, and 100,000 oxen had been trained for duty in animal traction. By early 1992, several projects of the PA were either suspended or curtailed; these included sugarcane drainage, rice planting, and irrigation dams. Castro (1992a) put it this way: "Really, the limitations of fuel supplies have curtailed some of the elements of the program." Why were such obvious limitations not anticipated in 1990 at the start of the socialist debacle?

From trivial levels in the early 1960s, Cuban imports of animal feeds reached 1.6 million metric tons in 1989 (400,000 tons of cereals and 1.2 million tons of soybeans), with over $120 million spent on cereals imports alone. Soybean fodder imports, on a per capita basis, tripled from 1975 to 1985. As a consequence, Cuba's animal fodder mixtures came to be largely elaborated with imported ingredients: 100 percent in the case of poultry and partially so for cattle (about 50 percent) and hogs (38 percent) (ANPP 1990, 59–60). No wonder that one of the basic goals of the livestock program of the PA is to establish a national fodder industry.

There is little change in the picture when the focus is shifted to human consumption. According to Pérez Marín and Muñoz Baños (1991, 1), "Undoubtedly, domestic agricultural-livestock production docs not satisfy the population's demand for food, which requires the importation of considerable volumes of [food] supplies" (see table 5-4). Finally, the research institute of JUCEPLAN, in a 1988 study on industrialization and foreign trade, concluded, "It is remarkable that we have maintained over time a very high dependency on the importation of basic foodstuffs, of both agricultural and livestock origin" (Fernández Font and Pico García 1988). Indeed, the authors found that only in the case of rice was the per capita import level lower in 1985 than in 1958 for a basket of eleven food products.

Rejection of Economic Tools

Last, the PA is also characterized by disregard for the traditional tools of socialist economic policy, such as prices, taxes, economic incentives, and limited private markets. Cuban ideology has long maintained that these instruments are to be used only in the breach, as a matter of last resort in confronting a major crisis. (Their use in the PA during the current economic crisis will be discussed below.) Thus, for theoretical and practical reasons, Cuba sees state control exercised through centralization and administrative means as representing optimal solutions. The rectification process, in parallel development with the PA, turned Cuban economic practice toward the radical-mobilizational model, which achieved its most complete form in the "moral economy" of the late 1960s (Roca 1977 and Mesa-Lago 1981).

Consider the following evidence of the contempt for economic mechanisms. The Fourth Party Congress voted "to ratify planning as the instrument par excellence for the economic management of the country, from the global to the enterprise levels" (Partido Comunista 1991). Throughout 1991, Castro criticized and ridiculed the market economy model, referring to it as "garbage," "craziness," and "fairy tale fantasies." In May 1992, Castro (1992c) equated market-clearing prices with theft: "To sell a banana for ten times its [government-fixed] price is tantamount to stealing it." In explaining his opposition to the reintroduction of MLCs, Castro alluded to the argument that competition among state enterprises, cooperatives, and private farmers in selling their output to the MLC would keep prices low. He retorted in a puzzled manner, "But all that is totally insane because then there would be no need for plans" (Castro 1992a, 5). What is the purpose of government policy: to produce food or to make plans? The centrality of the political motive in these policy positions is not difficult to ascertain. It is best exemplified by an earlier Castro (1987) statement: "If economic mechanisms were to solve everything, what would be left for the Party to do. . . . These ideas involved a negation of the Party."

Results of the PA

It is too early to conduct a full evaluation of the performance of the PA, especially with regard to production results. The first plantings started slowly in 1988, and the program absorbed a major exogenous shock in 1990 with the disruption of trade with the socialist countries. Production increases of beef and some fruits require many years, while poultry, pork, and rice are medium-term performers. Still, short-cycle crops (tubers, vegetables, plantains, and some fruits) already have had several rotations. Thus in its fifth year it is possible to assess the progress of the PA. Two factors make the task more complicated: data are given in two different forms ("total production" and "state sales"), and full time-series data through 1992 exist only for three products: tubers, vegetables, and rice. The presentation here will be in chronological order, with data from official statistical sources for the earlier periods giving way to leadership reports of more recent outcomes.

In general, production results in the early years were mixed with negative or stagnant tendencies in many sectors. Table 5-2 shows that total production of tubers and rice increased in 1988 and 1989, while vegetable and fish output rose in 1988 only to fall the following year. Milk, beef, and eggs remained essentially unchanged. Table 5-3, reporting state sales, indicates declining deliveries of tubers, vegetables, and rice from 1988 through 1990, with fruits being the only exception. The deep concern of the Cuban leadership was manifested in the report of the Council of Ministers to the National Assembly of People's Power in December 1990 (Díaz 1990), which stated that

> the low yields registered in some sectors of agricultural production . . . are due in great measure to organizational problems, lack of discipline, . . . lack of motivation of those who must directly guarantee better results, lack of adequate programming of tasks, lack of coordination between production units and managers and workers, . . . lack of optimal utilization of resources, water, soils, seeds, crop rotation, and lack of dynamic management. We also suffer from incorrect methods of distribution. All of the above limit yields, crop collection, processing and distribution with quality to the population.

Let us take a brief glance at the post-production inefficiencies affecting the PA. In December 1990, Castro admitted that "*acopio* [state procurement system] and distribution have been drenched in difficulties." According to Pérez Marín and Muñoz Baños (1991, 4), "conservative estimates" of harvesting losses alone for tubers, vegetables, and grains amounted to 225 kilograms per hectare in 1989, or the equivalent of 5 percent of the total annual needs of Cuba's population. Harvesting losses are defined as uncollected production left in the fields. There are four additional categories of agricultural losses: post-harvest, procurement, transportation, and marketing. These categories of agricultural losses amounted to roughly 20 to 30 percent of agricultural production in the former Soviet Union.

In February 1991, however, some retail food markets in the city of Havana were experiencing losses of 30 to 60 percent in yuca and 30 to 50 percent in lettuce because of the poor quality of the produce being delivered by truck from the farms (*Trabajadores* 1991). At the same time, journalist Alberto Pozo reported that at a seminar for key state-enterprise managers, participants agreed that "about 30 percent of the country's production is discarded, wasted or unused because of poor quality" (*Bohemia* 1991). One year later the problem had not abated. In early 1992, the main report of the Sixth Congress of the Union of Communist Youth stated, "The deficiencies found in the *acopio* and distribution of agricultural products . . . largely provoked by negligence, criminal activities and shipping delays, require a more energetic confrontation" (*Granma* 1992d).

Difficulties also continued to plague the agricultural production process itself. Orlando Lugo, president of the National Association of Small Farmers, admitted in May 1992 that "it is imperative to learn how to make production plans and acopio contracts that are adjusted to the possibilities of the lands worked by the cooperatives and individual farmers. We must accept the fact that our lands are not properly used" (*Granma* 1992e). After a tour of Guantánamo and Granma provinces in April 1992, Raúl Castro sternly criticized the "existing difficulties and deficiencies," which included "unfulfillment of output plans, irregularities in distribution, low level of application of scientific-technical findings, and poor coordination among enterprises" (*Granma* 1992f). At the same time, the Cuban president was clearly upset when he admonished young mobilized workers for requesting lower output norms and reduced work hours. He also reproached the youthful brigades for excessive talking during the workday and extensive partying in the night hours (*Juventud Rebelde* 1992 and *Granma* 1992g).

In light of all the above, the more recent production results of the PA should not have been unexpected. Table 5-2 indicates that in 1991, compared to 1989, total production of tubers declined 16 percent, with rice and vegetables registering output losses of about 25 percent each. The 1992 data, based on the official forecast released in May, show major production increases for all three items: tubers (32 percent), vegetables (18 percent), and rice (13 percent). Only tubers and vegetables, however, were later reported to have had successful campaigns. Through October, their combined production was put at 1.32 million tons (versus 1.29 million tons projected in May), with additional harvesting forthcoming (*Granma* 1992h). But, as will be discussed below, the outcomes for rice and other PA projects ranged from disappointing to disastrous.

Consider the following assessments from the top political leadership about the post-1990 performance of the PA. Early in 1992, Castro announced that several technical projects (sugarcane drainage, rice planting, and irrigation schemes) were either stopped or curtailed because of insufficient fuel. In November, Carlos Lage (1992b and 1992c), a member of the Politburo and the current spokesman on the economy, gave two extensive interviews to the national press that constitute the most comprehensive evaluation of the PA so far. What follows is a compilation of Lage's key points:

> [The PA] has not met the projections or the needs. It must be said that the food program which we approved . . . in December 1990, on which we had been working before then, has not had the minimum amount of necessary resources to meet the expectations and needs which Cuba has.
>
> I should say that in some activities and in some branches we are obtaining positive and encouraging results. In other activities of the food program, decreases have been small or non-existent and they have at least managed to maintain the production and consumption levels of some domestic products, and in others, such as beef and milk, there have been important production reductions from what we had in 1989–1990 . . . [Milk output is 50 percent below 1989].
>
> The production of tubers and vegetables is an area where we have begun to obtain positive results. On a national level, in 1992, compared to 1990, the production of tubers and vegetables increased 16 percent. . . . Almost the only production that has increased this year is the production of tubers and vegetables for the direct consumption of the population. Production of everything else has continued to decrease.

The PA as Projection of the Future

Despite the depiction above of the PA as a reflection of the Cuban past, there is some evidence of tests and trials of economic policies and instruments that, if further developed and implemented, could also signify a prominent role for the PA in projecting Cuba's future. To be sure, these are vague indications with ambivalent tendencies within a politically sensitive context accustomed to mixed signals. Furthermore, the ultimate goal of Cuba's reinsertion into the world economy on the basis of a self-sustaining national economy would require the adoption of some minimum but coherent version of the market model.

Clearly anathema to the Cuban leadership, the topic of the market is being discussed quietly but extensively in the island, especially among the elite. Indeed, the issue of promarket economic reforms may be a critical factor driving the dissension in the technocratic ranks of both party and government. It is the "soft parts" among the "leading circles," as Carlos Aldana (1992) put it before his fall from the pinnacle of power, who are searching for real solutions. It is impossible here to speculate about factions, extent or timing of reforms, and so on. What follows is simply an assessment of the indications of change in economic policy within the PA that may point the way to, or project toward, the future Cuban economic model.

The property system (state and quasi-state ownership) is an essential element of the socialist economic model for the purposes of regime definition and economic control. The property issue was the subject of a heated controversy in the island. In February 1991, Castro defined privatization as consecration of theft and indicated his strong support for the party to do away with private entrepreneurs. In October, though, after prolonged debate, the Fourth Party Congress approved a resolution allowing self-employment in selected service sectors but rejected the reinstitution of the MLCs. In addition, individual and community garden plots have been widely authorized to promote self-sufficiency in food consumption. For example, in 1990, over 85,000 families in Las Tunas province were growing tubers, plantains, corn, and fruits, while by 1992 the city of Havana had readied 17,000 plots covering 126 *caballerías* (about 1,700 hectares) in all fifteen municipalities (ANPP 1990, 18; *Granma* 1992, 2). And the private raising of hogs in the capital has been legal since 1990.

Granted that they are small and isolated exemptions to the grand rule of state ownership, still these decisions represent a departure from past practices and, more important, they open up potential options for future economic reform. Indeed, in a tantalizing manner, Gerardo González (1992, 19–20) has argued that "in thinking that a new model of development may include some elements of the market, we are not limiting ourselves to the possibility of rehashing the case for private property." He stated that there was "an economic rationality to ceding some space to the domestic private sector in those minor service industries in which the state has been traditionally inefficient."

Even more significant change has taken place in the realms of pricing decisions and financial equilibrium, again not without struggle. In late 1990 and early 1991, Castro rejected price increases as "craziness" and considered financial equilibrium to be "meaningless." But by November 1991, the Cuban president was defending price increases of selected agricultural commodities on the basis of economic criteria (that is, to help cover production costs, stimulate output, reduce subsidies, and increase workers' salaries). It is interesting to note that experts from the Ministry of Agriculture and the State Committee on Prices had been working since 1988 on proposals to raise producer and retail prices (*Granma* 1992i).

Prices of agricultural products were increased in early 1992. The retail prices of about twenty-five food items, mostly tubers and vegetables but including some fruits, were raised (*Granma* 1992j). Foremost among the reasons given for the price increases was the need to reduce food production subsidies, which in 1991 drained the state budget of 450 million pesos (excluding distribution costs). Other estimates of Cuba's food production subsidies are higher. For example, Pérez Marín and Muñoz Baños (1991, 10) give a figure of 600 to 800 million pesos a year, excluding processing and distribution costs. Since Cuban officials have indicated that distribution costs roughly equal production subsidies, then total annual food subsidy expenditures could amount to 1 to 1.6 billion pesos, about 10 percent of the state budget in 1989 (*Granma* 1992j). In addition, the price adjustments were designed to reduce waste (prevent people from using cheap farm products as animal feeds) and to increase productivity (provide funds to raise agricultural wages). That is, prices are being used as instruments in the pursuit of social-policy goals.

It is a welcome change to read in *Granma* about how price changes may have a beneficial impact on agricultural labor productivity. According to Raisa Pagés, a veteran economics reporter, the increase in wholesale or producer prices is intended "to provide private farmers with more adequate compensation for their efforts and to motivate them to produce different crops" (*Granma* 1992i). A similar policy is being implemented with regard to agricultural workers. Under experimental trials in several sectors (rice, livestock, and bananas) in 1992, the new system is designed "to improve efficiency in agriculture through stricter discipline and with salary compensation connected to individual effort" (*Granma* 1992k). In my recollection, until now positive references about material incentives and monetary rewards have been absent from the Cuban press since the middle 1980s.

Beyond the domestic agenda, the desiderata of Cuba's incipient price reform now include international considerations. World prices are to be Cuba's prices. According to Arturo Guzmán (1992), president of the State Committee on Prices, "Our leadership decided to introduce in the national economy the real prices at which the country exports and imports merchandise. The current system of wholesale/producer prices, conceived and applied under quite different circumstances, does not make it possible to accurately measure the cost of human and material resources which are spent in production. . . . [We] must insist on the fact that we are a small country that lives off the difference between costs and prices." Guzmán anticipated that the wholesale price level would increase by no less than 50 percent by early 1993.

Since price changes would presumably occur more frequently, Cuban officials were prepared to accelerate and extend the process of decentralization of pricing decisions, with some choices left to ministries and enterprises. Guzmán also noted that under the new pricing scheme, state enterprises would be forced to become truly profitable, as was not the case in the old practice of hiding subsidization through irrational prices. In coming forth with this policy package, Cuba may be moving toward accepting the economic value of relative prices in determining the allocation of resources. If the price program is fully implemented, Cuban policy makers will, in Guzmán's words, "know more precisely what enterprises are subsidized, what products to subsidize and to what extent, what to import and to export and at what prices it is reasonable to do it or not do it." At that point, more questions and tougher choices will come to the fore.

Finally, another illustration of the PA as a projection of things to come in Cuban economic practice may be found in the self-financing mechanism applied to selected export-oriented sectors, including fishing. Since 1990, the government has allowed certain export industries (nickel, biotechnology, tourism, and others) to retain part of the income generated by export earnings for use in acquiring needed imports and other resources for the enterprise. The system seeks to provide state enterprises with direct incentives to improve performance and expedite deliveries of supplies. According to Carlos Lage (1992c, 8), "[In 1992] the fishing industry has maintained the volume of past years and has even increased its freshwater fish production. There is also increased consumption of fish as the result of greater efficiency between fishing and the buying of fish on the world market." The program operates, however, under strict state supervision, including centralized control over the use of funds.

It may be wise to end this section with a word of caution. Many of the initiatives outlined above, though indicative of change and potential harbingers of reform, are at present tightly restrained in operational terms and highly constrained in their systemic impact. State enterprises, though given a wider range of managerial autonomy, must still cope with detailed instructions issued by the central administrators. At the same time that agricultural subsidies are reduced, increases in unemployment compensation and minimum pensions have largely offset the paring effect on the budget.

Summary and Conclusions

The PA is an economic project defensible in the short run as a program designed to deal with the socialist debacle, to overcome the "double-blockade" (U.S. and socialist) in foreign trade, and to guide the Cuban economy toward reintegration with the world economy. The strategic decision to implement the PA as part of the "special period" is essentially correct. In attempting to address the food consumption issue, a matter of sheer survival, Cuba had no viable alternatives. The operational practices of the PA leave much to be desired, however. The implementation of the PA has been fraught with inefficient methods and tools, inimical both to the fulfillment of the PA's production goals and to the transformation of the Cuban economy for participation in the global marketplace.

The PA and the special period are survival strategies that employ the mobilization model. To some extent, it is rational to use idle urban workers in agricultural tasks given that their opportunity costs are very low (that is, unemployed laborers in the cities receive partial wages, food, and social services anyway). However, labor mobilizations and the other PA practices and tools that were presented as reflections of the past do not lead to the first rung of the long ladder that is the carrier to economic efficiency. On the contrary, the modus operandi of the PA contributes to the continuation of the current Cuban economic model, implemented from the start of the revolutionary process with only slight deviations except for the period of experimentation with the Soviet-inspired Economic Planning and Management System (Sistema de Dirección y Planificación de la Economía, SDPE) in 1976–85.

But the rules of the world economy require a receptive, rather than a rejective, domestic economic structure and policy scenario for the incoming country to maximize the benefits of participation in global trade and finance. To capture the full rewards of insertion into the world market, Cuba's domestic economy must be made to respond to market signals in terms of resource allocation, production decisions, and distributional outcomes. Under a minimum but coherent market model, the Cuban government would have available, based on orthodox economic theory, policy prescriptions and specific tools to protect (and even to promote) the social achievements of the revolutionary process. Following a standard interventionist track, Havana policy makers would be able to implement distributional arrangements that ameliorate any unwanted results of the market.

To change long-standing political and economic patterns and modify deeply ingrained preferences and habits, however, are difficult, if not impossible, tasks. Fidel Castro has defined the struggle for Cuban survival as a nation and as a revolution to be inextricably bound with the retention of his brand of socialism. Carlos Lage said recently, "Our planned economy can be inserted in a planned, organized manner into the context of the global economy." According to him, Cuba has already adapted and changed and will continue to do so, but Lage drew the line at private property, capitalism, and a market economy.

If pressed to conclude on an optimistic note, I would venture to say that it is highly likely that Cuban officials will be forced by deteriorating economic conditions to extend the use of market-type policies and economic instruments in an attempt to achieve some efficiency gains. The key question is what influence such widespread but unrelated and uncoordinated elements of the market system would have in precipitating its more formal and generalized use in the rest of the Cuban economy. The relative success of the PA, especially those programs in which market criteria are prevalent, may have a substantial impact on the policy outcome. If that were the case, additional research would be required to explore the new Cuban economic model as a reflection of the PA.

Notes

1. For a detailed discussion of changes in economic policy, see Mesa-Lago (1988).
2. For alternative views and evaluations, see Deere (1992) and Mesa-Lago (1992).
3. In April 1992, after the Soviet economic debacle, Castro still referred to their "extraordinary, exceptional" achievements in strictly quantitative terms: production of 600 million tons of oil, 150 million tons of steel, and so on.
4. For a recent analysis of the issue, based on a 1985 survey of the supply of provincial farmworkers, see Artimes Canet and Sampedro González (1989).

References

Aldana, Carlos. 1992. *Granma*, January 1, 3–5.
Anuario estadístico de Cuba (AEC). 1989. Havana: Comité Estatal de Estadísticas. Annual.
Artimes Canet, Marianela, and María Virginia Sampedro González. 1989. "Algúnos problemas territoriales de la fuerza de trabajo agropecuaria." *Cuba: Economía Planificada* 4, no. 2: 113–35.
Asamblea Nacional del Poder Popular (ANPP). 1990. *Excepcional e inteligente esfuerzo: Programa alimentario*. Havana: Editora Política.
Bohemia. 1991. February 8, 44.
Boletín estadístico de Cuba (BEC). 1990. Havana: Comité Estatal de Estadísticas. January-June.
Cardet Hernando, Luis A. 1991. "El programa alimentario: Su estrategia económica." *Cuba Económica* 1, no. 1: 42–54.
Castro, Fidel. 1987. *Granma Weekly Review*, January 25, 3.
———. 1990. *Granma*, October 1, 4.
———. 1991a. *Granma*, February 25, 5.
———. 1991b. "Speech at the Provincial Assembly of the PCC in Havana." *Granma*, February 5, 3.
———. 1992a. "Speech at the Closing Session of Sixth Congress of the UJC." *Granma*, April 12, 5.
———. 1992b. *Ciencia, tecnología y sociedad, 1988–1991*. Havana: Editora Política.

———. 1992c. "Speech at the Closing Session of the Eighth Congress of ANAP." *Granma*, May 19, 5.
Deere, Carmen Diana. 1992. "Socialism on One Island? Cuba's National Food Program and Its Prospects for Food Security." The Hague: Institute for Social Studies. Working Paper no. 124.
Díaz, Adolfo. 1990. "Reporte sobre el programa alimentario." *Granma*, December 27, 2.
Fernández Font, Mario, and Nieves Pico García. 1988. "Consideraciones sobre la evolución de la industria y el sector externo de la economía cubana durante el período revolucionario." Instituto de Investigaciones Económicas de JUCEPLAN, *Compendio de Investigaciones* 5: 7–38.
González Núñez, Gerardo. 1992. "Los dilemas de la economía cubana mas allá del corto plazo." Paper presented at the 17th Conference of the Caribbean Studies Association, May 26–29, Grenada.
Granma. 1990a. September 25, 4.
———. 1990b. December 27, 2.
———. 1992a. February 22, 3.
———. 1992b. January 31, 1.
———. 1992c. March 7, 1.
———. 1992d. March 25, 5.
———. 1992e. May 9, 4.
———. 1992f. May 6, 3.
———. 1992g. May 1, 2.
———. 1992h. November 17, 1.
———. 1992i. August 1, 3.
———. 1992j. February 14, 4.
———. 1992k. August 5, 2.
Gunn, Gillian. 1992. "Cuba's Search for Alternatives." *Current History* (February).
Guzmán, Arturo. 1992. "Cambios radicales en la esfera de los precios mayoristas." *Trabajadores*, October 19, 5.
Juventud Rebelde. 1992. April 4, 2.
Kornai, Janos. 1992. *The Socialist System: The Political Economy of Communism*. Princeton: Princeton University Press.
Lage, Carlos. 1992a. "Lo que no es eficiente no es socialista." *Juventud Rebelde*, January 26, 6.
———. 1992b. *Granma*, November 10, 3–7.
———. 1992c. *Granma*, November 14, 3–8.
Mesa-Lago, Carmelo. 1981. *The Economy of Socialist Cuba: A Two-Decade Appraisal*. Albuquerque: University of New Mexico Press.
———. 1988. "The Cuban Economy in the 1980s: The Return of Ideology." In *Socialist Cuba*, edited by Sergio G. Roca, pp. 59–100. Boulder, Colo.: Westview Press.

———. 1992. "Cuba's Economic Policies and Alternatives for Confronting the Crisis." In *Cuba After the Cold War*, edited by Carmelo Mesa-Lago, pp. 197–257. Pittsburgh: University of Pittsburgh Press.
Ministerio de Agricultura. 1992. *Reporte a FAO*, May 6.
Morales Pita, Antonio, Luis Mirabal Barrios, and Luis Soto Esteva. 1989. "La rentabilidad de los CAI azucareros de la provincia de La Habana en el período 1983–1986." *Economía y Desarrollo* 19, no. 110: 34–46.
Partido Comunista de Cuba. 1991. "Resolución sobre el desarrollo económico del país." *Granma*, October 17, 3.
Pérez Marín, Enrique, and Eduardo Muñoz Baños. 1991. *Agricultura y alimentación en Cuba*. Havana: Editorial de Ciencias Sociales.
Rizo, Julián. 1991. *Granma*, November 23, 1.
Roca, Sergio G. 1977. "Cuban Economic Policy in the 1970s: The Trodden Paths." In *Cuban Communism* 3d edition, edited by Irving L. Horowitz, pp. 265–301. New Brunswick, N.J.: Transaction Books.
Trabajadores. 1991. February 9, 2.
Trinchet Viera, Oscar. 1990. "Rendimientos agrícolas de algunos cultivos." *Economía y Desarrollo* 20, no. 115: 140–57.
Zumaquero Posada, Ovidio, Lucía Santana Díaz, and Alberto Siles Denis. 1991. "Drenaje parcelario: Una metodología de evaluación económica." *Cuba Económica* 1, no. 2: 134–49.

SIX

Cuba's Labor Adjustment Policies during the Special Period

SERGIO DÍAZ-BRIQUETS AND
JORGE F. PÉREZ-LÓPEZ

One of the victims of the economic hardships associated with the "special period in time of peace" is the full employment policy that Cuba has pursued as a primary socioeconomic goal since the 1960s and that is enshrined in its Socialist Constitution.[1] Although the Cuban government admitted in the 1960s and 1970s that there were some "pockets of unemployment," it was not perceived as a major problem as the number of affected individuals was relatively small and the unemployment was deemed to be fractional. However, the job dislocations that have already occurred during the special period and are likely to occur in the future are much more substantial and the likelihood of reemployment rather remote given the overall condition of the economy and prospects. In spite of the economic woes of the special period, the revised Socialist Constitution approved by the National Assembly in September 1992 left unchanged the article that guarantees a job to every able-bodied worker ("Constitución" 1992).

Cuba's policies to deal with workers who have lost their jobs as a result of plant shutdowns or the reduction in work hours during the special period have been set forth in a number of resolutions issued by the State Committee on Labor and Social Security (Comité Estatal de Trabajo y Seguridad Social, CETSS). These regulations establish rules whereby dislocated workers in some enterprises may be shifted to other areas of the economy where labor demand is on the upsurge (primarily agriculture), maintain and even expand the already generous safety net, deal with labor disputes associated with the dislocations, and reduce the size of the civilian labor force. Although these special rules have purportedly been promulgated to deal with an emergency situation and therefore can be expected to be temporary, there is no reason to be optimistic about an economic turnaround in the near term that would reverse the trend toward continued worker dislocations.

In this chapter we survey Cuba's labor adjustment policies during the special period, most of which were ratified during the Fourth Congress of the Cuban Communist Party. In the first part of the chapter we describe the set of regulations that Cuba has issued since 1990 to address worker dislocations. In the second part we describe the main characteristics of the Cuban labor force and assess the impact of the current changes on the labor market, focusing on the ability of growth sectors (agriculture and tourism) to absorb surplus labor. We conclude the paper with some general observations on worker dislocations and adjustment and prospects in the near term.

Emergency Legislation to Deal with Dislocations

The Fourth Congress of the Cuban Communist Party, held in October 1991, addressed the problem of worker dislocations and adopted the following as part of its resolutions on economic development: "A basic income for each family or worker will be assured, maintaining the right of each citizen to work. Nevertheless, transfers and movements of human resources will be inevitable in order to adjust to the country's needs and possibilities. In those cases where it is not possible to keep someone working, the worker will retain the right to the post and will receive a percentage of his or her salary, according to current legislation" ("Resolución" 1991).

The adoption of this policy merely formalized at the highest political level a series of initiatives formulated to cope with the labor dislocations arising from the special period. These initiatives took the form of emergency resolutions issued by the CETSS and other agencies beginning in September 1990. Taken together, the emergency labor resolutions constitute a comprehensive package of measures to deal with the labor dislocations induced by the economic crisis by:

- reallocating dislocated workers from sectors affected by economic disruptions to emergency and high priority production sectors where labor demand has increased;
- maintaining, and even expanding, Cuba's already generous economic safety net;
- creating the institutional mechanisms to resolve the many labor disputes that such major labor realignments are likely to produce; and
- reducing hours of work and the size of the civilian labor force.

Cuban officials have described their approach to the worker dislocations as an antishock policy. This is a jab at the stabilization measures (often referred to as shock treatment) implemented by Eastern European nations early in their transition to market economies to bring inflation and government spending under control and at the package of adjustment measures often recommended by the International Monetary Fund (IMF) and other international institutions for adoption by developing countries facing financial imbalances. These measures are generally associated with substantial unemployment and reduction in free services to the population.

Taking a few liberties with definitions, President Castro (1990a, 9–10) described the Cuban approach to the economic crisis and contrasted it with approaches used elsewhere:

> Not a single citizen was left without a job. Not a single youth, adolescent, or child has been left out of school. Not a single school has been closed. The first thing they do elsewhere is to look into the education budget and close down 30 to 40 percent of the schools. Thousands of teachers are left without jobs. They also close down 20 or 30 percent of hospitals and dismiss doctors, nurses, and health workers. We have not dismissed a single employee. . . . Not a single factory has been closed because of lack of fuel or raw materials. Not a single worker has been left unemployed. I ask myself if this happens elsewhere in the world. If the number of days are to be decreased, days are given off. If Friday has to be given off, it is given off, but no worker is dismissed. Not a single retired worker has been left without his pension.

A Cuban analyst (Recio 1992, 7) has put it as follows:

> In view of the tremendous shortage of resources that has suddenly befallen the country due to circumstances beyond its control, the Cuban state

opted not to employ a shock policy. This would have left hundreds of thousands of workers and their families out in the cold and would have abandoned social accomplishments such as education and health, which are an essential part of the citizens' standard of living. An antishock policy, which leaves no one unprotected and distributes hardships among everyone, was the way Cuba chose to deal with this difficult economic situation. It accepted the challenge of maintaining the population's income at levels that by far exceed the supply of goods.

In this section of the chapter we briefly describe and analyze the main emergency labor resolutions touching on the four general topics mentioned above: dislocations and reallocation of workers, safety net, institutional mechanisms to resolve disputes, and reduction of hours of work and the size of the labor force. The measures are discussed in chronological order so that we can relate them to the changing economic situation underlying their issuance. Objectives and key concepts of the principal emergency labor regulations are summarized in table 6-1.

Dislocations and Reallocation of Workers

In July 1990, the Executive Committee of the Council of Ministers approved Decree No. 157 (Comité Ejecutivo 1990), derogating existing legislation regulating the treatment of available (*disponibles*) workers that had been in place since 1977.[2] It also authorized the CETSS to issue new regulations on the placement and compensation of workers affected by anticipated economic dislocations.

CETSS Resolution No. 13/90 (CETSS 1990a), issued on September 3, 1990, dealt specifically with the reassignment of workers who might be affected by the elimination (*amortización*) of their jobs. In general, the new resolution tracks the regime for available workers set forth in Decree No. 13 of 1977 (Consejo de Ministros 1977). Unlike the previous instrument, however, CETSS Resolution No. 13/90 sets up a very structured methodology for reassignment and singles out agriculture as one of the likely sources of employment for dislocated workers.

According to the resolution, circumstances that might lead to the elimination of jobs include structural or institutional changes in state organization, changes that promote the more rational use of the labor force, the merger or partial or complete shutdown of workplaces, technological changes, and other justifiable reasons. It also states that, in

Table 6-1. Objectives and Key Concepts Relating to Principal Cuban Emergency Labor Resolutions, 1990–92

Resolution No. and Date Issued	Objective	Labor Concepts
CETSS No. 13/90 (September 1990)	Sets rules for the transfer of workers affected by the elimination of their jobs.	Available worker (*trabajador disponible*): A worker not reassigned to another job or who is not undertaking training.
CETSS No. 17/90 (October 1990)	Addresses labor and salary situation of workers made redundant by reductions in supplies of raw materials and fuels.	Surplus worker (*trabajador sobrante*): A worker who, for a variety of reasons, cannot be reassigned to another job.
CETSS No. 4/91 (March 1991)	Consolidates worker relocation and compensation rules of CETSS Resolutions No. 13/90 and 17/90.	Reverses the definition of the available worker and the surplus worker labor concepts.
CETSS-CEF No. 3/91 (September 1991)	Regulates worker transfers from their original workplaces to high economic priority sectors (e.g., agriculture).	Mobilized worker (*trabajador mobilizado*): Sending (*cedente*) and receiving (*receptora*) worker centers.
CETSS No. 1/92 (January 1992)	Facilitates transfer of workers to work centers near their residences.	Job swaps (*permutas laborales*).
CETSS No. 3/92 (January 1992)	Sets rules for the temporary reassignment of workers affected by the temporary shutdown of workplaces.	Work interruptions (*interrupciones laborales*).

determining which jobs are to be eliminated, efforts should be made to retain jobs occupied by men 50 years old or older and women 45 years old or older.

Reassignment Alternatives. A worker who becomes dislocated as a result of the elimination of a job has the right to the following reassignment options:

- permanent transfer to another position or occupation within the same workplace;
- permanent transfer to another position or occupation in another workplace within the same municipality (where the original work-

place or the residence of the worker is located) or, when feasible, in another municipality;
- temporary transfer to jobs temporarily vacant because of military, agricultural, and social mobilizations or the assignment of personnel to internationalist missions (or permanent transfer if a temporary vacancy becomes permanent);
- temporary transfer to another workplace;
- transfer to the agricultural sector, microbrigades, or other priority activities; and
- enrollment in training or retraining courses in the worker's workplace or another workplace, or in one of the schools of the national education system.

Workers whose jobs are slated for elimination must be informed in person by management in the presence of a representative of the union and given a set of reassignment options. The worker has seven calendar days to decide which option he or she wishes to pursue.

A dislocated worker who is reassigned to a permanent job at a lower salary than the one he or she held at the time of dislocation will retain the former salary for one year. In cases of temporary reassignments, the worker will continue to draw the former pay until a permanent reassignment has been made. Workers who choose not to accept reassignment offers (including retraining) or who fail to complete retraining will draw pay for only one month.

Available Workers. Dislocated workers who are not reassigned to another job or do not enter training become "available workers" (*trabajadores disponibles*). Such workers are permanently removed from the rolls of their former workplace and placed under the jurisdiction of the Labor Directorate (Dirección de Trabajo) of each municipality.

As the economic situation deteriorated, and the lack of imports of raw materials and fuels became more generalized, CETSS proclaimed a new set of emergency measures. CETSS Resolution No. 17/90, issued on October 17, 1990, dealt with "labor regulations and salary applicable to permanent workers who, as a result of the reduction in fuels and supplies of raw materials and manufactured goods, have become redundant in workplaces throughout the nation" (CETSS 1990b). Unlike Resolution No. 13/90, which offered a menu of reassignment options to dislocated workers, Resolution No. 17/90 authorizes management, with the consent of the union, to direct redundant workers to another job within the enterprise or a different enterprise, or to the construction or agricultural sectors. Workers who are thus reassigned retain a nexus with their former place of employment, however.

The labor affiliation issue is significant because it serves as one of the possible criteria to determine salary level after reassignment. Reassigned workers have the right to choose whether to retain their original salaries, provided they meet work norms in their new occupation, or to receive the compensation associated with jobs to which they have been reassigned. CETSS Resolution No. 17/90 also clarifies how workers are to be penalized or rewarded for under- or overfulfillment of work norms in their new labor assignments.

Surplus Workers. Resolution No. 17/90 introduces a new term, "surplus worker" (*trabajador sobrante*), one that was not used in CETSS Resolution No. 13/90, the labor emergency resolution issued just a month earlier, or in earlier legislation. Surplus workers are defined as those who cannot be reassigned to a similar job or to agricultural or construction activities because of the lack of job opportunities, health or physical impediments, the presence of minor children at home who require care, or other justifiable reasons. The addition of the surplus worker category to the dislocated worker taxonomy seems to have been dictated by the severity of the labor disruptions and by the authorities' recognition that temporary or permanent reassignment of many workers over the short- and medium-term was unfeasible.

Surplus versus Available Workers. CETSS Resolution No. 4/91 (CETSS 1991a), issued in March 1991, consolidated the worker reallocation and compensation rules first proclaimed by CETSS Resolutions No. 13/90 and 17/90. It is interesting that CETSS Resolution No. 4/91 formally reversed the definitions of the two categories of dislocated workers (available workers and surplus workers) that had been separately described in the two earlier resolutions.[3] According to CETSS Resolution No. 4/91,

- a surplus worker (*trabajador sobrante*) is one who must be reassigned to a new position as a result of (a) fuel or material input shortages that affect production; (b) elimination of his or her job because of the reorganization of state institutions or enterprises; and (c) the consolidation or elimination of positions resulting from measures implemented to enhance labor utilization; and
- an available worker (*trabajador disponible*) is a surplus worker

that has not been reassigned to another workplace, is under the jurisdiction of the Labor Directorate of his or her municipality, and is collecting compensation at the rate of 60 percent of his or her former salary.

CETSS Resolution No. 4/91 does not break any new ground regarding the procedures for the reassignment of workers, but it does state that surplus workers who have become dislocated as a result of lack of fuels and raw materials can only be reassigned to temporary jobs in other workplaces "in order to preserve, to the extent possible, the workforce of the unit until the time when normal conditions return." Surplus workers who are reassigned temporarily to other jobs retain a nexus with their former workplace.

CETSS Resolution No. 4/91 is a harbinger of a later resolution (CETSS Resolution No. 1/92) establishing the rules whereby surplus and available workers would be permitted to swap jobs according to proximity to their place of residence since it states a preference for reassigning surplus workers to workplaces near their homes.

Mobilized Workers. A joint resolution of the CETSS and the State Committee on Finance (Comité Estatal de Finanzas, CEF) issued in September 1991, CETSS-CEF Joint Resolution No. 3/91 (CETSS-CEF 1991b) deals with yet another category of workers affected by the special period: mobilized workers (*trabajadores movilizados*). Mobilized workers are those who are shifted from their normal occupations to high-priority areas, most likely agricultural activities. Mobilizations may be for short periods of time or may extend for more than eleven months. Mobilized workers may originate from any sector of the economy, including industry, transportation, construction, administration, services, and agriculture.

Job Swaps. Clear recognition of the difficulties associated with transportation facing the Cuban labor force during the special period was provided by the issuance of CETSS Resolution No. 1/92 (CETSS 1992a) on January 2, 1992. This resolution builds on the notion of taking into account the proximity of a worker to his or her workplace in making reassignment decisions, a notion that appeared almost as an afterthought in Resolution CETSS No. 4/91 (CETSS 1991a).

CETSS Resolution No. 1/92 explicitly provides for voluntary job swaps (*permutas*) between workers in similar or different occupations in order to reduce the distance they have to travel between home and work. The resolution encourages state institutions to facilitate the implementation of job swaps and defines the rules that must be followed, as well as the rights and obligations of workers involved in swaps. The efficiency consequences of this resolution can only be guessed at, given the many other current adverse developments in the Cuban economy, but they could be massive since the resolution allows swaps even between workers in different occupations. It is difficult to conceive, however, that the swaps would have more than a marginal adverse impact on overall economic performance since material and fuel shortages have already taken a major toll on production.

Preliminary information suggests that job swaps have not been very popular with Cuban workers. Through early March 1992, CETSS officials had visited 4,000 workplaces in the city of Havana, employing over 118,000 workers who required the use of public transportation to travel to and from their jobs. Only 13 percent of those workers had indicated an interest in exploring the possibility of swapping jobs (Pégles González 1992).

Work Interruptions. CETSS Resolution No. 3/92, issued on January 31, 1992, recognizes that equipment breakdowns and shortages of energy, raw materials, semifinished goods, or spare parts could lead to the temporary shutdown of workplaces, whether for a few hours or for a few days at a time (CETSS 1992b). Workers affected by these work interruptions (*interrupciones laborales*) may be reassigned temporarily to other duties or may remain idle awaiting the restart of the production process. When it is not possible to arrange reassignments, management and the union have the authority to decide whether the workers remain at the workplace or are released from work and sent home. When it is evident that a given work interruption will last for more than 30 days, affected workers receive the same treatment as surplus workers ("Interrupción laboral" 1992).

It is interesting that CETSS Resolution No. 3/92 raises the issue of work interruptions caused by negligence or willful action of workers. It orders management of the workplace to investigate whether a work interruption is attributable to any of the workers; if so, appropriate penalties are to be applied.

Compensation

CETSS Resolution 13/90 and Decree No. 13 of 1977 are very similar with respect to compensation to dislocated workers. In both cases, the maximum time period for drawing compensation payments is one year. However, CETSS Resolution No. 13/90 relates the length of time in which workers are eligible for compensation payments to seniority as follows: workers with seniority of one year are eligible for compensation payments equivalent to one month's pay; those with seniority from 2 to 5 years, four months' pay; those with seniority from 6 to 10 years, six months' pay; and those with seniority of more than 10 years, one year's pay.

Available workers draw full pay for the first month of dislocation, 70 percent of the former pay for the second month, and 50 percent for all subsequent months. An exception is made for internationalist workers whose jobs might have been eliminated while they were abroad; these workers will draw 100 percent of their former pay for the time period for which they are eligible to do so. The workplace is responsible for payment of the first month's compensation; subsequently, responsibility shifts to the municipal labor directorates and therefore to the state budget.

In a major departure, CETSS Resolution No. 17/90, issued in November 1990, modified the compensation system and provided that surplus workers would be eligible to draw 100 percent of their former salary for the first month of dislocation and 60 percent for each subsequent month "while they have not been reassigned to other productive endeavors." In instances in which compensation at this level is not sufficient to meet the needs of the family unit, supplementary social assistance can be provided. These guaranteed compensation payments represent an open-ended measure that carries to its maximum limit—unsustainable over the long term—the socialist safety net.

Major compensation rules were essentially unchanged by CETSS Resolution No. 4/91, although three telling refinements were introduced. First, the resolution explicitly set forth that the 100 percent compensation payment would be payable only once to each worker, suggesting that workers might have been affected by multiple dislocations because of shutdowns of workplaces to which they had been reassigned after the original dislocation. Second, it provided that workers who have been dislocated because of energy and raw material shortages and refuse reassignment or retraining may receive compensation for only one month (at 100 percent of the former salary), although they retain their nexus to their original workplace; similar behavior by workers whose jobs have been eliminated for other reasons results in the same level of compensation but in the severing of the nexus to the former workplace. And third, workers who are permanently reassigned to other jobs at lower pay than they formerly received retain their higher salary indefinitely unless they are promoted to a job drawing the same or a higher salary than they drew before; previously, salary retention was only for a twelve-month period.

CETSS-CEF Joint Resolution No. 2/91 (CETSS-CEF 1991a), a complement to CETSS Resolution No. 4/91, elaborates on compensation of surplus and available workers and sets some rules regarding their fringe and social security benefits. Surplus workers who are reassigned for up to 60 days to another workplace will continue to draw the salary and benefits associated with their original job; they will also have the right to earn and use paid vacation. Those taking assignments beyond 60 days are governed by the compensation and vacation rules applicable to their new place of employment. Surplus workers who are not placed in another job (available workers) or those undertaking retraining do not earn vacation benefits, however. Surplus and available workers who receive social security payments because of partial incapacitation can continue to draw such payments in addition to the guaranteed compensation for which they might be eligible.

Pursuant to CETSS Resolution No. 3/92 (CETSS 1992b), workers affected by work interruptions continue to draw 100 percent of their daily salary whether they are reassigned temporarily to another job or remain idle for the first 30 days. When work interruptions exceed 30 days, workers will be compensated at 60 percent of their daily wage for any lost time after the 30th day. This compensation schedule differs from the one proclaimed in 1979 (Consejo de Ministros 1979b; "El financiamiento" 1988) to deal with job interruptions, which was aimed more directly at short interruptions (three days or shorter) and did not fully compensate workers in the event of such short work interruptions.

As a point of interest, one resolution issued by CETSS in 1991 actually does reduce the level of benefits to workers. CETSS Resolution No. 13/91 (CETSS 1991d), issued on October 23, 1991, regulates worker cafeteria benefits during the special period. It permits workplaces to modify their work shifts to avoid providing workers with a midday meal. Among the alternatives open to workplaces are scheduling work in two half-day shifts, with a break in between to allow workers to provide lunch on their own; reducing the work shift from eight hours to seven hours and twenty minutes, providing no heavy meal and a snack only if it is available; or maintaining the regular eight-hour shift some days of the week with cafeteria service and having a seven-hour shift on other days without such service.

Institutional Mechanisms for Dispute Settlement

Fuller (1992:125–44) has documented that labor-management disputes are quite common in Cuban workplaces. Major labor dislocations associated with the special period and the complex regulations issued to accommodate a growing number of available workers increase the potential for labor-management disputes, particularly since decisions have to be made on issues such as which jobs are eliminated and which are maintained; which workers are reassigned to other duties, retrained, or laid off; rights to vacation and other benefits; and so on. Reassignments and job swaps affect seniority rosters, a very sensitive issue for workers.

CETSS Resolution No. 18/90 (CETSS 1990c) provides the basic rules and mechanisms governing labor-management relations at a time of widespread labor reallocations caused by the special period. It formalizes the Commissions for the Selection, Evaluation and Promotion of Workers (Comisiones para la Selección, Evaluación y Promoción de los Trabajadores). These commissions, to be established within each workplace, are to be composed of three members: a representative of management, a representative of the union, and a worker of high prestige elected by the workers' assembly.

The functions of the commissions are varied and include (a) selecting, on the basis of background and experience, the best qualified worker to occupy, on a temporary or permanent basis, an existing or newly vacant job; (b) selecting the workers that should be proposed for training; (c) when there is a reduction in force, determining which workers should retain their jobs, which should be assigned to training, and which should be reassigned; (d) determining which workers are not qualified to carry out their work assignments and recommending whether they should receive additional training, be transferred, or be removed from their jobs; and (e) selecting those workers who should remain at their posts when long-term labor interruptions occur. The resolution sets forth some of the criteria that the commissions must use in making such determinations.

CETSS Resolution No. 18/90 also sets forth the appeal process that management as well as affected workers may follow if they disagree with decisions made by the commission. Management has the right to request that the commission reconsider a given decision but has no further appeal rights. A worker's scope for appeal is broader, since he or she can seek reconsideration by the Labor Council (Consejo de Trabajo) or the local Labor Justice Organ (Organo de Justicia Laboral).

Finally, CETSS Resolution No. 18/90 establishes the procedures to be followed when establishing seniority rosters. These rosters will be used when necessary to make assignments regarding shifts and other work conditions. This is far from a straightforward procedure since, during the special period, some workplaces have shut down and their workforces merged with workforces of others.

CETSS-CEF Joint Resolution No. 3/91 sets forth in detail the rules governing the relationship between the sending (*cedente*) and receiving (*receptora*) entities regarding mobilized workers. These include rules regarding, among other things, computation of time of service, fringe benefits, and which entity should provide the worker with vacation benefits. Mobilized workers retain their affiliation with the sending entities; which of the two entities compensates the mobilized worker will depend on the length of time for which the worker is mobilized. The resolution also regulates how and under what conditions receiving entities must compensate sending entities for services provided (for example, equipment to transport the mobilized workers).

By late 1992, the commissions were active throughout the island. The emergency measures appear to have caused a significant increase in labor disputes. Meanwhile, the national problem with lack of work discipline persisted. In this regard, the Fourth Congress of the Cuban Communist Party approved the following resolution regarding worker discipline ("Resolución" 1991):

> Under current conditions, it is of decisive importance to confront squarely and with resolve the lack of labor discipline. Such lack of discipline manifests itself in absenteeism, poor use of the work shift, and the violation of the many rules regarding the production of goods and services. These deficiencies are reflected, aside from objective difficulties, in the misuse of material and human resources, rises in costs, the very low level in the introduction of scientific and technical innovations, the decline in labor productivity, corruption, and other economic crimes. . . .
> A general climate of order and discipline is essential for the effective functioning of any economic activity at any time, but it becomes crucial during the special period in order to face the challenges it has brought and a very high priority for the work of the party.

In July 1990, the Council of State (Consejo de Estado 1990) approved Law Decree No. 121, establishing a pilot program of workplace-level labor courts (Organos de Justicia Laboral de Base, OJLB) in Villa Clara province. These grassroots labor courts, with representation from management and labor, were authorized to resolve disputes over such issues as vacation, wages, social security payments, and the like and also to impose disciplinary measures. Disciplinary measures that result in dismissals or transfers are appealable to the municipal labor courts.

The experience in Villa Clara, where disciplinary measures involving workers increased by 32 percent and those involving management increased by 36 percent, was deemed a success after its first year of implementation ("Valoración" 1992; "Panel Discusses" 1992, 3). As a result, the experiment was extended to the entire nation by Law Decree No. 132 of April 9, 1992 (Consejo de Estado 1992; Lafita Navarro 1992). Subsequently, CETSS, the Ministry of Justice (Ministerio de Justicia, MINJUS), and the Popular Supreme Tribunal (Tribunal Supremo Popular, TSP) issued CETSS-MINJUS-TSP Joint Resolution No. 1/92 (CETSS-MINJUS-TSP 1992), setting forth very detailed rules and regulations for the operation of the OJLB.

Work and Workforce Reductions

In early January 1991, the CETSS did away with the half-day work shift on Saturdays and adopted in its place a policy of having a full shift work on alternate Saturdays. The logic for this change was that it would reduce transportation and fuel needs. Later in the year, shortages of fuel and other raw materials became quite severe and brought about the suspension of Saturday work altogether in many enterprises. For 1992, CETSS Resolution No. 19/91 formally continued the practice of full shifts on alternate Saturdays (CETSS 1991c), although it is clear that the practice of no Saturday work was generalized and therefore work hours were reduced from 44 to 40 per week for a large number of workers.

Two resolutions issued in late 1991 had the effect of easing labor market pressures by removing workers from the labor force. A joint resolution between CETSS and the Cuban Academy of Sciences (Academia de Ciencias de Cuba, ACC), ACC-CETSS No. 1/91, was issued on November 18, 1991.[4] It facilitates retirement of workers who are otherwise eligible but have incomplete work histories by permitting them to provide documentation attesting that they have fulfilled the required 25 years of service.[5]

CETSS Resolution No. 10/91, while not as far-reaching as ACC-CETSS Joint Resolution No. 1/91, equally eased labor market pressures by allowing mothers of infants of up to six months of age to remain at home while drawing 60 percent of their salaries (CETSS 1991b). This measure may have been intended to accommodate the child care problems of economically active new mothers, caught between the need to meet home and work obligations in light of the severe transportation problems Cuba is currently facing.

Summary of Labor Adjustment Measures

As has been set out above, since 1990 the Cuban Government has enacted numerous measures to deal with labor adjustment matters in a quickly deteriorating economic environment. Because some of the measures have derogated earlier ones, there is considerable confusion regarding which are actually in effect at a given point in time. Table 6-2 draws on the earlier discussion in this chapter and on an interview given in early 1992 by CETSS President Francisco Linares (Lee 1992) to summarize the main labor emergency measures in effect in late 1992.

Labor Dislocations during the Special Period

Cuba has not released systematic information on the magnitude or distribution of labor dislocations that have occurred during the special period. Considering the sharp contractions in imports of raw materials and fuels, however, it is reasonable to assume that the dislocations have been sizable and that they have been generalized, although their impact has probably been strongest in the industrial sector and urban areas.

In this section of the chapter we attempt to put the labor dislocations in perspective. First we present the broad contours of the Cuban labor force, relying on official statistics. Second, we try to identify sectors of the economy that might have been particularly affected by the lack of imports and attempt to put together what information is available on the magnitude and distribution of worker dislocations. Third, we discuss

Table 6-2. Emergency Labor Measures in Effect in Cuba in Late 1992

Issue	Measures
Job dislocations due to permanent closures and/or restructuring	• Worker eligible for retraining or reassignment • Link with former workplace is severed • If reassigned to another job, maintains salary; older workers given preference in reassignments • If not reassigned, maintains full salary for one month, and 60 percent of salary for subsequent months
Job dislocations due to shortages of fuel, raw materials, and spare parts (*interrupciones laborales*)	• Worker subject to temporary reassignment • Link with former workplace is maintained • Workers draw full salary if reassigned to another job • If not reassigned, maintains full salary for one month, and 60 percent of salary for subsequent months
Job swaps (*permutas*)	• Swaps encouraged between workers in similar or different occupations to reduce distance they have to travel to work • Workers who have swapped jobs receive the salary of the job they have transferred into, but historical salaries are maintained
Work hours	• Work shift may be adjusted to eliminate cafeteria (i.e., lunch and snacks) benefits • Permits working split shifts with a break for workers to go home for a meal • Permits reduction of the work shift from 8 hours to 7 hours and 20 minutes per day, or to a mix of 8-hour and 7-hour days during the work week • Half-day shifts on Saturdays replaced with full-day shifts every other Saturday
Workforce reductions	• Simplification of retirement process allows workers to substitute attestations for other documents in building up their work histories • Mothers of infants up to 6 months allowed to remain at home drawing 60 percent of pay

very briefly the alternatives that are available to dislocated workers, focusing on tourism and agriculture.

The Cuban Workforce

At year-end 1989, total civilian employment in Cuba amounted to nearly 3.9 million workers (*Anuario estadístico de Cuba* [AEC] 1989, 111). Reflecting the overwhelming role of the state in the economy, private sector employment was very small, amounting to some 230,000 workers or less than 6 percent of total employment; most private sector employment consisted of small farmers (3.2 percent of total employment) and cooperative members (1.6 percent).

Employment. According to official statistics (AEC 1989, 111), in 1989, the latest year for which such data are available, the state civilian workforce in Cuba averaged slightly over 3.5 million workers; about 70 percent of the workforce was employed in the so-called productive sphere of the economy (producing goods and some services) and the remaining 30 percent in the nonproductive sphere (producing services). Leading sectors in terms of employment in 1989 were industry (767,500 workers or 21.8 percent of total employment), agriculture (690,300 workers or 19.6 percent), education (396,400 workers or 11.2 percent), and commerce (395,300 workers or 11.2 percent).

Cuba does not publish comprehensive data on the distribution of employment by well-defined industries. However, such data are published for broadly defined industries within the industrial sector (AEC 1989, 147). The largest industrial employer in 1989 was the sugar industry, which employed 146,700 workers or 19.1 percent of industrial employment. Other significant industries in terms of employment were food processing (100,800 workers or 13.1 percent), nonelectrical machinery (87,300 workers or 11.4 percent), construction materials (57,600 workers or 7.5 percent), and beverages and tobacco (51,100 workers or 6.7 percent).

Wages. Since 1962, wages of Cuban workers have been set on the basis of a uniform, nationwide wage scale for the various categories of jobs (Ghai et al. 1988, 15). Prior to a wage reform carried out in 1981 to stem the flight of workers from agriculture, average earnings of agricultural workers were substantially below those of other sectors of the economy (for example, an average of 108 pesos per month for agricultural workers compared to an overall average of 135 pesos in 1975, and 127 pesos per month compared to an overall average of 148 pesos in 1980). After 1981, the gap between agricultural and nonagricultural workers was closed, and by 1988–89, average monthly earnings of agricultural workers were at or very near the average for workers in the productive sphere and higher than the average earnings of workers in several other sectors within the productive sphere such as commerce and communications.

In 1989, average monthly earnings of Cuban workers in each of the main economic sectors, in pesos per month, were as follows (AEC 1989, 116):

Industry	186
Construction	201
Agriculture	186
Forestry	184
Transportation	211
Communications	176
Commerce	163
Community and personal services	164
Science and technology	217
Education	191
Culture and arts	223
Public health, social security, and tourism	195
Finance and insurance	190
Administration	201

Within the industrial sector, average monthly earnings ranged from 237 pesos a month for workers in electricity production and distribution to 141 pesos a month for workers in the apparel industry (AEC 1989, 147).

At that time, the average agricultural monthly earnings of 186 pesos exceeded by 46 percent the maximum agricultural monthly wage rate allowed (127 pesos) under the 1981 wage scale guidelines (Ghai et al. 1988, 39) As noted, the improvement in agricultural wages followed from the government's desire to increase the appeal of agricultural work.

Unemployment. Cuba does not publish statistics on open unemployment on a regular basis. The only official unemployment statistics that are available are those associated with population samples or censuses. Although Cuba officially describes those unemployed as "between jobs" (that is, fractionally unemployed) rather than as long-term unemployed, analysts (for example, Ghai et al. 1988, 100) are not so sanguine.

The 1970 population census recorded a rate of unemployment of 1.3 percent of the labor force, probably the lowest in Latin America at that time (Mesa-Lago 1981, 122). A sample survey of the labor force taken in 1979 reported open unemployment at 5.4 percent in that year (CEE 1981b). According to the 1981 population census (CEE 1981a), 3.4 percent of the labor force was unemployed; when adjusted to account for the number of people searching for work for the first time, the open unemployment rate rises to about 5.5 percent. Over the period 1981–89, average state civilian employment in Cuba rose from 2.8 to over

3.5 million workers, or at an average annual growth rate of 2.8 percent.[6] Since the economically active population was projected to grow at a rate of 1.9 percent over this period (Ghai et al. 1988, 101), this would suggest that open unemployment prior to the current economic crisis may have been lower than at the beginning of the decade.

Worker Dislocations

In October 1990, shortly after the special period began, President Castro stated that dislocations associated with plant shutdowns resulting from the lack of imports would be "in the hundreds of thousands" ("Entrevista" 1990). Considering that Cuba's import crisis has worsened since the beginning of the special period—with, as noted earlier, imports in 1992 estimated to be 70 percent below 1989 levels—shortages of fuels and raw materials must have had a very significant impact on employment, particularly in the industrial sector, which used nearly 60 percent of total consumption of oil and oil products.[7] In September 1992, President Castro (1992, 4) stated that in the previous two years, 500,000 workers from the city of Havana alone had been "mobilized" to support agricultural activities.

Cuba has not published detailed trade statistics since 1989. However, the Central Intelligence Agency (CIA 1992) has reconstructed Cuban imports and exports through 1991 from published trade data from partner countries. These estimates reveal that Cuban imports in 1991 were 54.6 percent lower than in 1989, with significant reductions across all categories of importation. Food imports (–28.8 percent) received the smallest cut. Imports of several types of commodities and equipment that are critical to the functioning of the economy and the maintenance of employment suffered sizable cuts:

- Machinery and equipment imports fell by 67.6 percent between 1989 and 1991. This category of imports includes not only new capital goods, whose importation can be deferred without affecting current employment, but also transportation equipment, office equipment, ball bearings, electronic components, and spare parts for all machinery and equipment, affecting such industries as nonelectrical machinery and electronics with employment in 1989 estimated at 100,000 workers (AEC 1989, 147).
- Raw materials imports, which include imports of cotton, news-

print, paper, lumber, metals, and so on, fell by 54.4 percent, affecting the ferrous metallurgy, metal products, paper and cellulose, printing, wood products, construction materials, glass and ceramics, textiles, and apparel industries, with 1989 employment of nearly 200,000 workers.
- Chemicals imports fell by 49.1 percent, affecting employment in the chemical industry, with 1989 employment of 30,500 workers.
- Oil imports fell by 47.7 percent, directly affecting employment in the electricity and oil refining industry, with combined employment in 1989 of nearly 28,000 workers. In addition, reductions in oil imports affected production in many other energy-intensive industries such as nonferrous mining and metallurgy (with 1989 employment of 15,000 workers) and construction materials (57,600 workers).

Scattered information from the Cuban press since 1990 confirms that worker dislocations have been significant:

- In September 1990, President Castro announced that as a result of the breakdown of trade relations with the Soviet Union, several recently completed investments would remain idle. In this category were a nickel production plant at Las Camariocas, built with Soviet assistance, and an oil refinery in Cienfuegos. An existing nickel production plant, at Moa, would remain idle because of the lack of fuel (Castro 1990b, 3).
- In mid-October 1990, the Ministry of Light Industry reported that 321 factories under its purview were operating at a rate of 24 hours per week because of shortages of imported raw materials and spare parts. In addition, 26 factories (6 producing leather products, 10 producing textiles, and 10 producing wooden furniture) had been shut down altogether for the same reasons ("Paralización" 1990).
- In December 1991, the Cuban press reported that 1,700 of 4,000 workers (42.5 percent) in Textilera Hilatex, a giant textile plant, had been dislocated from their jobs because of lack of fuel (Sánchez 1991).
- CETSS reported in early 1992 that approximately 155,000 workers had become dislocated from their jobs as a result of the lack of imports (Dávalos 1992, 30); trade union official Ross Leal ("Se reactiva" 1992) reported at roughly the same time that 120,000 workers had lost their jobs.

- In July 1992, Havana Communist Party Chief Jorge Lezcano stated that fuel shortages would necessitate that 600 workplaces in that city halt work temporarily during the months of July and August; during the hiatus, the workers would be reassigned primarily to the agricultural sector ("18,000 habaneros" 1992; "Work Centers" 1992, 4).
- Cienfuegos, one of the provinces with the highest industrial concentration, has been one of the hardest hit by the special period. According to Castro (1992, 5), numerous industrial plants were shut down or were operating below capacity in September 1992 because of the lack of raw materials. Shut down altogether were a nitrogen plant and a new oil refinery; a large cement plant was operating well below capacity. The decision to discontinue construction of the Juraguá nuclear power plant because of the inability to enter into an agreement with Russia for the supply of components will idle the bulk of the 6,000 to 7,000 workers still working there in September 1992 (Castro 1992, 6).
- Communist Party officials in Pinar del Río province announced that 50,000 workers (including dislocated workers and students) would be mobilized within that province from November 1992 to February 1993 to participate in the cultivation and harvest of coffee, tobacco, citrus, fruits, and vegetable crops ("Pinar del Río" 1992).
- According to a report by the Ministry of Labor (Ministerio del Trabajo), the breakdown of the transportation system—because of the lack of equipment, spare parts, and fuel—had led to a quadrupling of the absenteeism rate in the first half of 1992 compared to 1991 ("Crisis de transporte" 1992).

Information is similarly very scanty regarding how the dislocated workers have been redeployed. A CETSS official reported in mid-1981 that 87 percent of dislocated workers had been assigned to other jobs; 10 percent had been deemed not suitable for reassignment because of illnesses, handicaps, family responsibilities, and so on; and 3 percent refused reassignment and were taken off the payroll. Those workers who were reassigned were almost equally divided between those who took new positions within the same workplace and those who took positions outside of the workplace. Of the latter, 65 percent were reassigned to agricultural jobs and 6 percent to construction jobs ("Majority of Surplus Workers" 1991). Referring to the same period, a trade union official has stated that 87 percent of dislocated workers had been placed in other jobs, principally in agriculture, and the remaining 13 percent were idle and at home, receiving 60 percent of their salary ("Se reactiva" 1992). Another source has reported that 131,000 of 155,000 workers dislocated in early 1992 (85 percent) had been reassigned to other jobs (Dávalos 1992, 30).

Sources of Employment

In the mid-1980s, most unemployed workers were assigned to the construction industry as part of the microbrigade movement. This is not a viable option during the special period because of the shortage of construction materials.

Cuban officials have identified tourism and agriculture as the two sectors of the economy that can absorb workers whose jobs have been eliminated during the special period. To what extent can these two sectors provide productive, good jobs for dislocated workers?

Tourism. The Cuban leadership has singled out tourism as one of the main prospective sources of hard currency earnings. Thus Cuba has taken a number of steps to promote international tourism, especially the creation of joint ventures with foreign investors.

These efforts have borne some fruit. As is discussed by Espino in chapter 7, between 1981 and 1991 earnings from tourism rose from $43.6 million to $287.0 million, or at an average annual rate of 20.7 percent. Cuban tourism officials have reported that the number of tourists visiting the island rose by 25 percent in the first half of 1992 compared to a like period in 1991 and that earnings rose by 30 percent ("Cuba dice" 1992).

As to what extent tourism can absorb those workers who are being laid off from their jobs during the special period, it appears that, despite the industry's impressive growth, it has very limited potential to create a large number of productive jobs quickly, commensurate with the level of dislocations.

Cuban statistical sources do not provide data on employment in the tourism industry; they are grouped with employment data for public health, social security, and sports. Espino reports in chapter 7 that Cuban tourism officials have estimated that their industry employed 42,000 workers in 1988, or roughly 1.2 percent of total state employment that year. According to a Cuban trade union official, tourism joint ventures with foreign investors created approximately 30,000 new jobs during the second half of 1990 and the full year 1991, and these enterprises were expected to generate an additional 20,000 to 40,000 new jobs by the end of 1992 ("Se reactiva" 1992). While these employment gains are not insignificant, they are dwarfed by the magnitude of the actual and potential dislocations throughout the economy.

Moreover, tourism jobs are mostly seasonal, involve low productivity, and are menial (the industry needs waiters, attendants, and so on), not the types of jobs that well-educated Cuban workers aspire to (Díaz-Briquets 1993). The peak of the international tourism season is during the fall and winter in the Northern Hemisphere (November through April), a period that coincides with the sugarcane harvest season, and harvesting draws many workers into that sector.

Agriculture. The centerpiece of Cuba's current economic strategy is a national food production program (programa alimentario, PA), the aim of which is to increase rapidly the output of agricultural products that can be produced in Cuba and consumed by the population or exported ("Resolución" 1991). Although the beginning of the PA can be traced back to the mid-1980s, as Roca discusses in chapter 5, its profile was raised by the special period because (1) it filled the gap created by the reduction in food imports; (2) unlike other endeavors, it permitted the replacement of capital and energy by manual labor; (3) it had the potential for generating exports; and (4) it provided an alternative place of employment for dislocated workers.

The PA is characterized by the return to manual agricultural activities. The lack of fuel has ruled out the use of tractors and other mechanized equipment. Work formerly carried out with mechanized equipment is currently being done by teams of oxen or by manpower. Between mid-1990 and mid-1992, some 81,000 oxen had been trained and were already displacing gas-guzzling tractors, while another 36,500 were being trained; the plan was for an additional 100,000 oxen to be trained and devoted to such activities ("Adiestran en Cuba" 1992). Similarly, shortages of fertilizers, pesticides, and herbicides have forced a return to more labor-intensive cultivating techniques.

Unlike tourism, the PA can, in principle, absorb unlimited amounts of labor. There are some limits, however, on the number of workers that can be mobilized into the agricultural sector because of transportation and housing problems. Workers who are mobilized and assigned to agricultural tasks must be transported to their workplaces, a requirement that taxes the already strained transportation system. They also have to be fed and housed. To house workers overnight, lodging facilities must be built at considerable expense and using scarce resources. The alternative is to transport workers daily to the agricultural tasks, an expensive proposition in terms of fuel.

In the Havana experiment with food self-sufficiency, which is part of the PA, approximately 20,000 mobilized workers from urban areas are rotated every two weeks to the fields. They are housed in 60 or 61 campsites built by microbrigades with a capacity of about 300 workers each (Castro 1990b, 7, and 1990c, 119). Because these workers—previously office workers, store clerks, teachers, musicians, singers, dancers, and the like—are unaccustomed to agricultural work, their productivity is much lower than that of agricultural workers ("Notas para un recuento" 1991, 25). To increase productivity, CETSS and the unions have made arrangements to relax certain worker safety and health rules applicable to mobilized workers; for example, mobilized workers were permitted to weed irrigation canals serving rice fields after severe rainstorms, an activity that normally would not be permitted because of its hazardous nature under such conditions (Martínez 1991). President Castro has admitted that the mobilizations to agriculture would not be sufficient to absorb all of the idle personnel in Havana, however ("Entrevista" 1990).

Conclusions

Since the mid-1980s, the Cuban economy has been mired in a recession. The recession deepened in the late 1980s and became a full-blown depression in 1989–90, in large part because of the breakdown of trading arrangements between Cuba and the former socialist nations. At the time of this writing, there is no reason to believe that the economic tailspin has ended and the economy has bottomed out. Thus it can be anticipated that worker dislocations will continue to be a serious problem in the near future.

Consistent with its stated antishock policy, the Cuban government has chosen not to dismiss workers who are dislocated as a result of the reduction in economic activity associated with the special period. Instead, it has expanded its safety net to provide compensation (cash payments) to idle workers at quite generous levels and has tightened discipline. Considering that the average Cuban worker earned 188 pesos a month in 1989 (AEC 1989, 116), payments at the 60 percent level imply outlays of 113 pesos per worker a month, a very large burden on the already strained state budget, whose main source of revenue— activities of state enterprises—is down. Increasing shortages of imported fuels, intermediate goods, raw materials, and spare parts, coupled with a crumbling transportation system, are creating large numbers of idle workers receiving transfer payments form the state while not performing productive work. According to a Cuban official ("Cerradas" 1993), about 60 percent of Cuba's factories were idle in May 1993 because of shortages of fuels, raw materials, and spare parts. It remains to be seen how long Cuba can continue to sustain the current set of labor adjustment policies.

Notes

The authors are grateful to Carmelo Mesa-Lago for very helpful comments on an earlier version of this chapter.

1. Article 8(b) of the Socialist Constitution (*Constitución* 1976, 8) guarantees "that every man or woman able to work have the opportunity to a job through which he or she could contribute to society and to the satisfaction of his or her own needs."

2. In addition to derogating Decree 13 of 1977 (Consejo de Ministros 1977) dealing broadly with the treatment of available workers whose jobs were eliminated as a result of organizational changes, productivity gains, technological changes, mergers of enterprises, and so on, Decree No. 157 also derogated portions of Decree 41 of 1979 (Consejo de Ministros 1979a) dealing with workers whose jobs were eliminated while they were overseas carrying out internationalist military missions.

3. Cuban workers are also confused by the terminology. See, for example, the August 1992 response by a columnist from the newspaper *Trabajadores* to a reader ("No es lo mismo" 1992).

4. The Social Security Archive (Archivo de Seguridad Social), the institution responsible for maintaining the social security records of all workers, is part of the National Archive of the Cuban Academy of Sciences (Archivo Nacional de la Academia de Ciencias de Cuba). Therefore the joint resolution is between CETSS and ACC.

5. In addition to 25 years of service, other requirements for retirement are

attainment of the minimum retirement age (60 years for males and 55 for females); having a record of at least 15 years of recorded work service since January 1, 1969; and being employed at the time of submitting the retirement application.

6. Calculated from official data in AEC (1989, 111).
7. This is based on statistics from CEE (1989). Oil and oil products consumption, by economic sectors, in 1988 was as follows: industry, 59.3 percent; transportation, 11.2 percent; personal consumption, 7.9 percent; construction, 6.2 percent; agriculture, 4.2 percent; and unspecified (which may include military), 10.2 percent.

References

Academia de Ciencias de Cuba and Comité Estatal de Trabajo y Seguridad Social (ACC-CETSS). 1991. "Joint Resolution 1/91." *Gaceta Oficial*, November 20, 349–51; "Presunción de tiempo de servicios." *Trabajadores* 32, no. 47 (November 25): 11.
"Adiestran en Cuba 81,000 bueyes ante la escasez de combustible." 1992. *Diario las Américas*, August 13, A1.
Anuario estadístico de Cuba (AEC). 1989. Havana: Comité Estatal de Estadísticas.
Castro, Fidel. 1990a. "Speech at the Closing Ceremony of the Fourth Congress of the Federation of University Students (FEU), on December 20, 1990." Havana Cubavisión Network (December 22), reproduced in *FBIS-LAT-90-250*, December 28, 3–18.
———. 1990b. "Speech at the Ceremony Marking the 30th Anniversary of the Committees to Defend the Revolution, on September 28, 1990." *FBIS-LAT-90-190*, October 1, 1–16.
———. 1990c. "Conclusiones del VIII Período Ordinario de Sesiones de la Asamblea Nacional del Poder Popular." In *Excepcional e inteligente esfuerzo: Programa alimentario*, pp. 115–34. Havana: Editora Política.
———. 1992. "Discurso pronunciado en el acto por el XXXIX Aniversario del Asalto al Cuartel Moncada y el XXXV del Levantamiento de Cienfuegos, el 5 de septiembre de 1992." *Granma*, September 8, 2–6.
Central Intelligence Agency (CIA). 1992. *Cuba: Handbook of Foreign Trade Statistics*, ALA92-10033. Washington, D.C. September.
"Cerradas más de la mitad de las fábricas." 1993. *Nuevo Herald*, May 8, 3A.
Comité Ejecutivo del Consejo de Ministros. 1990. "Decreto No. 157." *Gaceta Oficial*, August 7, 482–83.
Comité Estatal de Estadísticas (CEE). 1981a. *Censo de población y viviendas 1981: Cifras preliminares*. Havana.

———. 1981b. *Principales características laborales de la población de Cuba: Encuesta demográfica nacional de 1979*. Havana.

———. 1989. *Compendio estadístico de energía 1989*. Havana.

Comité Estatal de Trabajo y Seguridad Social (CETSS). 1990a. "Resolución No. 13/90." *Gaceta Oficial*, September 3, 553–56.

———. 1990b. "Resolución No. 17/90." *Gaceta Oficial*, November 7, 680–81. Also "Dictan Resolución sobre el tratamiento laboral y salarial a trabajadores reubicados." *Granma*, November 24, 1.

———. 1990c. "Resolución No. 18/90." *Gaceta Oficial*, November 17, 710–14.

———. 1991a. "Resolución No. 4/91: Reglamento para el tratamiento laboral y salarial a los trabajadores sobrantes." *Trabajadores* 32, no. 13 (April 1): 5; "Tratamiento salarial para trabajadores declarados sobrantes." *Trabajadores* 32, no. 14 (April 8): 5; "Procedimiento para la declaración de trabajadores sobrantes y disponibles." *Trabajadores* 32, no. 15 (April 15): 5. Translated as "Text of Regulations for Excess Workers." *FBIS-LAT-91-106*, June 3, 5–9.

———. 1991b. "Resolución No. 10/91." *Gaceta Oficial*, July 24, 250–52.

———. 1991c. "Resolución No. 19/91." *Trabajadores* 33, no. 1 (January 6): 3.

———. 1991d. "Resolución No. 13/91." *Gaceta Oficial*, November 7, 329–330. Also in *FBIS-LAT-91-227*, November 25, 12–13.

———. 1992a. "Resolución No. 1/92." *Gaceta Oficial*, January 7, 1; "Regulaciones sobre la permuta laboral." *Trabajadores* 33, no. 31 (January 20): 9.

———. 1992b. "Resolution No. 3/92: Labor and Salary Treatment for Work Interruptions." *FBIS-LAT-92-089*, May 7, 9–10.

———, and Comité Estatal de Finanzas (CEF). 1991a. "Resolución Conjunta 2/91." *Gaceta Oficial*, September 30, 287–89.

———, and ———. 1991b. "Resolución conjunta 3/91: Tratamiento salarial y financiero para el pago a trabajadores movilizados." *Trabajadores* 32, no. 41 (October 14): 5.

———, Ministerio de Justicia, and Tribunal Supremo Popular (CETSS-MIN-JUS-TSP). 1992. "Resolución conjunta 1/92: Bases y normas procesales para los Organos de Justicia Laboral de Base." *Trabajadores*, May 4, 9; "Aplicación y medidas disciplinarias y procedimientos para solucionar conflictos laborales." *Trabajadores*, May 11, 9; and "Solución de inconformidades y rehabilitación de trabajadores sancionados laboralmente." *Trabajadores*, May 18, 9.

Consejo de Estado. 1990. "Decreto-Ley No. 121." *Gaceta Oficial*, July 19, 19–20.

———. 1992. "Decreto-Ley No. 132." *Trabajadores*, April 20, 9.

Consejo de Ministros. 1977. "Decreto No. 13." *Gaceta Oficial*, December 10, 33–35.
———. 1979a. "Decreto No. 41." *Gaceta Oficial*, March 17, 215–17.
———. 1979b. "Decreto No. 43." *Gaceta Oficial*, May 31, 16–18.
Constitución de la República de Cuba. 1976. Havana: Editorial de Ciencias Sociales.
"Constitución de la República." 1992. *Granma*, September 22, 4–10.
"Crisis de transporte afecta la producción." 1992. *Nuevo Herald*, October 3, 3A.
"Cuba dice turismo aumentó en un 25 por ciento." 1992. *Nuevo Herald*, August 1, 4A.
Dávalos, Fernando. 1992. "Nadie en desamparo." *Bohemia* 84, no. 14 (April 3): 30–33.
Díaz-Briquets, Sergio. 1993. "Collision Course: Labor Force and Educational Trends in Cuba." *Cuban Studies* 23.
"18,000 habaneros a trabajos agrícolas." 1992. *Nuevo Herald*, July 11, 3A.
"Entrevista con Fidel." 1990. *Bohemia* 82, no. 40 (October 5): 36.
"El financiamiento de las interrupciones laborales." 1988. *Finanzas y Crédito* 13 (January-March): 61–66.
Fuller, Linda. 1992. *Work and Democracy in Socialist Cuba*. Philadelphia: Temple University Press.
Ghai, Dharam, Cristóbal Kay, and Peter Peek. 1988. *Labour and Development in Rural Cuba*. London: Macmillan.
"Interrupción laboral." 1992. *Trabajadores*, August 10, 5.
Lafita Navarro, Caridad. 1992. "Doce preguntas sobre el Decreto-Ley No. 132." *Trabajadores*, April 27, 9.
Lee, Susanna. 1992. "Precisiones acerca de las implicaciones laborales y salariales de las últimas medidas acordadas por el Gobierno." *Granma*, February 1, 3.
"Majority of Surplus Workers Said Relocated." 1992. *Juventud Rebelde*, June 2, 2. As reproduced in *FBIS-LAT-91-141*, June 2, 4.
Martínez, Magda. 1991. "Atemperar la protección al período especial." *Trabajadores*, June 24, 5.
Mesa-Lago, Carmelo. 1981. *The Economy of Socialist Cuba: A Two-Decade Appraisal*. Albuquerque: University of New Mexico Press.
"Metodología para la constitución de los Organos Laborales de Base." 1992. *Trabajadores*, May 25, 8.
"No es lo mismo sobrante que disponible." 1992. *Trabajadores*, August 24, 8.
"Notas para un recuento." 1991. *Bohemia*, August 16, 24–26.
"Panel Discusses New Grassroots Labor Courts." 1992. *FBIS-LAT- 92-186*, September 24, 3–4.

"Paralización de la industria ligera." 1990. *Nuevo Herald*, October 18, 3A.
Pégles González, Pedro. 1992. "Algunas reflexiones sobre la permuta laboral." *Trabajadores*, March 30, 6.
"Pinar del Río May Mobilize 50,000 Workers." 1992. Havana Radio Rebelde Network, September 17. As reproduced in *FBIS-LAT-92-182*, September 18, 3.
Recio, Renato. 1992. "Economic Difficulties, Gains Reviewed." *Trabajadores*, August 17. As reproduced in *FBIS-LAT-92-190*, September 30, 6–7.
"Resolución sobre el desarrollo económico del país." 1991. *Granma*, October 17, 3.
Sánchez, Sonia. 1991. "Obreros interruptos, pero no desempleados." *Trabajadores* 32, no. 48 (December 2): 3.
"Se reactiva el sector turístico de Cuba." 1992. *Novedades* (México), April 29, B7.
"Valoración de una experiencia." 1992. *Trabajadores*, March 2, 5.
"Work Centers to Halt Work Due to Fuel Shortage." 1992. Havana Radio Rebelde Network, July 9. As reproduced in *FBIS-LAT-92-133*, July 10, 4–5.

SEVEN

Tourism in Cuba
A Development Strategy for the 1990s?
MARÍA DOLORES ESPINO

Beginning in 1986, the Cuban economy entered a deep crisis from which it has yet to emerge. The Cuban crisis has been the subject of numerous studies by economists, both inside and outside Cuba (Roca 1991; Rodríguez 1990b; Ritter 1988). It is not my purpose in this essay to add to that body of work. Rather I will focus on the international tourism industry, a sector of the Cuban economy that has maintained a positive performance throughout the crisis.

International tourism has been targeted as a key export sector and is a major component of the Cuban economic adjustment program, the *período especial en tiempo de paz* (special period in time of peace). Just recently, the Fourth Communist Party Congress reasserted the official commitment to development of international tourism and identified the sector as "an important source of revenues for economic development" (*Granma* 1991). In this essay I explore the performance of international tourism in Cuba. In the first part I examine the development of the international tourism industry in Cuba. In the second I analyze the impact of tourism on the Cuban economy and explore the possibility for tourism-led economic development on the island.

Development of International Tourism in Cuba

Tourism in pre-1959 Cuba was a major industry and a primary source of hard currency and employment for the nation. In 1957, 347,508 foreigners visited Cuba (Truslow 1950; Grupo Cubano de Investigaciones

Económicas 1963; Martín Fernández 1988). Tourist expenditures amounted to 62.1 million pesos in that year. By 1957, hard-currency earnings from tourism had surpassed those from the tobacco industry (Banco Nacional de Cuba, 1960b, 1960c). Tourism had become the second-largest earner of foreign currency in the Cuban economy.

In the early years of the Revolution, international tourism all but disappeared from the island. Although the major reason for the demise of international tourism can be attributed to the U.S. embargo, internal ideological concerns also contributed. Tourism was perceived as too closely associated with the capitalist evils of prostitution, drugs, gambling, and organized crime. The revolutionary government discounted tourism as a vehicle for economic growth and development. During the 1960s and early 1970s, no major investment in tourism was undertaken. The vast tourism infrastructure built up during the prerevolutionary years was left for the use of Cuban citizens and international guests from socialist and other friendly countries or simply abandoned. Some sixteen hotels were closed down, and hotel capacity was reduced by 50 percent (Ayala Castro 1991, 15).

By the mid-1970s, visitors from capitalist nations started trickling back. In 1974, 8,400 visitors from capitalist countries visited Cuba. By 1991, this figure had increased to about 398,400.

In 1976, recognizing Cuba's comparative advantage as a vacation spot and realizing the potential economic benefits to be derived from international tourism, the Cuban government created the Instituto Nacional de Turismo (INTUR). INTUR became the agency primarily responsible for developing policy for both national and international tourism as well as for collecting data on tourist arrivals and tourist expenditures.

In recent years, Cuba has started promoting tourism strongly in capitalist countries. In 1987, another tourism development agency, Cubanacán, S.A., was created. Cubanacán is the primary Cuban corporation that engages foreign capital in joint-venture investments in the Cuban tourism industry. A smaller corporation, Gaviota, S.A., with ties to the Cuban military, also operates in Cuba and engages in joint ventures.

Indicators of International Tourism Activity

The most reliable statistics that can be used as indicators of international tourism activity are the number of foreign travelers arriving in a given country. Though the tourism literature uses various definitions of what constitutes a traveler or tourist, the international community has accepted a standard definition recommended by the United Nations Conference on International Travel (World Tourism Organization 1981). The United Nations defines a visitor as "any person visiting a country other than that in which he has his usual place of residence, for any reason other than following an occupation remunerated from within the country visited." Visitors are classified as either tourists or excursionists. The term *tourist* is defined as a visitor staying at least twenty-four hours in the country visited whose purpose in making the journey can be classified as (1) leisure (recreation, holiday, health, study, religion, or sport), (2) business, (3) family, (4) mission, or (5) meeting. *Excursionists* are temporary visitors staying less than twenty-four hours, such as sea-cruise travelers. Following international guidelines, the Cuban government collects two different sets of data on international visitors' arrivals.

One series includes only visitors who arrive in the country through a travel agency. This series is compiled by the Cuban tourism corporations (INTUR, Cubanacán, and so on) and is published in the *Anuario Estadístico de Cuba*. A second, much broader series is compiled by the Dirección de Inmigración y Extranjería and includes all foreign visitors arriving at the border. This latter series is published by the World Tourism Organization in the *Yearbook of Tourism Statistics* and by the Banco Nacional de Cuba in its *Informe Económico*.

All sources point to a rapid growth in international tourism in Cuba in the 1980s (see table 7-1). International visitors more than tripled from 132,900 in 1981 to 424,000 in 1991, while international visitors arriving through travel agencies increased from 129,500 in 1980 to 275,600 thousand in 1989.

The majority of international visitors to Cuba come from capitalist nations (see table 7-2). In 1991, Western Europe, North America, and Latin America accounted for over 90 percent of visitors to the island. The country generating the highest number of visitors to Cuba is Canada, with 81,100 in 1991, 19.1 percent of all foreign visitors to the island.

Though the United States is the largest generator of tourism to the Caribbean, accounting for over 60 percent of all foreign visitors to the area, U.S. policy restricting pleasure and business travel to Cuba has forced Cuba to seek alternative markets. In 1991, only 2.6 percent of all visitors were from the United States. Of these, the majority were

Table 7-1. International Visitors to Cuba, 1982–91 (thousands)

	Total Visitors	Percent Change	From Capitalist Nations	Percent Change
1982	150.7	—	101.5	—
1983	174.1	15.5	124.9	23.1
1984	218.3	25.4	168.5	34.9
1985	243.0	11.3	193.2	14.5
1986	281.9	16.0	217.9	12.8
1987	293.3	4.0	237.3	8.9
1988	309.2	5.4	246.9	4.0
1989	326.3	5.5	289.4	17.2
1990	340.3	4.3	310.3	7.2
1991	424.0	24.0	398.4	28.4

Source: Dirección de Inmigración y Extranjería, *Estadística de Frontera*, unpublished series; and Banco Nacional de Cuba, *Informe Económico*, various issues. Author estimates for 1989–91.

Cuban nationals residing in the United States who made family visits to the island, a category of U.S. travelers exempt from the U.S. Treasury Department limitations.

Western Europe is Cuba's top source of tourists, representing over 40 percent of all visitors in 1990. European countries sending significant numbers of tourists to Cuba are Germany, Spain, Italy, Austria, and France, in that order. Cuba is one of the few nations in the Caribbean that have been able to tap the European market on a broad basis, attracting visitors even from countries with which it has no historical or cultural ties.

Many visitors to Cuba also come from Latin America, which provided 27 percent of all visitors to Cuba in 1991. Mexico, Venezuela, Argentina, and to a lesser extent Brazil accounted for the highest numbers of visitors from Latin America.

During the 1980s most visitors to Cuba were tourists—that is, their stay in the island lasted longer than twenty-four hours. Very few excursionists visited Cuba during that period. In 1989, Cuban statistics show only 5,259 excursionists compared to 270,359 tourists (Comité Estatal de Estadísticas [CEE] 1989, p. 396). The tourist/excursionist breakdown in the 1980s is quite different from that prevailing in prerevolutionary Cuba and from the current pattern in most of the Caribbean. During the 1950s a major portion of the tourist trade to Cuba could be attributed to excursionists: 75,200 in 1957 and 90,000 in 1958. The low number of excursionists today can be attributed to the island's exclusion from

Table 7-2. International Visitors to Cuba through Travel Agencies, by Area of Origin, 1980–89

	1980	1981	1982	1983	1984	1985	1986	1987	1988	1989
Socialist Nations	29,696	34,634	28,363	20,007	23,909	28,322	34,083	31,446	31,393	28,647
Percent of Total	22.9	32.7	27.2	16.9	15.1	16.4	17.5	15.1	12.7	10.4
Capitalist Nations	98,678	69,543	75,562	95	126,796	139,856	152,005	166,606	205,326	237,277
Percent of Total	76.1	65.6	71.1	79.5	80.2	81.0	78.1	80.0	83.1	86.1
Other	1,217	1,859	1,814	4,208	7,330	4,398	8,443	10,189	10,361	9,694
Total	129,591	106,036	106,399	118,308	158,035	172,578	194,531	208,241	247,080	275,618
Percentage of Growth										
Socialist Nations	n.a.	16.6	-16.4	-30.9	-19.5	18.5	20.3	-7.7	-0.2	-8.7
Capitalist Nations	n.a.	-29.5	8.7	24.4	34.8	10.3	8.7	9.6	23.2	15.7
Total	n.a.	-18.2	0.3	11.3	33.6	9.2	12.7	7.0	18.7	11.6

Source: CEE, 1986-89.

the sea-cruise circuit. During 1989, the rest of the Caribbean reported 6.7 million visits from sea-cruise passengers and 7.4 million in 1990. (Caribbean Tourism Organization 1990)

Cuba's share of the Caribbean tourism market is very small. Over the period 1982–90, Cuba accounted for only about 3 percent of all tourist visits to the region, whereas estimates of Cuba's share of the Caribbean tourism market in the late 1950s ranged from 18 to 21 percent.[1] After reaching a peak of nearly 3.3 percent in 1986, the island's share of Caribbean tourist arrivals began falling in the later 1980s. Preliminary data suggest, however, that in 1991 Cuba's share of the Caribbean market increased to about 3.5–3.7 percent.

It is unlikely that Cuba's share of the Caribbean tourism market will grow significantly as long as the U.S. trade embargo remains in effect. First, the embargo prohibits U.S. citizens from traveling to Cuba for pleasure. This denies Cuba access to the U.S. travel market, though the United States is its "natural partner" and the major source of tourists to the Caribbean, supplying over 60 percent of all visitors to the area. Cuba has tried to overcome the handicap of U.S. travel restrictions by catering to the Canadian and European market. Canada, however, does not have the depth of the U.S. market, and the distance between Europe and Cuba significantly raises the cost of a Cuban vacation for Europeans, once travel fares are included.

Second, as long as the embargo is in place, Cuba will continue to be left out of the lucrative Caribbean sea-cruise industry, based in Miami. The U.S. embargo prohibits cruises from including Cuba in their itineraries.

Finally, the U.S. embargo prohibits U.S. citizens, corporations, or overseas affiliates from investing in Cuba. This closes the door to important sources of foreign investment just when Cuba is seeking funds to build and restore its tourism infrastructure. Failure to expand existing facilities may seriously constrain the growth of international visits to Cuba.

Investment in Cuba's Tourism Infrastructure

The Cuban government has targeted tourism infrastructure as a priority investment area. During the 1980s, tourist accommodations expanded across the island. New hotels and motels were built and others renovated. In 1988, 321 hotels and motels were operating in the island, 54

Table 7-3. Cuba's Capacity for International Tourism, 1989–91

	1989		1990		1991	
	Installations	Rooms	Installations	Rooms	Installations	Rooms
INTUR	91	10,815	92	10,551	108	13,357
Cubanacán	17	2,069	22	3,600	37	6,307
Gaviota	3	126	7	465	10	609
Other	6	536	6	536	6	536
Total	117	13,561	127	15,151	161	20,809

Source: Unpublished INTUR statistics. Installations include hotels, motels, villas, cabins, etc.

more than at the beginning of the decade (CEE 1986, 610; 1987, 619; 1988, 614). Hotel and motel capacity increased at an even faster pace, with 21,108 rooms available at the end of 1988, almost double the number available in 1980.

Accommodations in establishments other than hotels and motels (villas, houses, apartments, cabins, camps, and so on) increased only minimally. In 1988, there were only 470 more beds available in these establishments than in 1980 (CEE 1986, 609; 1987, 611; 1988, 614). In total, 30,697 rooms were available in the island at the end of 1988. Of this number, 43 percent were in Havana and 9.3 percent in the traditional beach resort of Varadero (CEE 1988, 613). The Cuban tourism development plan calls for stepped-up expansion of tourist accommodations and the development of new tourism centers throughout the island.

Of the rooms available at the end of 1988, around 8,000 were reserved for international tourists.[2] Of these, about 6,500 (81.3 percent) were managed by INTUR.[3] Through new construction and renovation, INTUR planned to increase its accommodation capacity by 60 percent by the end of 1991. The task of renovating existing facilities in Havana and Varadero falls mainly to INTUR (Castells García 1989).

The bulk of new construction of tourist accommodations has been undertaken by Cubanacán, S.A. Cubanacán's plan for 1988–92, as reported in 1989, called for an expansion of 16,800 rooms throughout the island (Mena 1989). The development of new tourism resorts on the northeastern coast of Cuba and near Santiago de Cuba and the Sierra Maestra will primarily be under Cubanacán's leadership.

Capacity for international tourism in 1989 and 1991 is displayed in table 7-3. Though INTUR seems to have met its reported plans for expanding room capacity, Cubanacán has fallen well short of the 18,500 rooms it planned to have completed by the end of 1992. Plans for expanding hotel capacity continue to be ambitious. By 1995, Cuba expects to more than double its present hotel capacity and to have 50,000 rooms available for international guests (Banco Nacional de Cuba 1991).

Fulfillment of this ambitious investment plan hinges to a large extent on Cuba's ability to attract foreign investment to finance hotel and motel construction. In fact, one of the main tasks assigned to Cubanacán upon its creation in 1987 was to attract foreign capital for joint ventures in tourism.

Foreign investment in the form of joint ventures has been allowed in Cuba since Law Decree no. 50 was enacted in February 1982. Under Law Decree no. 50, mixed corporations with up to 49 percent foreign ownership are allowed to operate in Cuba (Pérez-López 1985).

It is clear that one of the objectives of the joint venture law was to open up the tourism industry to foreign capital. The decree established significantly more favorable provisions for foreign investment in tourism than for other industries. In particular, joint ventures in tourism may be exempt from all taxes and licenses and subject to less regulation. Additionally, foreign managers of joint ventures in international tourism are allowed to lease Cuban installations and to hire Cuban workers directly. Finally, it has been rumored for years, and recently reported by Cuban tourism officials, that the 1982 joint venture law is being amended to allow majority foreign ownership in approved international tourism ventures ("Trade Winds" 1990; French 1991)

Cuba has been somewhat successful in attracting joint ventures in the tourism industry. In 1990, two hotels constructed and operated under joint venture agreements opened their doors in Varadero. The Sol Palmeras Hotel is a joint venture between Cubanacán, S.A., and the Spanish conglomerate Grupo Sol; the Tuxpán Hotel is a joint venture between Cubanacán and German interests, managed by the German company LTI International Hotels (Cabrera 1991). In 1992, Grupo Sol opened its first five-star hotel in Varadero, the Meliá Varadero, with 490 rooms.

There is at present no way to estimate accurately the total amount of foreign investment that Cuba has attracted to the tourism sector. Some joint venture projects on the way, however, involve one more five-star hotel in Varadero: the Meliá Las Américas, also to be constructed by the Grupo Sol, with 250 rooms (*Cuba Business* 1991). The Cohiba

Hotel, under construction in Havana, is a joint venture with the Spanish company Royal Tours of Spain. The Jamaican firm Super Clubs is currently operating a hotel in Santa Lucía, in northern Cuba, and it plans to renovate and operate the Cactus Hotel in Varadero, as well as to construct a new hotel in the same area (French 1991). Though no details have been provided, Cubanacán claims that it has finalized other joint venture agreements with a number of European and Latin American hotel companies.

An important type of joint venture deal is foreign management of existing hotels, restaurants, and clubs. For example, Royal Tours of Spain, which is constructing the Cohiba Hotel in Havana, operates sixteen other hotels across the island (*Cuba Business* 1991). In establishing these agreements, the Cuban government seeks to improve the quality of service offered to international visitors and to train Cuban workers. The quality of tourist services has been notoriously poor, which accounts for the low return rate to Cuba, only about 2 percent. This is the lowest rate in the Caribbean (Pozo 1987).

The Economic Impact of International Tourism in Cuba

The economic importance of international tourism lies in its ability to generate benefits for the host country. Tourism brings an improved balance of payments, generates government revenues, enhances income, creates jobs, and promotes economic growth and development.

International Tourism Receipts

Because international tourism represents the consumption of domestic goods and services by foreigners, it is considered an export activity. Cuba's tourist exports are recorded in the services (or invisibles) category of Cuba's balance-of-payment accounts.

Unlike international arrivals, which are relatively easy to account for, receipts from international visitors are hard to estimate. Two identifiable and distinct series of hard-currency visitors' receipts exist in Cuba, though they are often reported interchangeably (Martín Fernández 1988). The first series reports visitors' expenditures following international guidelines, which include money spent on lodging, food, entertainment, travel within the country, and the like but exclude interna-

Table 7-4. Cuba's Hard Currency Visitors' Expenditures and Gross Revenues from Visitors, 1977–91 ($US millions)

	Expenditures	% Increase	Gross Revenue	% Increase
1977	16.7			
1978	26.2	56.8		
1979	87.6	234.4		
1980	39.6	−54.8		
1981	43.6	10.1		
1982	50.9	16.7	61.1	
1983	59.4	16.7	74.3	21.6
1984	75.7	27.4	95.5	28.5
1985	87.3	15.3	102.6	7.4
1986	97.7	11.9	124.6	21.4
1987	111.7	14.3	145.0	16.4
1988	146.9	31.5	189.0	30.3
1989	166.0	13.0	260.0	37.6
1990	198.0	19.3	310.0	19.2
1991	287.0	45.0	400.0	29.0

Source: Martín Fernández, (1988); Banco Nacional de Cuba, Informe Económico, various issues; Banco Nacional de Cuba, unpublished series; World Tourism Organization (1990).

tional travel fares. The second series is much broader and refers to gross revenues; it includes hard-currency revenues from activities related to international tourism such as international communications and aviation.

Both series (table 7-4) indicate strong growth in international tourism receipts during the 1980s. Visitors' expenditures increased from $43.6 million in 1981 to $198.0 million in 1990. Gross revenues from tourism increased from $61.1 million in 1982 to $310.0 in 1990. Preliminary figures for 1991 show expenditures at $287 million and gross revenues at $400 million.

During the latter half of the 1980s, visitors' receipts increased at a higher rate than visitors' arrivals. This is reflected in table 7-5, which shows average expenditure per visitor. After declining for the first half of the 1980s, average expenditure per visitor increased from $448 in 1986 to $638 in 1990. Considering that a large share of Cuba's tourists are Latin Americans who tend to have relatively little money to spend, it is unlikely that the increase in average spending is due to an expansion in real expenditures per tourist. It can probably be attributed to price increases for international tourists.

Table 7-5. Visitor' Arrivals from Capitalist Nations and Hard Currency Expenditures in Cuba, 1982–91

	1982	1983	1984	1985	1986	1987	1988	1989	1990	1991
Visitors from Capitalist Nations (thousands)	101.5	124.9	168.5	193.2	217.9	237.3	246.9	289.4	310.3	398.4
Visitor Receipts in Hard Currency ($US millions)	50.9	59.4	75.7	87.3	97.7	111.7	146.8	166.0	198.0	287.0
Average Receipts per Visitor from Capitalist Nations ($US)	501	476	449	452	448	470	595	574	638	720

Source: Author's calculations.

Raising prices might prove detrimental to Cuba's tourism industry, however. Cuba has attracted visitors from capitalist countries partly because prices are lower in Cuba than in other comparable vacation spots. During 1986, Cuba had the lowest average receipts per visitor night of all major Caribbean countries (Espino 1992). This is true whether calculations are made on the basis of all visitors or on the basis of only visitors from capitalist countries. Average receipts per visitor night in Cuba were $42.59 for all visitors, and $50.54 when calculated for visitors from capitalist countries only.[4] The highest figure in the Caribbean is the one estimated for Puerto Rico: $117.67 per visitor night, more than twice the Cuban figure.

It is impossible from the available data to calculate receipts per tourist and receipts per tourist night, two indicators that would give a better comparative picture of costs in Cuba vis-à-vis other Caribbean vacation areas. Because of the small number of excursionists who visit Cuba, however, the figures for tourists would be very close to those calculated for all visitors. This is not true of the rest of the Caribbean, where a great percentage of visitors are excursionists, who do not spend money on lodging. Excluding receipts per day for excursionists from our calculations would therefore have significantly increased the average receipts per day for most countries in the Caribbean, but not for Cuba. While this would further emphasize Cuba's price advantage within the region, any future price increases might erode that advantage.

It is unlikely that real expenditures per visitor to Cuba will expand significantly in the near future, since the vast majority of visitors arrive through prepaid package deals, which limits their spending potential.

Though the exact percentage of tourists traveling through package plans is not available after 1990, we do know that 84.5 percent of all visitors to the island in 1989 arrived through travel agencies.[5]

Tourism Exports and Cuba's Balance of Payments

Tourism exports are fast becoming a major source of hard-currency receipts for Cuba. The increasing importance of tourism as an export industry is best seen by comparing visitors' receipts with hard-currency receipts generated by other industries. In 1981, visitors' expenditures were $43.6 million, or 3.1 percent of hard-currency receipts from total merchandise trade. By 1988, visitors' expenditures had reached $146.9 million, or about 13.2 percent of hard-currency receipts from total merchandise trade. In that same year, gross revenues from tourism were 17 percent of total merchandise hard-currency receipts.

By 1987, tourism receipts were the third-largest earner of hard currency in Cuba, excluding oil reexports (Banco Nacional de Cuba 1988, 10). Only sugar and fish products exports generated more hard currency for the Cuban economy than did international tourism (Zimbalist and Brundenius 1989, 149).

Tourism receipts are forecast to reach $1 billion by the year 2000. Cuban government officials project that by the end of the century, the international tourism industry will be the most significant generator of hard currency in the island's economy (McManus 1990, 55). Even if tourism receipts fall short of the $1 billion forecast by Cuban tourist officials, the relative importance of tourism as an export industry is sure to increase in the future, considering the poor prospects for Cuba's other major hard-currency-earning industries.

Gross receipts, however, do not accurately reflect the true contribution of international tourism to Cuba's balance of payments. A better measure would be net receipts—that is, gross receipts minus the associated hard-currency imports. The import component of tourism receipts includes the cost of imported goods and services used by tourists; the foreign exchange cost of capital investment; payments that leave Cuba in the form of profits, interest payments, royalties, management fees, payments to foreign travel agents, and so on; the cost of publicity and promoting travel to Cuba; and the cost of overseas training of service personnel.

Cuban sources, citing INTUR studies, report that between 23.0 and 64.9 percent of the cost of providing goods and services used by tourists and up to 50 percent of the cost of capital investment in the tourism sector is in hard currency (Canovas Rada 1990, 50). On average, the import component is calculated at 30–38 percent (Ayala Castro 1991, 23).

The INTUR estimates fall within the range estimated for other Caribbean countries, 25.2–44.8 percent (Pearce 1989, 197). There is no way to confirm these estimates, however, or to ascertain whether profits, internal payments, and management fees repatriated by foreign partners in joint ventures are included in them. The present practice of promoting foreign capital participation in the tourism sector and giving more and more concessions to foreign interests will further increase the import component of tourism receipts in Cuba.

International Tourism and Government Revenues

A major economic benefit of international tourism is that it generates revenues for the government. Direct and indirect revenues derived from tourism include aircraft landing fees, airport departure taxes, hotel occupancy taxes, sales taxes on tourist purchases, import duties on goods and services used by tourists, corporate taxes and profit repatriation taxes, and other licenses and fees.

Revenues generated by international tourism allow the host nation to export a portion of its tax burden. The portion of government revenues contributed by foreign visitors in Caribbean countries is estimated to be quite high, ranging from 20 percent in Saint Lucia to 62 percent in the Bahamas (Caribbean Tourist Research and Development Centre [CTRC] 1987, 11).

It is hard to ascertain the impact of international tourism on government revenues in Cuba. Whereas Cuba does not have a comprehensive tax structure, the majority of Cuba's factors of production are government-owned.

It is worth noting that Cuba's concessions to foreign investors regarding guaranteed profit repatriation and waiver of import tariffs might seriously curtail the potential benefits from international tourism. As Cuba moves toward a mixed economy, it should take care to create a tax structure that will increase government revenues from tourism.

International Tourism's Impact on Income and Employment

Spending by tourists directly injects foreign money into the local economy, creating income and employment for those who sell their goods and services to tourists. Partial estimates of the impact of international tourism in Cuba, made by INTUR, report that in 1988 entities under INTUR control contributed 455.9 million pesos to the national economy and employed 42,000 workers (Ayala Castro 1991, 23).

In 1988, INTUR operated around 80 percent of all the rooms available for international tourists in Cuba. Assuming that the total share of income and employment generated by tourism is also 80 percent, the total direct impact of international tourism in Cuba can be estimated at 547 million pesos and 50,400 jobs. These estimates represent only 2.1 percent of Cuba's total global social product (GSP) and 1.4 percent of total employment in 1988.

Tourist spending has more than a direct impact, however. Those who profit from it in turn purchase other goods and services. As spending circulates through the economy, a multiplier effect is created, generating more income and jobs.

The total impact of tourist spending on the local economy is a combination of direct and induced effects. It is calculated by multiplying tourist expenditures by a tourist income and/or employment multiplier. The value of the multiplier depends on the portion of income that leaks out of the local economy at each round of circulation. These leakages include payments for import of raw materials, rent and profits paid to nonresidents, and savings by residents. The larger and more diversified the economy in question, the lower the leakages and the larger the multiplier value.

Tourist income multipliers have been estimated for a number of countries in Asia, the Pacific, and the Caribbean (Archer 1982). For Hong Kong and Indian Ocean islands, they have been estimated at 1.02 and .95–1.03 respectively, at .65 for Fiji, and at .90–1.30 for Hawaii. Estimated values of the tourist income multiplier for small island economies in the Caribbean range from .58 for the British Virgin Islands to 1.58 for Jamaica; for other Caribbean island nations the estimated tourist income multipliers are Cayman Islands, .65; Bahamas, .78; Antigua, .88; Bermuda, 1.03; and Dominica, 1.20. The differences in these estimates result in part from different methodologies underlying their calculation.

Making a number of assumptions, the value of the tourism multiplier for Cuba can be estimated to be in the range of .74 to .84, one of the lowest values in the literature (See Appendix). This low value results primarily from Cuba's high propensity to import from both tourism receipts and income as a whole.

The expansionary effect of the multiplier is also affected by supply constraints. The multiplier concept rests on the premise that demand stimulates supply, but the Cuban economy does not facilitate this process. The multiplier effect of tourist expenditures is further curtailed by government policies designed to keep the tourism sector separate from the rest of the economy. The total impact of tourism expenditures on the Cuban economy is probably not much larger than the direct income and employment that these expenditures create.

In recent years many developing countries have turned to international tourism to promote economic growth. Tourism exports offer several advantages over other Third World exports, whether traditional or nontraditional. First, international tourism is a growth industry. Worldwide tourist arrivals increased at an annual average rate of 6.5 percent during the 1980s. Second, long-run prospects for international tourism are bright. Tourist demand is highly income-elastic. Third, tourism exports are more stable than those earned from traditional primary commodities; and, finally, developed nations place very few restrictions and barriers on international travel by their citizens, which is not the case with trade in manufactures.

Strong growth in an export sector, however, will not by itself promote economic growth and development in a nation. The sector's ability to stimulate economic growth depends on its linkages to the rest of the economy. A number of researchers have expressed serious doubts about whether the international tourist sector can establish linkages among industries (Bryden 1973; Griffith 1989). Establishing such ties is especially problematic because the international tourism sector is separated from the rest of the Cuban economy. Only when such segregation is abandoned and mass tourism is promoted will the possibilities for interindustry linkages increase. The experiences of the Mediterranean countries demonstrate that mass tourism can stimulate economic growth and development (Williams and Shaw 1988).

Establishing effective interindustry contacts between the tourist sector and the rest of the economy also depends on other factors, such as the structure of the economy, the skills of the labor force, internal demand,

162 ▪ María Dolores Espino

and a nation's capability for income substitution. At present, the tourism enclave model adopted by the Cuban government and the structure of the economy curtail the establishment of linkages between industries.

Concluding Remarks

In spite of the slowdown in the later 1980s, tourism to Cuba will probably increase in the next few years. Travelers will continue to be attracted to Cuba by low prices.

The primary economic benefit that Cuba currently derives from tourism is that it generates hard currency—and this seems to be the main motivation behind Cuba's tourism policy. The economic impact of tourism on the island's national income and employment is still very small both in absolute terms and in relation to national levels. This is due to two factors: (1) the low value of the tourism income multiplier and (2) constraints on supply. If international tourism is to become a vehicle for economic development in the 1990s, it must first become a leading generator of income and employment. For this to happen, in turn, the value of the tourism multiplier must increase—that is, Cuba must reduce its imports in all sectors. Second, effective linkages must be established with other sectors of the Cuban economy, in particular agriculture, services, and retailing.

The present policy of keeping the tourism sector separate from the rest of the economy hinders both the expansionary effect of the income multiplier and discourages linkages between tourism and other industries. Unless government policy changes, Cuba will continue to forgo the potential economic benefits from international tourism.

Appendix: Tourism Income Multiplier for Cuba

To a large extent, the choice of methodology to estimate tourism income multipliers has been governed by the availability of data and the existence of economywide econometric or input-output models. Lack of data and of economywide models has led many researchers to estimate a tourist income multiplier using an ad-hoc method.[6] They start by assuming an aggregate Keynesian multiplier of the following type:

$$T = \frac{1}{1-(c-m)}$$

In this model c is the marginal propensity to consume economywide and m is the marginal propensity to import nationwide. Since tourist expenditures might well be subject to leakages before undergoing the multiplier expansion, researchers have transformed the aggregate Keynesian multiplier into a tourist income multiplier as follows:

$$TM = \frac{1-a}{1-(c-m)}$$

In this model c and m are the same as above and a is the marginal propensity to import out of tourist receipts (the import component of tourist receipts).

At this time the values of c and m for the Cuban economy are not available, but estimates of the Cuban economy's average propensity to consume and average propensity to import can be found in the *Anuario Estadístico de Cuba*. Using the average values for 1989 of c and m and letting a range from .30 to .38 percent, a tourist income multiplier for Cuba can be estimated as follows:

$$TM = \frac{1-.30}{1-[.69-.525]} \text{ to } \frac{1-.38}{1-[.69-.525]} \; . \; = \; .84 \text{ to } .74 \; .$$

Notes

1. Calculation of Cuba's share of the Caribbean tourism market is hindered by lack of comparable data. Leal cites Cuba's share at about 18 percent; my calculations place it at around 21 percent.
2. This figure is cited by McManus (1990) and by Casanova and Monreal (1989).
3. Author's calculations. Of the 8,000 rooms available for international tourism in 1988, Cubanacán managed 1,562 (Mena 1989).
4. Visitors' receipts reported for Cuba are hard-currency receipts, so the correct calculation of both receipts per visitor and receipts per visitor night should be based on only visitors from capitalist countries, the only ones who generate hard currency.

5. Author's calculation based on CEE 1989, 396; and Dirección de Inmigración y Extranjería, *Estadística de Frontera*, unpublished data series on visitor arrivals.

6. For a review of the ad hoc multiplier and its application to tourism research, see Espino 1986.

References

Archer, B. H. 1982. "The Value of Multipliers and Their Policy Implications." *Tourism Management* 3, no. 4.
Ayala Castro, Héctor. 1991. "Notas Sobre el Turismo." Serie de Estudios Sobre la Economía Cubana, Universidad de la Habana. (June).
Banco Nacional de Cuba. 1960a. *Informe Económico*. Havana.
———. 1960b. *Memoria 1958–1959*. Havana.
———. 1960c. *Programa de Desarrollo Económico*. Informe no. 4, Havana.
———. 1991. "El Turismo en Cuba." Unpublished manuscript.
Bryden, J. 1973. *Tourism and Development: A Case Study of the Commonwealth Caribbean*. New York: Cambridge University Press.
Cabrera, Carlos. 1991. "A Challenging 12 Months." *Granma Weekly Review*, January 13.
Canovas Rada, Iveliz. 1990. "Evaluación de la Eficiencia Económica de los Polos Turísticos." *Planificación Física/Cuba*, no. 1.
Caribbean Tourism Organization. 1990. *Caribbean Tourism Statistical Report*. Barbados.
Caribbean Tourism Research and Development Centre (CTRC). 1987. *The Contribution of Tourism to Economic Growth and Development in the Caribbean*. (October).
Casanova Montero, Alfonso, and Pedro Monreal González. 1989. "Cuba and the United States: The Potential of Their Economic Relations." In *U.S.-Cuban Relations in the 1990s*, edited by Jorge I. Domínguez and Rafael Hernández. Boulder, Colo.: Westview Press.
Castells García, Jesús. 1989. "Tourism in Revolution." In *Cuban Foreign Trade*, no. 1.
Comité Estatal de Estadísticas (CEE). 1986, 1987, 1988. *Anuario Estadístico de Cuba*. Havana.
Cuba Business. 1991. 5, no. 4 (August).
Espino, María Dolores. 1986. "The Impact of Tourist Exports on Florida's Economy." Ph.D. dissertation, Florida State University.
———. 1992. "International Tourism in Cuba: An Economic Development Strategy?" In *Cuba in Transition*, pp. 193–220. Miami: Florida International University.

French, Howard W. 1991. "Cuba's New Hotels Dream of Dollars." *New York Times*, March 31, travel section.
Granma. 1991. October 16.
Griffith, Wiston. 1989. "Tourism in the Commonwealth Caribbean: A Case Study." In *The Troubled and Troubling Caribbean*, edited by Roy Glasgon and Wiston Langley. Lewiston, N.Y.: Edwin Mellen Press.
Grupo Cubano de Investigaciones Económicas. 1963. *Un Estudio Sobre Cuba*. Coral Gables, Fla.: University of Miami Press.
Leal, María M. 1990. "El turismo y su aporte a la economía mundial." Paper presented at the WAPTT/AMFORT Conference, Havana. (November).
Martín Fernández, Ramón. 1988. "El turismo y su desarrollo." *Economía y Desarrollo*, no. 5.
McManus, Jane. 1990. "Cashing in on the Caribbean." *South Survey* (June).
Mena, Jesús. 1989. "Quality Service for International Tourism." *Granma Weekly Review*, May 7.
Pearce, Douglas. 1989. *Tourist Development*. New York: John Wiley.
Pérez-López, Jorge. 1985. *The 1982 Cuban Joint Venture Law: Context, Assessment and Prospects*. Institute of Interamerican Studies, University of Miami, July.
———. 1988. "Cuban Hard-Currency Trade and Oil Reexports." In *Socialist Cuba: Past Interpretations and Future Challenges*, edited by Sergio G. Roca. Boulder, Colo.: Westview Press.
———. 1990. "Sugar and the Cuban Economy: Implications After Thirty Years." Paper presented to the Association for the Study of the Cuban Economy. Washington, D.C., October 18.
Pozo, Alberto. 1987. "Gallina de Huevos de Oro." *Bohemia* (February 6).
Ritter, A. R. M. 1988. "Cuba's Convertible Currency Debt Problem." *CEPAL Review* 36 (December): 117–40.
Roca, Sergio G. 1991. "Cuba y la nueva economía internacional: Tiempos duros, decisiones difíciles." Paper presented at the Latin American Studies Association meeting, Washington, D.C. (April).
Rodríguez, José Luis. 1990a. "Una imperiosa necesidad de cambios." *Cuba Internacional*. June.
———. 1990b. "The Cuban Economy: A Current Assessment." In *Transformation and Struggle: Cuba Faces the 1990s*, edited by Sandor Halebsky and John M. Kirk. New York: Praeger.
"Trade Winds: Cuba." *Miami Herald*. 1990. December 10, Business Monday section.
Truslow, Adam Francis. 1950. *Economic and Technical Mission to Cuba*. Washington, D.C.: International Bank for Reconstruction and Development.

Williams, Allan M., and Gareth Shaw, eds., 1988. *Tourism and Economic Development: Western European Experiences*. London: Belhaven Press.
World Tourism Organization. 1981. *Technical Handbook on the Collection and Presentation of Domestic and International Tourist Statistics*. Madrid.
———. 1986, 1988, 1989, 1990. *Yearbook of Tourism Statistics*.
Zimbalist, Andrew, and Claes Brundenius. 1989. *The Cuban Economy: Measurement and Analysis of Socialist Performance*. Baltimore: Johns Hopkins University Press.

EIGHT

Cuban Biotechnology
A First World Approach to Development
JULIE M. FEINSILVER

The Fourth Congress of the Cuban Communist Party, held during one of the most difficult times in the history of the Cuban revolution, gave further impetus to Cuba's long-standing strategy of using science to promote socioeconomic development. Although Fidel Castro first stated in 1961 that Cuba must not only take advantage of the scientific-technical revolution but also be a part of it, Cuban scientific development did not really take off until the mid-1980s. There were a number of scientific achievements in the 1970s, but there was a quantitative and qualitative leap forward in the 1980s, which included the establishment of a large scientific-industrial complex based around the campus of the Center for Genetic Engineering and Biotechnology (CIGB).

When Castro proclaimed a "special period in time of peace" in 1990, he designated biotechnology and medicine as priority sectors in which investments would continue despite a severe economic crisis and fiscal retrenchment. Castro stipulated that the country's scientists and technicians would make a concerted effort to increase food production, develop alternative exports, and seek ways to reduce imports (*Granma Weekly Review* 1990, 4). The Fourth Party Congress made imperative the application of science, particularly biotechnology and genetic engineering, to the most pressing problems of the population's and the regime's survival.

Biotechnology and genetic engineering were seen as creating export products, particularly pharmaceuticals, as well as products for domestic use that would substitute for imports the country could no longer afford. Their use developed from Cuba's highly advanced medical system, which, since 1980, had fostered health tourism, also a facet of the high-priority tourist sector (Feinsilver, 1992, 1993a).

The application of biotechnology and genetic engineering to agriculture to increase crop yields through the production of disease-resistant seeds and strains of plants, biofertilizers, biopesticides, and more productive strains of plants, and to improve animal health and milk and meat yields, would save millions of dollars of scarce hard currency (*Granma* 1991, 3). Likewise, the introduction of genetically engineered industrial enzymes into various production processes would also result in considerable savings and improve output. Because Cuba had previously taken a First World approach to the rapid generation and application of science and technology to economic development, the groundwork had been laid to meet the challenges of the Fourth Party Congress's dictates.

The appeal of science as an instrument of societal transformation has been common in developing nations with socialist ideologies because of socialism's "scientific" analysis of the movement of history and because science itself provides rational means by which to achieve development goals which then legitimate the regime (Apter 1964, 23–30). Only Cuba, however, has raised science to the highest priority and made it one of the most important weapons in the struggle to overcome underdevelopment and a severe economic crisis.

It is, indeed, rather astounding that Cuba should make biotechnology such a high priority in its development plans. No other country has done so, with the exception of Japan, which has the necessary industrial, scientific, and technological infrastructure and the capital to finance long-term projects that may or may not be fruitful (Bialy interview February 1991). This emphasis on biotechnology is clearly a First World approach to development. It is highly risky but also potentially highly rewarding, and it places Cuba in a position to take advantage of future developments that will be inaccessible to all but a handful of developing nations.

In what follows I shall briefly discuss the development of the Cuban biotechnology industry, then examine the products it has produced (particularly recent developments), their market potential, the effect of the special period on the biotechnology industry, the industry's performance in accordance with the resolutions of the Fourth Party

Congress, and the viability of this First World development strategy in a developing country with few resources and no benefactor.

The Cuban Biotechnology Industry

As I have discussed elsewhere, Cuban biotechnology and genetic engineering evolved from clinical medicine, which from the outset of the revolution was a key area of development (Feinsilver 1989, 1992, 1993a, 1993b). By 1980, when Castro decided to invest heavily in biotechnology and use the development of interferon as a model for advanced molecular biology procedures, Cuba already had a national network of health-care delivery facilities, medical schools, research institutes, and pharmaceutical and medical products factories that could be put at the service of this incipient scientific sector.

Considerable investment was made in biotechnology in the mid to late 1980s, so much so that in June 1992 a Cuban Academy of Sciences biotechnology database listed 53 centers that conducted biotechnology research. Twenty-six worked on agricultural, marine, and forestry biotechnology, 4 on industrial biotechnology, 12 on human medical and pharmaceutical biotechnology, 3 on both agricultural and human medical and pharmaceutical biotechnology, and 2 on agricultural and industrial biotechnology. Six did research on and developed support services and facilities, such as the development of specific pathogen-free laboratory animals, software design, databases, production automation processes, equipment and factory design and production, and scientific translation (Centro de Intercambio Automatizado de Información 1992). These do not include test sites and purely production facilities such as the eight biofactories for accelerated seed production and the 228 Biological Pest Control Production Centers that have been established across the nation (Foreign Broadcast Information Service [FBIS] 1992, 6).

Criticisms of Cuba's biotechnology effort revolve around two issues: 1) the cost of the project and 2) the focus on applied research rather than basic science. Cuba's investment in physical plants for biotechnology and genetic engineering is impossible to calculate because so many facilities have participated in the process over the years and not all of them were designed for or solely conduct biotechnology research. Moreover, data are not available for most facilities, and the Cubans do not include in their accounting process a number of factors such as the cost of land and surrounding infrastructure.

Cuban officials have repeatedly stated that the entire biotechnology industry is self-financing and that the initial investment has been recovered (Smith interview 1990; *Granma Weekly Review* 1991, 3; and FBIS 1992, 13). They fail, however, to state exactly what that investment was, to what facilities they refer, what their past and current sales are, and what their profits have been. Some of this information is available, but there is far too little for an accurate assessment.

Incomplete and at times contradictory data abound. Economic czar Carlos Lage, for example, has stated that from 1989 through 1992, over $300 million was invested in "121 objectives in the medical, pharmaceutical, and biotechnical industries in new incentives such as expanding goals and the modernization of important goals" and that this investment has been recovered through these centers' exports earnings in hard currency (FBIS 1992, 13). It is not at all clear to what objectives and goals he refers, and there is no mention of exactly what was exported.

Investments in science and technology for construction, equipment, feasibility studies, and advisory services have increased from 11.8 million pesos in 1977 to 65.2 million pesos in 1989. Construction and equipment costs alone skyrocketed from 1984 through 1986, the years in which CIGB was under construction. Costs for construction (68.5 million pesos) and equipment (73.3 million pesos) totaled 141.8 million pesos for those years. Investment declined somewhat between 1986 and 1989, but only by less than 20 percent. Current operating expenses for science and technology in general more than doubled between 1980 and 1989 (71.6 million pesos to 166.7 million pesos) (Comité Estatal de Estadísticas [CEE] 1991, 304). It is uncertain what percentage of these investments and expenses can be attributed to biotechnology, but one can assume that it is significant, given the government's policy of promoting biotechnology during that period.

Data are not available for later years in which considerable investment in new construction and equipment has been made. One European biotechnology laboratory equipment vendor confided in June 1992 that the past few years had been the best he had had in sales to Cuba and that the government had recently purchased equipment from him valued at over U.S.$500,000 (Anonymous source no. 89 interview 1992). He was not the only vendor pleased with Cuba's recent scientific expansion.

When pressed on the issue of recouping all costs, CIGB director Manuel Limonta admitted that no one pays off capital costs all at once and that CIGB was no different in this respect. He said that they were amortizing the capital costs but were self-financing in operating costs (Limonta Vidal interview 1992). This is certainly more believable than the less specific rhetoric that generally surrounds this subject.

Funding for Cuba's biotechnology enterprise has come from the United Nations Development Program (UNDP), the United Nations Industrial Development Organization (UNIDO), the Pan American Health Organization (PAHO), UNESCO, and the sale of biotechnology and pharmaceutical products. According to the United Nations agencies represented in Cuba (the above and the World Food Program [WFP]), they provided Cuba with $210 million from 1976 through 1991, and funds available for the 1992–96 period total $91 million, of which $32 million is not yet committed but is potentially available on a bilateral or multilateral basis (FAO et al. 1989). Although data are not available as to how much of this funding goes to biotechnology, it, along with previous Soviet aid, certainly has allowed the Cubans to divert funds from elsewhere to invest in biotechnology.

Daniel J. Goldstein, professor of biological sciences at the University of Buenos Aires, argues that the failure to do basic research limits Cuba's potential to create new technology. Cubans are, in his words, technicians rather than scientists (Goldstein 1991). Cuban scientists at CIGB recognize the importance of basic research and would do more of it if they had the resources, but they contend that their whole project is geared toward producing immediate, usable results rather than delving into questions of basic science (Smith 1990; Smith interview 1990; Herrera interview 1988). They do some basic research, such as work on transgenesis, but their aim has always been to harness science for socioeconomic development.

Biotechnology Products and Markets

Cuban researchers have developed over 160 medical-pharmaceutical biotechnology products and a number of agricultural and industrial biotechnology products, some innovative and others merely derivative. These products fall into four broad categories: human medical-pharmaceutical products (including diagnostics and therapeutics), industrial enzymes and bioremediation (for example, the use of microorganisms to clean up oil spills), agricultural applications (for example, plant and animal genetics), and research laboratory equipment and supplies. Whereas biotechnology companies in the United States are primarily concerned with human diagnostics (28 percent) and therapeutics (35 percent), the most lucrative market segments, only 8 percent work on agricultural biotechnology (Burrill and Lee 1990, 16). In Cuba the primary focus is on medical applications as well, but agricultural biotechnology is far more important than in the United States, particularly during the special period. As a result, there has been an exponential increase in research on and production of biopesticides, biofertilizers, disease-resistant seeds, and tissue cultures to clone *in vitro* seedlings.

Agricultural Biotechnology

Cuban researchers have been working on improving crop strains and livestock breeds since the 1960s, but it was not until the big push in biotechnology in 1981 that a more concerted effort was made. Finally, with the prioritization of biotechnology in 1989, vast resources, both human and fiscal, were dedicated to addressing the country's economic development problems through the rapid application of research results, a policy reaffirmed in 1991 at the Fourth Party Congress.

For two decades scientists at the Tropical Agricultural Research Institute have been producing strains of soybeans for local conditions; they have aimed for resistance to heat, rain, and pests. They have recently developed a new type of soybean, Cubasoy 23, that takes only 100 days from planting to harvest. It also makes the soil ready for other crops with which it will be rotated (sugarcane and tobacco) because it does not deplete the soil of moisture and nitrogen but rather enhances their retention, thereby saving time and resources. In spring 1992, 16,500 acres of soybeans were planted by 142 sugar mills in 13 provinces. The following spring, the new Cubasoy 23 was to be planted on 19,800 acres (Radio Havana Cuba, August 10, 1992).

In the Cuban Sugar Research Institute's pilot study of ifopol, the biological bactericide they developed to preserve sugarcane after cutting, the product was found to increase industrial yield by 0.54 percent. The Cuban reporter writing about this claimed that when the seemingly insignificant increase is extrapolated across the country, it would generate considerable savings ("El recurso" 1991). This appears to be a bit hyperbolic.

Although less immediately useful, Cuban researchers are also working on plant, animal, and fish transgenesis; that is, the introduction of foreign DNA into cells to modify their structure. They claim to have successfully produced the first transgenic sugarcane in the world, but Harvey Bialy, research editor of *Bio/Technology*, the scientific journal to which they have submitted their findings, said that their data are "not terribly convincing." He contends that Cuban scientists are much less advanced in this field than in other areas of biotechnology and that transgenesis does not provide immediate dividends because whether a crop is disease resistant or pest resistant is not immediately evident (Bialy interview 1993).

The current benefit of agricultural biotechnology is clearly import substitution. Cuba has saved millions of dollars a year through import substitution and increased productivity. Genetic engineering laboratories produce disease-resistant seeds for more than five basic crops (FBIS 1991, 4). Cuba's National Research Center (CENIC) biochemists have produced dry cells for poultry feed by extracting lysine from yeast (Ubell 1983, 746). Center for Biological Research (CIB) scientists innovatively isolated a toxin that causes hemorrhagic bovine disease and developed a vaccine for it (Miller 1986, 22). A fertilizer for sugarcane produced from *cachaza*, a sugar byproduct, was first used massively in the 1991–92 harvest, with 80,000 tons applied. In the 1992–93 harvest, 1 million tons were to be used (FBIS 1992, 6).

Perhaps the most important biofertilizer is Rhizobium, which is used as an inoculant in legume seeds to promote nodulation and nitrogen fixation. Yields of crops on which Rhizobium has been used have reportedly increased by 30 to 75 percent, depending on the soil type and species planted. Savings on imported nitrogen-based fertilizers for legumes are between 80–150 kilos per hectare, which in the case of soybeans amounts to up to US$92 a hectare. Extrapolating from the 1991 soy planting of 16,500 acres, one may say that potential savings for that year alone would come to US$614,575. Moreover, Rhizobium increases the amount of protein in the soybean by 8 percent and the amount of fodder (used as a high-protein animal feed) by 15 percent when the plant is harvested in 65 days (Añe 1992, 15).

Tissue culture research is a major area of concentration and has led to the establishment of six biofactories with the capacity to propagate *in vitro* 3.5 to 5 million plantain seedlings. The Villa Clara biofactory produces sugarcane somaclones of various varieties on an industrial scale as well. By June 1991, four biofactories had cloned 4.7 million plantain seedlings from tissue culture, which has led to substantial savings. Tissue culture research is also being conducted on potatoes, pineapple, tobacco, grazing grasses, garden vegetables, and fruits, including citrus (Añe 1992, 14; Radio Havana Cuba August 6, 1992).

Although it is difficult to calculate the significance of Cuba's total savings from import-substitution without more data, the magnitude of the effort and of prior imports is noteworthy. Since the beginning of the special period, the Cuban government has created 228 Biological Pest Control Production Centers and eight centers for the accelerated production of seeds (FBIS 1992, 6). Data are not available on their total output, but, according to Rosa Elena Simeón, president of the Cuban Academy of Sciences, in 1990 Cuba had already saved US$7 million a year on potato seeds alone (FBIS 1991, 4). Given the scientific infrastructure already in place and the rush to implement research results, total savings are probably considerable and sufficient to make the second CIGB, located in Camagüey and devoted to agriculture, self-financing in operating costs.

In 1989 Cuba imported 1.3 million tons of fertilizers (nitrogen, phosphorus, and potassium), but in 1992 it could afford to import fewer than 250,000 tons. The development of biofertilizers capable of nitrogen fixation, such as azotobacter, produced by CENIC through fermentation, should enable Cuban farmers to fertilize their fields with a significant reduction in hard-currency expenditures. Azotobacter was used for the first time in Cuba in 1992, when 6 million liters were applied (FBIS 1992, 5).

Trade data for 1989 and 1992 indicate that Cuba spent 157.7 million pesos on imported fertilizers in 1989 and 80.8 million pesos on herbicides and pesticides, but only US$30 million on herbicides and pesticides in 1992 (FBIS 1992, 5; and CEE 1991, 283). What portion of that can be substituted by nitrogen fixation, biofertilizers, inoculants, and biopesticides is unclear. The point, however, is that over time the savings could be substantial, and production could be increased to make possible exports to other developing countries, all of which could benefit from these biotechnology products.

Industrial Biotechnology and Bioremediation

Biotechnology is being used both as an input into various industrial processes and to improve the industrial efficiency of sugar mills through the addition of enzymes at various junctures in the production process (FBIS 1991, 4). Various genetically engineered enzymes such as alpha-amylase, beta-galactosidase, invertase, dextranase, alkaline, and rennin are used in other Cuban industrial processes. Alpha-amylase and invertase are used in the beverage industry (alpha-amalyse in soft drinks and brewing and invertase in soft drinks and liquors); and alpha-amylase, which breaks down starches, among other things, is also employed in the textile and sugar industries. Alkalines are part of the soap and perfume production processes.

Beta-galactosidase aids in the digestion of dairy products by those who are lactose intolerant, and recombinant rennin is a critical part of the cheese-making process. Both products have been singled out as being perfect vehicles through which to foster cooperation with and integration into Latin America. It is suggested that these products have considerable market potential because the world supply does not satisfy the demand and, in the case of beta-galactosidase, that a large percentage of the world population has some type of lactose intolerance. Natural rennin is scarce, and the development of other types of natural starter cultures is often quite slow. An investment of about US$4 million is needed to develop these two products on a large industrial scale, and the Cubans are analyzing various types of economic associations with foreign entities that might provide the initial capital. Anticipated profits are expected to be greater than those from traditional exports, and the investment should be recouped in a short time (Añe 1992, 16).

Bioremediation, the use of microbes to clean up oil spills, is important but has received considerably less attention than medical and agricultural biotechnology. Cuban researchers, however, have been studying various types of surfactants (surface-active agents), such as oil-eating microbes. They have also developed anticor, an anticorrosive agent to chemically clean sugar mill equipment ("El recurso" 1991).

The Institute of Oceanology has researched surfactants for some years now and is currently testing five types of autochthonous marine bacteria and microbial groups to see which is most active in breaking down hydrocarbons. In tests the microbes have already proven effective in breaking down petroleum in twenty days, leaving behind fewer complex hydrocarbons with less molecular weight. These microorganisms have other important applications in the oil industry, such as to decrease the viscosity of Cuban crude and make it easier to extract oil and to clean oil tanks and tanker ships. The microbes can also be employed in the textile and cosmetics industries (Salazar 1992).

Human Medical-Pharmaceutical Products

It is in the field of human medical-pharmaceutical product development that Cuban biotechnology has excelled so far. The major results of this endeavor are recombinant alpha 2b interferon, natural interferons, interleukin-2, colony-stimulating factors, recombinant hepatitis B vaccine, recombinant streptokinase, 39 monoclonal antibodies, mathematical modulation of the micromolecular structure of antibodies, reagents, 40 restriction endonucleases, 8 modification enzymes, 4 other enzymes for use in molecular biology, recombinant epidemeral growth factor, diagnostic kits (for HIV, hepatitis B, allergies, congenital malformations, infectious diseases, and so on), and human transfer factor (Feinsilver 1993a, 1992). (Researchers are currently working on a recombinant meningitis B vaccine but have not yet achieved it.) Most of these products, however, have been patented in the major markets by transnational pharmaceutical companies.

Of the products listed above, perhaps three have the greatest commercial potential: recombinant hepatitis B vaccine, recombinant streptokinase, and interferons. The Cuban hepatitis B vaccine has proven effective in clinical trials in Cuba, Colombia, Venezuela, Russia, and Eastern Europe, and the results show good seroconversion and titer of antibodies.[1] If this vaccine is certified, it can be provided to all UN organizations, including UNICEF, which provides vaccines to the Pan American Health Organization (PAHO) and other regional and state Expanded Immunization Programs (EPI). The EPI have recently included hepatitis B vaccine because hepatitis leads to chronic liver disease.

PAHO and other international organizations buy vaccines from the least expensive World Health Organization (WHO)–certified bidder. The successful laboratory must meet WHO criteria for hygiene, good manufacturing practices (GMP), standard operating procedures, technical operations data, and scientific data. Moreover, the lab must allow WHO to make inspection visits to the production site. Cuba should be able to meet these criteria because of recent large investments in quality control, adherence to U.S. and international standards, the presence of a well-qualified group of people working in the area, and first-class production facilities (Herrera interview 1992; anonymous source no. 87 interview April 30, 1992, and 1993). These conditions are the result of the government's high priority on biotechnology exports in the special period, which entails rigorously meeting international standards (something they were less wont to do in the past).

There is, however, stiff competition for the Cuban recombinant hepatitis B vaccine because it is also produced by such pharmaceutical giants as Smith-Kline, Merck-Sharpe, RIT Belgium, and at least three Japanese companies. Smith-Kline has licensed its technology to China and North Korea as well, making potential barter deals for Cuba's sale of the vaccine to China rather unlikely unless China cannot produce a sufficient quantity for domestic purposes.

When questioned about possible violation of intellectual property rights, CIGB deputy director Luis Herrera stated that they changed the process of obtaining recombinant hepatitis B vaccine and its genetic structure, and the immunological effect increased as a result. Cuba has therefore requested patents in the European Community (Herrera interview 1992). The vaccine's developer, Eduardo Pentón Arias, said in June 1992 that it was registered in Russia and Colombia and was at various stages in the registration and patent process in Venezuela, Brazil, Mexico, India, and the European Community (Pentón Arias interview 1992). Cuba has sold recombinant hepatitis B vaccine to Colombia, and the vaccine was also part of Cuba's trade package with the former Soviet Union for 1990 and 1991, but political and economic difficulties prior to the USSR's dissolution nullified the exchange (Pentón Arias interview 1992; FBIS 1990, 7–8).

Recombinant streptokinase, used to dissolve blood clots during heart attacks and to prevent cerebral embolisms, is innovative, but natural streptokinase is relatively inexpensive ($76-$300 per dose) and readily available. The recombinant form would be attractive to buyers primarily if it were less expensive than the natural form or if it were more stable or more active (Anonymous source no. 74 interview 1991; *New York Times* 1992, A16). Cuba's prices for most medical-pharmaceutical products have been below market prices, sometimes considerably below. To enter the world market and compete in it, Cuba must charge a price well below what the transnational pharmaceutical companies charge. The current attitude of some Cuban decision makers, however, is to charge as much as possible, even if it means a lower volume of sales and a short time horizon (Anonymous Cuban source no. 36 interview 1992).

Heber Biotec, the commercial arm of CIGB, did not list prices in its 1992–93 product catalog, and I am not aware of any source for them. Manuel Limonta, the director of CIGB, and Carlos Mella, the president of Heber Biotec, have repeatedly stated that they will consider any type of deal to get their products on the market as long as it is beneficial to Cuba (Limonta interview 1992; Mella interview 1991). As the economy continues to deteriorate rapidly, the Cubans have become more aggressive about trying to market their wares and thus will probably be more inclined to sell at a lower price.

The worldwide market for interferons began to expand in the 1990s as clinical results indicated their increasing utility. According to a U.S. pharmaceutical industry securities analyst, "Alpha interferon is at the springboard of several antiviral and anticancer indications that make it look like it could be a $1 billion drug" (New York Times 1990, C1 and C17). Worldwide sales were already over $300 million annually according to 1990 estimates and are expected to triple by 1994 partly because the drug is used to treat hepatitis (ibid.).

Alpha interferon has also recently been proven effective in halting the progression to AIDS in people who are HIV-positive but asymptomatic and in treating Karposi's sarcoma, an AIDS-related cancer. This should vastly increase the market. Schering-Plough, however, already sells alpha interferon in 51 countries, and Hoffman-LaRoche is also a major supplier (New York Times 1991). It is rumored that the Cubans have made a deal with a European firm to distribute Cuban interferon and genetically engineered vaccines, but no data are available. The export manager of Heber Biotec affirmed that they were selling interferons and recombinant hepatitis B vaccine, among other products, and that they were close to having most of their biotechnology products registered in Colombia, Venezuela, Argentina, and Mexico. Heber Biotec was not, however, looking at the Russian market, but only those of Latin America, Asia, and Europe (Miró interview 1992).

Equipment and Supplies

Domestic need and economic difficulties led to import-substitution production of various types of equipment and supplies for genetic engineering such as the diagnostic process SUMA, electrophoresis and gas chromatography equipment, restriction endonucleases, nucleic acid reagents, DNA molecular weight markers, diagnostic kits (for human and plant diseases), monoclonal antibodies (for human, plant, and veterinary diagnostics), computer software, databases such as a worldwide directory of biotechnology enterprises, and specific pathogen-free (SPF) laboratory animals, among other things.

Perhaps the most commercially viable advance in this area is the development of a less expensive than the universally standard diagnostic process ELISA (enzyme-linked immunosorbent assay). According to an international expert, the Cuban-developed SUMA (Ultra-Micro ELISA System) shows "an impressive array of performance characteristics" (Bialy 1987). The first model of SUMA, made in 1981, used only a tenth of the reagents of a standard ELISA (the most expensive part of testing), making SUMA suitable for cost-effective mass screenings of individuals for HIV, hepatitis B, alpha fetoprotein, hyperthyroidism, and allergies; mass screening of blood supplies for HIV and hepatitis B; and diagnosis of viral diseases in plantains, sugarcane, potatoes, and tobacco (Heredia del Portal interview 1988; Añe 1992, 15). Sixth-generation SUMAs made in 1992 required only between one- twentieth to one-sixtieth of the reagents the standard ELISA used, thereby further reducing test costs (Centro de Inmunoensayo n.d., 14–15).

Because of Cuba's inexperience in selling in an unprotected market, little attention was paid to marketing techniques until late 1991. As a result, the Brazilian biotechnology firm Vallee Diagnósticos, which produces diagnostic kits for AIDS, hepatitis, and syphilis, purchased its technology in 1988 from a U.S. firm for more than twice the price it would have had to pay Cuba for the same technology only because it was unaware of the Cuban products at that time (*Folha de São Paulo* 1988).

By 1990, however, seven SUMAs had been sold to Brazil, and in 1992 a Brazilian importer that markets SUMA and other high-technology Cuban medical equipment (electrocardiograph and electromyographic analysis systems) made more sales in two weeks than would have been expected in two months. Brisk sales resulted from the comparatively low prices and large volumes of sales to the state secretaries of health. Brazilian companies are now seeking a joint production arrangement with the Cubans for their medical equipment (Panisset interview 1993).

Problems and Prospects

Problems facing all biotechnology producers worldwide are the high costs of research and development, the long lead time required to get products to market, stiff competition, intellectual property rights disputes, the lack of uniform patent legislation, and complex and changing regulatory processes (Burrill and Lee 1990, 4–8). Like most producers of biotechnology products worldwide, the Cubans are seeking strategic alliances with companies that can provide what they lack: capital, marketing expertise, distribution networks, and name recognition and reputation in the marketplace (ibid, pp. 1–2, 20–21).

Foreign investment in Cuba's biotechnology industry should offer good returns if distribution problems are solved, because, unlike most U.S. biotechnology firms, the Cuban industry has not just one tested product ready to market but 160 products, some of which should give Cuba a comparative advantage. A foreign analyst suggested that this advantage could be "worth several billion dollars per year in product sales over the long term" (Diamond 1991). U.S. companies have managed to attract investment with only the promise of products to come; thus it would seem that investment in Cuban biotechnology should be forthcoming. Mexican investors are reported to have expressed interest in, and invested in, Cuban biotechnology recently (Radio Havana Cuba 1992).

There are, however, various reasons why Cuba may not be able to capitalize on its biotechnology investments in the manner suggested by Fidel Castro both before and during the Fourth Party Congress. Since I and a few others have made most of these criticisms previously, the Cubans have made considerable progress in rectifying their errors and deficiencies (Feinsilver 1993a, 1993b, 1992; Diamond 1991). They are eager to learn and to change, but they have not yet solved all of their problems related to marketing, sales and distribution networks; competition; patents (others and theirs); credibility in the marketplace; the U.S. embargo; their overall economic situation and economic practices (including the lack of strategic planning); scarcity of resources (for biotechnology and in general); and a stressful environment overall in which young scientists must come up with solutions to extraordinarily difficult economic problems.

Industrywide problems affect the Cubans, but differently in some cases from the way they affect private companies in market economies. For example, costs are much less for the Cuban biotechnology industry (research, production, packaging, and marketing) because salaries and domestic inputs are only a fraction of those paid by private concerns elsewhere, as are some of the capital costs, and because the functions from initial research to sales are now integrated (Limonta interview

1992). Despite Cuba's integrated development approach, however, a strategic alliance is still a necessary condition for ultimate success in the market.

In the biotechnology industry in market economies, small start-up companies do the initial research and then merge with, are acquired by, or enter into some other type of strategic alliance with transnational pharmaceutical companies to market and distribute their products. Even the most successful U.S. biotechnology company, Genentech, made a deal a few years ago with Hoffman-LaRoche in which the latter acquired a majority stake in Genentech (Burrill and Lee 1990, 1).

Nowhere is Cuba's need for a strategic alliance more evident than in marketing and distribution. Until late 1991, the Cubans thought marketing was simply a matter of offering a good product at a lower price than that charged by the competition. They did not realize that marketing is both a science and an art and that it requires strategic planning. They were unaware of the need to identify a niche in the market into which they could reasonably insert their products.

Because of their lack of attention to strategic planning, the Cubans have invested considerable time and resources in the development of existing products or products under development elsewhere rather than seeking a niche for themselves. This results from the fact that the Cuban biotechnology industry has been based on learning by copying others, the method successfully employed by the Japanese and the Asian tigers in other economic sectors. Moreover, Cuban biotechnology developed not from some global strategic plan but from unrelated scientific advances, particularly in clinical medicine. The original impetus, as I have argued elsewhere, was to make Cuba a world medical power and accumulate symbolic capital (prestige, influence, credit, and goodwill) that could ultimately be converted into material capital (trade and aid) (Feinsilver 1993a, 1989).

In the 1990s Cuban scientists are focusing more on finding innovative products and methods of expression of genes. Because all science builds on the work of others, most biotechnology companies do work on products that others are developing as well. It is a race against time to see who gets to the market first.

Without the slick marketing techniques, the distribution networks, and the follow-up and service of the established producers, it is unlikely that Cuba can gain a foothold in the market unless it finds a partner (perhaps in a joint venture) to market and distribute its products. Recognizing this problem, the industry is currently pursuing a strategy of seeking local partners in each market and being flexible as to the type of deal that is worked out (Herrera interview 1992; Miró interview 1992; Lage interviews 1993).

The need to do market research to analyze the prospects for each product in each market, to design a specific strategy to develop each product and market, and to find a suitable partner in each market did not become part of Cuban strategy until 1992 (Limonta interview 1992). To aid in this endeavor, the Center for Automated Information Exchange of the Cuban Academy of Sciences has developed a worldwide descriptive database, Biotec (which is patented and marketed abroad), which lists all types of organizations, associations, firms (suppliers and vendors), and consultants in the biotechnology field and provides information on the activities they conduct. The database, which is available on CD/ROM, covers 114 countries and had over 6,800 entries in June 1992 (Centro de Intercambio Automatizado de Información, 1992).

Access to this information is a good start, but Cuban planners and policy makers also need confidential information about strategic planning in biotechnology companies elsewhere in order not to waste time and money on products that have little likelihood of success in competition with producers that have a well-established global market presence (Diamond 1991). This information is extremely difficult for them to get, but not impossible.

On a positive note, the principal biotechnology marketing firm, Heber Biotec, has made a dramatic improvement in product catalogs since 1991. Their 1992–93 catalog and promotional materials approached international standards. None of the Cuban biotechnology centers or firms, however, has the large expense accounts for marketing activities that the transnational vendors have, and this too makes a difference in sales potential.

The global biotechnology market is small and largely divided among the major transnational pharmaceutical and chemical corporations. Cuba cannot compete with the transnationals and gain a share of the world market for most products primarily because it cannot sell to countries that recognize U.S., European, and Japanese patents. Cuba, like most developing countries, has copied patented products without license and markets them. Cuban interferons, for example, could only be sold for research use rather than medical use in those markets because all interferons are already patented there (Bialy interview June 17, 1991). For this reason CIGB is currently looking for new ways of expressing interferon and other products, which would allow them to apply for a patent for a new process (Herrera interview 1992).

Even if Cuba could compete with the transnationals, it could not supply the U.S. market because of a three-decade-old trade embargo against its products and those made with Cuban components. This embargo has been tightened with the passage of the Cuban Democracy Act of 1992, which encourages Cuba's trading partners to restrict trade with Cuba, forbids entry into U.S. harbors of any vessel that has been to Cuba within the previous six months, and precludes U.S. government aid and debt forgiveness for any country that assists Cuba by granting Cuba any type of preferential treatment in the market. Moreover, the law specifically forbids exports to Cuba that will aid its biotechnology industry (*Cuban Democracy Act* 1992, 692–94 and 698).

Another serious problem is that the entire Cuban economy has been geared to uncompetitive (subsidized and protected) production for the past three decades, and considerable time will elapse before substantive change can be made. It is difficult to have a highly efficient productive enclave in the midst of an inefficient economy. Even more worrisome is the vast deterioration of the Cuban economy in general in the special period. Although the biotechnology sector is spared much of the hardship, the general environment negatively affects everyone to some degree.

The ongoing economic crisis has led to the rapid commercialization of products, often before they have been extensively tested. Foreign critics are not the only ones who believe that Cuba has rushed biotechnology and medical products to the market. Cuban scientists have also decried marketing agencies' rush to sell their discoveries.[2] This initially led to problems of quality, but these have reportedly been solved with the implementation over the past two years of rigorous quality control procedures and equipment (Anonymous source no. 87 1993). Cuba's credibility in the international market, however, is linked to its ability to disseminate convincing scientific information about its products and counteract attempts to discredit Cuba in the media. Cuban scientists are working on this through efforts to increase publications in scientific journals and by their participation in international conferences, but the U.S. government has denied visas to Cuban biotechnology scientists on a number of occasions and most recently barred their attendance at the annual biotechnology meetings in Miami in 1992 (Bialy interview 1993). This policy, however, may change with the new administration.

Cuba may get around some of these difficulties by concentrating on the Third World market and that of the former Soviet republics until these countries agree to recognize patents, and by agreeing to barter trade, countertrade, or clearing accounts rather than hard currency payable in cash. Developing countries, however, may be unable to afford Cuba's biotechnology products because their governments have other, more pressing priorities for their scarce resources. On the other hand, because Cuba's products are often less expensive than those otherwise available, their purchase would be a wise use of scarce resources if these products are needed. It can be argued that most are needed and would result in long-term savings for the purchaser, but the purchaser may not have the option to think long-term because of the current economic crisis.

Barter, countertrade, and clearing accounts are still at the heart of Cuba's recent trade and cooperation agreements with various African, Latin American, and Middle Eastern countries and with China and the republics of the former Soviet Union. These agreements have included an increase in cooperation (which means aid and trade, particularly barter) in the health sphere whereby Cuba provides medical, pharmaceutical, and biotechnology products and the other party furnishes whatever it can (agricultural or industrial goods) that Cuba either needs or can sell elsewhere, through triangular deals, for something more useful.

Finally, Cuba's biotechnology investment may provide large dividends if the extensive scientific infrastructure and human resources are leased to a transnational pharmaceutical company. Because of the enormous costs of their development, Cuba's installed capacity and research and development capabilities should be very attractive to a foreign investor. The question is whether a deal can be struck that the Cuban government believes is beneficial for the development of both the industry and the country and whether a partner can be found that is farsighted enough to make the investment now. Agustín Lage, the director of the Center for Molecular Immunology, suggested that from the Cuban perspective, this was a possibility (Lage interviews 1993).

Biotechnology and the Special Period

Scarcity of resources in the special period has accentuated the government's desire for scientists to solve all of the problems of development, which in turn would further stratify society by scientific ability and ultimate ability to produce something exportable or for import substitution. As a result, increased competition among research centers in Cuba may be inevitable unless research efforts are consolidated and interrelated rather than separated. There is some indication that, in fact, consolidation of efforts is taking place as the university faculties are becoming involved in projects with research institutions and scientists affiliated with those institutions are participating in the teaching and training of university students (Trueba González 1991).

On the other hand, the special period is forcing many entities to be self-financing. They must therefore compete with each other for scarce resources and for markets. Although Heber Biotec represents CIGB and also markets some products made elsewhere, such as monoclonal antibodies, the other research institutes also market their products independently. It is not clear if they are working together as part of a team that is casting a wide net to capture as many customers as possible or if each is simply trying to finance its own institute's operations. The latter appears to be the case.

Whether Cuba can continue to maintain a highly privileged scientific sector in a country that in many areas is rapidly returning to the preindustrial era is questionable. Tensions are bound to arise between workers in this sector and in the nonprivileged sectors of society, particularly those workers who become marginally employed or unemployed because of the energy and raw material shortages and have to work in agriculture.

The special period has affected resources for biotechnology in the sense that cost accounting is now being done and greater effort is made to prevent the wasting of reagents and other supplies. In fact, a scientist can no longer get supplies without approval from the department head and the division chief. At the same time, equipment orders and construction projects to boost research, development, and production are given high priority. European vendors have seen an increase in equipment sales to Cuba for biotechnology development during the special period.

Conclusions

The overall policy of capitalizing on the development of biotechnology is a sound, First World approach to development, but the current economic circumstances make short-term success difficult, though not impossible. Cuban biotechnology was developed primarily to meet domestic needs; thus import-substitution in agriculture, industry, and medicine makes biotechnology worth the investment. Perhaps most important, Cuba must maintain its commitment to biotechnology to be in a position to take advantage of the breakthroughs that are yet to come in this field, otherwise the country will see the technological gap widen between itself and the developed world.

Agricultural biotechnology should hold great promise, particularly in Cuba, where research results can be implemented immediately, as suggested by the Fourth Party Congress. It is not, however, a panacea for all of the woes that face Cuban agriculture. Biotechnology can decrease the need for imported pesticides and fertilizers but as yet cannot entirely replace them. It can provide disease-resistant seeds, and seedlings from tissue cultures, but agriculture still depends more on weather conditions than on science, as recent devastating floods and storms have proven.

Recombinant epidermal growth factor, recombinant hepatitis B vaccine, interferons, reagents and restriction endonucleases, and recombinant streptokinase have been sold in Latin America and Europe, and most of those and other products as well have been sold to Russia and China. These products, like SUMA and the industrial enzymes beta-galactosidase and rennin, should be attractive on the world market, but the competition is stiff. Finally, Cuba has great prospects as an offshore production facility if it can find an appropriate strategic alliance.

Some international biotechnology experts who are sympathetic to Cuba admit privately that they see no hope, not just for Cuba, but for biotechnology companies in general, primarily because of the complex regulatory environment and the financial ill health of much of the industry. On the other hand, industry analysts in the United States predict billion-dollar sales for some products that Cuba produces. If Cuba can get into the market, it should be able to make biotechnology a success. Rumor has it that some marketing agreements have already been made for sales in Europe and Latin America, but no details are available at this time. It is highly unlikely, however, that Cuba will have time to see the fruits of its investment.

Notes

1. The following discussion of hepatitis B vaccine is based on interviews with anonymous source no. 87, August 8, 1991, April 30, 1992, July 13, 1992, and November 23, 1992.

2. Dr. Alejandro Silva, head of the microbiology laboratory at CIB, and Dr. Silvio Barcelona, one of the directors of CIB, cited in "Cuban-made interferons" 1986; Pan American Health Organization, internal memorandum HSD/MGP/92.18 1989; Pan American Health Organization, internal document HSD/BIO program 1989, 1 and 3; Anonymous source no. 87, November 12, 1991.

References

Published Sources

Añe, Lia. 1992. "La biotecnología en la agricultura cubana: análisis preliminar." *Boletín de Información sobre Economía Cubana* 1, no. 1 (January): 14–16.
Apter, David E., ed. 1964. *Ideology and Discontent*. New York: Free Press.
Bialy, Harvey. 1987. "Cuba to Market an Ultra-Microelisa System." *Bio/Technology* 5 (July): 663.
Burrill, G. Steven, and Kenneth B. Lee, Jr. 1990. *Biotech 91: A Changing Environment: Fifth Annual Survey of Business and Financial Issues in America's Most Promising Industry*. San Francisco: Ernst and Young.
Centro de Immunoensayo. N.d. Brochure on the Immunoassay Center and SUMA.
Centro de Intercambio Automatizado de Información. 1992. *Biotec* data base. July 12.
Centro de Intercambio Automatizado de Información. N.d. Promotional literature on Biotec and a sample printout for Cuba.
Comité Estatal de Estadísticas (CEE). 1991. *Anuario estadístico de Cuba 1989*. Havana.
Cuban Democracy Act of 1992. PL 102–484, 1992 HR 5006, pp. 692–94, 698. Weslaw fax.
"Cuban-made Interferons Reach Out for World Markets." 1986. *Biotechnology Newswatch* 6, no. 6 (March 17): 3.
Diamond, Stuart. 1991. "Cuba: The Biotechnology Industry Second Report on International Opportunities. Key Issues in Marketing and Strategy." United Nations Center for Transnational Corporations Informe al Gobierno de la República de Cuba. Unpublished manuscript.
"El recurso de la tecnología." 1991. *Bohemia* (January 15): 32.
FAO, OMS, PMA, PNUD, UNESCO. 1989. "Informe de las agencias de las Naciones Unidas representadas en Cuba preparado para una reunión con el presidente de los Consejos de Estado y de Ministros de Cuba, Fidel Castro Ruz," November 24. Unpublished manuscript.

Feinsilver, Julie M. 1993a. *Healing the Masses: Cuban Health Politics at Home and Abroad.* Berkeley and Los Angeles: University of California Press.

———. 1993b. "Can Biotechnology Save the Cuban Revolution?" *NACLA Report on the Americas* 26, no. 5 (May): 7–10.

———. 1992. "Will Cuba's Wonder Drugs Lead to Political and Economic Wonders? Capitalizing on Biotechnology and Medical Exports." *Cuban Studies* 22: 79–111.

———. 1989. "Cuba as a 'World Medical Power': The Politics of Symbolism." *Latin American Research Review* 24, no. 2: 1–34.

Folha de São Paulo. 1989. April 6, 1988, A17; cited in Ulysses B. Panisset. "Health Diplomacy in Latin America: A Case Study of Health Technology Cooperation between Brazil and Cuba." Unpublished manuscript.

Foreign Broadcast Information Service. *Latin America Daily Report,* FBIS-LAT-90-083, April 30, 1990, 7-8; FBIS-LAT-91-007, January 10, 1991, 4; and FBIS-LAT-92-219, November 12, 1992, 5–13.

Goldstein, Daniel J. 1991. Personal communication, July 21.

Granma, 1991. October 17, 3.

Granma Weekly Review, 1990. August 5, 4, 12; 1991. January 13, 3.

"International Trade: Bush's Signing of the Cuba Embargo Law May Trigger GATT Complaint, EC Warns." 1992. *Daily Report For Executives,* October 28.

Miller, Julie Ann. 1986. "Cuba's Commitment to Genetic Engineering Grows in Size and Scope." *Genetic Engineering News* (May): 22.

New York Times, August 16, 1990, C1, C17; February 26, 1991, D1; March 27, 1992, A16.

Organización Panamericana Sanitaria. 1989. "Reunión operativa interpaises OPS/OMS en cooperación técnica entre paises (CTPD/CTP) en el contexto del presupuesto programa de la OPS/OMS 1990–1991." Havana, November.

Pan American Health Organization. Internal memorandum HSD/MGP/92.18, August 17, 1989; and HSD/BIO program, May 1989.

Radio Havana Cuba, August 6, 1992; August 10, 1992; December 26, 1992.

"Resolución sobre el desarrollo económico del país." 1991. *Granma,* October 17, 3.

Salazar, Alberto. 1992. "Bacterias que comen petroleo." Electronic mail from Movimiento Cubano por la Paz, December 17.

Smith, Issar. 1990. "Report on NACSEX 1/28-2/7/90 Trip [to Cuba]." Unpublished manuscript.

"Summary of International Response to Torricelli Bill." 1992. *NotiSur-South American and Caribbean Political Affairs,* October 27.

Tecnosuma Internacional. Leaflet on SUMA. N.d.

Trueba González, Gerardo. 1991. "Política científica y biotecnología en Cuba: Quinto curso de planificación de C & T en América Latina." Havana, March. Unpublished manuscript.

Ubell, Robert N. "Cuba's great leap forward." 1983a. *Nature* 302, no. 28 (April 28): 745–48.

———. 1983b. "High-Tech Medicine in the Caribbean: 25 Years of Cuban Health Care." *New England Journal of Medicine* 309, no. 23 (December 8): 1468–72.

Interviews

Anonymous Cuban source no. 36. July 13, 1992.

Anonymous source no. 74. September 17, 1991.

Anonymous source no. 87. August 8, 1991; November 12, 1991; April 30, 1992; July 13, 1992; November 23, 1992; July 19, 1993.

Anonymous source no. 89. June 11, 1992.

Bialy, Harvey, research editor, *Bio/Technology*. February 15, 1991; June 17, 1991; January 7, 1993, New York.

Heredia del Portal, Lorenzo, subdirector, Centro de Inmunoensayos. November 25, 1988, Havana.

Herrera, Luis, director of production, Centro de Ingeniería Genética y Biotecnología (CIGB). November 25, 1988; June 13, 1992, Havana.

Lage, Agustín, director, Centro de Inmunología Molecular. August 3 and 6, 1993, Washington.

Limonta Vidal, Manuel, director general, CIGB. June 13, 1992, Havana.

Mella, Carlos M., president, Heber Biotec, S.A. June 19, 1991, Havana.

Miró, José, export manager, Heber Biotec, S.A. June 11, 1992, Havana.

Panisset, Ulysses, consultant. January 6, 1993, Washington.

Pentón Arias, Eduardo. CIGB, June 11, 1992, Havana.

Smith, Issar, North American-Cuban Scientific Exchange. October 16, 1990, New York.

SUMA exhibitor at Biotecnología 1992 international conference. June 12, 1992, Havana.

Vela, Osvaldo, deputy director, MediCuba. January 16, 1990; June 13, 1991, Havana.

NINE

Islands of Capitalism in an Ocean of Socialism
Joint Ventures in Cuba's Development Strategy
JORGE F. PÉREZ-LÓPEZ

Cuba's rejection of market-oriented economic reforms, at the same time that it steps up promotion of incoming foreign investment, has given rise to a curious phenomenon: the proliferation of economic enclaves subject to capitalist rules—"islands of capitalism"—within a centrally planned economy—"an ocean of socialism."

The chaos in the external sector attributable to political and economic changes in Eastern Europe and the former Soviet Union and the consequent loss of overseas sources of goods, technology, and financing have forced the Cuban leadership to rethink its economic strategy. The economic resolutions approved by the Fourth Congress of the Cuban Communist Party ratified the drive to attract foreign investment and formally recognized this activity as one of the strands in the nation's current economic strategy ("Resolución" 1991): "As a complement to the investment efforts that the country must effect, foreign investment will be stimulated in the areas of the economy and geographic zones where it would be appropriate in terms of its contribution to capital, technology, and markets. Different modalities to attract foreign investment will be used, such as joint ventures, joint production arrangements, marketing agreements, etc., as provided for in domestic legislation."

As chief economic strategist Carlos Lage ("Estamos decididos" 1991) has made clear, however, Cuba does not equate the promotion of foreign investment from capitalist countries with a shift away from socialism: "Our opening is not an opening toward capitalism, but rather a socialist opening toward a capitalist world. It is based on certain principles that guarantee the preservation of socialist order over our economy and our ability to meet our economic and social objectives."

In this chapter I explore the role of the promotion of foreign investment, particularly in the form of equity joint ventures, within Cuba's current development strategy. In the first part of the chapter I briefly review the legal framework regulating involvement by foreign investors, emphasizing de jure and de facto changes that have been made in recent years to stimulate incoming investment. In the second I examine foreign investment activity to date in the form of equity joint ventures, exploration agreements, joint production agreements, and the like. In the third part I analyze the feasibility of a foreign investment–led economic development strategy within a centrally planned economy, drawing on the experiences of China. I close the chapter with some tentative conclusions.

Legal Framework

The legal framework for foreign investment in socialist Cuba was established by Law Decree No. 50, approved by the Council of State in February 1982 (Consejo de Estado 1982).[1] The decree authorized the creation of joint ventures between Cuban entities and foreign interests for the specific purpose of engaging in profit-making activities that promote Cuba's economic development.

Each joint venture is governed by a memorandum of association and statutes developed jointly by the prospective partners. The memorandum of association contains the basic agreements regarding management strategy of the joint venture; it must contain provisions that "guarantee" management or comanagement of the joint venture by the Cuban partner as well as explicit commitments regarding the markets each partner will provide for selling the goods or services produced by the joint venture.

Contributions to joint ventures can take the form of cash or assets. Contributions of the latter kind by the Cuban partner may include the temporary use of land, buildings, and structures. Partners may also contribute raw materials, tools, equipment, and so on. Foreign ownership is limited to 49 percent of the value of the assets of the joint venture; this limit may be exceeded if authorized by the Executive Committee of the Council of Ministers.

The Cuban government "guarantees" foreign partners the unrestricted ability to remit abroad, in hard currency, their share of profits or dividends earned by a joint venture or the proceeds from liquidation of a joint venture. Income of joint ventures, shareholders' dividends, and income of joint venture executives are exempt from the national system of taxation. Instead, the following taxes and levies, payable in hard currency, are applicable: 30 percent on net income (that is, net profit), payable annually within the first two months following the end of the calendar year; 25 percent payroll tax, levied on the total compensation (excluding payments from incentive funds) of Cuban workers employed by the joint venture (this tax includes the employer's contributions to social security); import duties; personal property taxes on automobiles; and levies and fees generally associated with obtaining or renewing certain legal documents.

Joint ventures must employ Cuban workers except in those management, technical, and highly skilled positions that both partners agree can be filled only by foreign citizens. Joint ventures do not employ Cuban workers directly. A Cuban entity hires workers for the joint venture; this entity then contracts with the joint venture to provide manpower in return for a monthly fee, in hard currency, that covers workers' wages and benefits. Joint ventures are subject to all legislation regarding worker safety and health.

Cuban workers are paid according to the official wage scale as established by the State Committee on Labor and Social Security (Comité Estatal de Trabajo y Seguridad Social, CETSS), except for Cuban management workers, whose remuneration is comparable to that received by foreign management personnel. Although joint ventures make payment to cover workers' wages and benefits to the domestic hiring entity in hard currency, Cuban workers are paid in domestic currency. The Cuban entity is responsible for wages and benefits due workers who are separated from the joint venture. Joint ventures must also establish an incentive fund for the benefit of its Cuban workers.

Statutory Changes

In its current drive to attract foreign investment, Cuba has made two significant statutory changes to its legal framework for foreign investment: (1) a special labor regime for international tourism and (2) changes to the Constitution recognizing some forms of private property.

Labor Regime for International Tourism. Law-decree No. 122, passed in August 1990 (Consejo de Estado 1990; "Dictan" 1990), together with regulations issued by the CETSS (1990a and 1990b) and the National Tourism Institute (Instituto Nacional del Turismo [INTUR] 1990), created a special labor regime applicable to workers in international tourism, including tourism joint ventures, different from that which applies to Cuban workers at large (that is, the 1984 Labor Code).

Generally speaking, the special labor regime for workers in the international tourism industry provides for higher levels of compensation than apply to other Cuban workers (Pérez-López 1993). International tourism workers also face longer probationary periods, have less job security, work longer hours, are more likely to work abnormal schedules, and may be forced to complete specialized training as a condition for obtaining or maintaining employment.

The special labor regime also differs from the Labor Code with regard to discipline and the process for disputing disciplinary actions. The special regime is more restrictive than the Labor Code on both counts: it provides for more reasons to apply disciplinary measures, shortens the time periods for disputing such measures, and rules out the possibility of appeal through normal administrative or judicial channels.

Finally, the special labor regime places heavy emphasis on the suitability of the worker, an ill-defined concept that seems to relate to personal qualities and behavior both on and off the job. Since lack of suitability is sufficient reason for dismissal or reassignment and the procedures to contest suitability decisions are not effective, job security of workers in the international tourism industry is undermined.

Recognition of Private Property. In mid-July 1992, the National Assembly of People's Power passed a number of constitutional amendments that went a long way toward providing assurances to foreign investors that they could safely invest in the island (Rúa and Monreal 1993, 3). First, a new Article 23 was inserted in the 1976 Socialist Constitution setting out that "the State recognizes the ownership of property by joint ventures, corporations, and associations established in accord with domestic law." Second, Article 14 was modified to clarify that socialist ownership of the means of production was limited to "fundamental" means of production rather than to their totality. Third,

Article 15 was modified to provide a Constitutional basis for the transfer of state property to the private sector.

Flexible Application

There is evidence that Cuba has applied Law-decree No. 50 very flexibly, negotiating aggressively with prospective foreign investors on a case-by-case basis to land foreign investment. According to a foreign investor who has negotiated with Cuba on tourism projects, the Cuban government often negotiates more liberal deals than those contemplated in its formal legislation: "They have a joint venture law that is published and is open knowledge, but the government will do what it chooses.... What they're willing to give depends a lot on what the overseas partner brings to the deal."[2] The Vice President of the Cuban Chamber of Commerce has stated that "everything is open to consideration."[3] For example, according to official rules, international tourism joint ventures may be granted twenty-five-year leases on land, renewable for another 25 years; yet a businessman who has negotiated a long-term lease to prime beachfront property has indicated that "the [Cuban] government as of now gives leaseholds on land for a negotiable term of up to 99 years, not unlike what companies are offered in other places like the Cayman Islands."[4]

Cuba has modified its joint venture law in several different ways to attempt to compete more effectively with other nations seeking incoming foreign investment:

- In late 1990, Cuba announced for the first time a willingness to consider majority ownership by foreign investors in priority areas like tourism (French 1990). Chamber of Commerce President Julio García Oliveras told journalists in January 1991 that he "would not answer negatively" to the possibility of foreign capital representing 100 percent of mixed enterprises or creating new firms in the island ("Chamber of Commerce Invites" 1991; Gil 1991).
- President Castro (1991a, 50) indicated at the Guadalajara Summit of Iberoamerican Leaders that Cuba would be willing to grant "preferential treatment" to Latin American investors, presumably including 100 percent ownership of investments.
- In October 1991, the Fourth Congress of the Cuban Communist Party reportedly decided "to allow joint ventures to export and

import directly and free from tariffs and duties" (Kaplowitz and Kaplowitz 1992, 5).
- In November 1991, at the opening ceremony of the Ninth Havana International Fair, Castro (1991b, 10) expounded on the benefits of investing in Cuba, telling the assembled crowd that "I do not believe any country in the world offers the tax facilities we offer here" and that investors "will repatriate their capital [profit] more easily than in any other part of the world because the repatriation of capital [profit] is automatic."
- In May 1992, Cuban officials announced that the sugar industry would no longer be off-limits to foreign investors ("Ofensiva de Cuba" 1992).
- For the first round of open bidding for rights to explore for oil onshore and offshore held in early 1993, Cuban officials announced that the anticipated 11 percent royalty fee on hydrocarbons produced would be waived in order to provide "additional incentives to invest in Cuba now" (Brogan 1993).

Foreign Investment In Cuba

Thorough analysis of the number of foreign investments in Cuba, and of their significance to the domestic economy, is not possible because of the lack of data. As is discussed below, some information is available on specific projects. This information, however, is very sketchy: it is often difficult to sort out whether specific arrangements have been consummated or are still under discussion, or whether they entail an equity joint venture or some other form of arrangement (for example, a cooperative processing agreement).

Cuban officials candidly admit that detailed information inter alia on the nature of foreign investment projects, the names of the foreign partners, the value of the investments, and terms of the agreements is privileged and not subject to disclosure. The rationale behind this policy of "minimum reporting," as articulated by a high-ranking Cuban official ("Carlos Lage" 1992, 9), is "the pressure which everyone who comes to invest in Cuba is subjected to [by the United States]," aiming to discourage them from doing so. An unstated and perhaps equally important reason for the secrecy is the desire on the part of Cuban officials to improve the investment climate by giving the impression that many parties have already invested or are eager to invest in Cuba.

Information on the overall number or value of foreign investments in Cuba is available only from statements by government officials, who are not disinterested parties. With regard to specific projects, however, fragmented information is available from multiple sources. In what follows, this information has been brought together to provide a preliminary sketch of the depth and breadth of activities involving foreign capital.

Equity Joint Ventures

A visitor who met with high-level officials around 1983, shortly after the passage of Law-decree No. 50, reported that Cuba sought foreign participation in eight factories purchased from Japanese or European suppliers that were operating at less than full capacity because of shortages of raw materials or lack of export markets. Foreign investors were expected to provide capital, raw materials, technology, management expertise, and overseas markets for the output of the joint ventures (Zorn 1984, 19).

Factories mentioned in the press during the early 1980s as potential candidates for joint ventures included those producing pharmaceutical products; automobile batteries; cable and wire; construction materials; toilet tissue; steel wool and detergent; medical equipment and instruments; aluminum castings; nuts, screws, and washers; hydrosulfuric acid; sheet glass and bottles; nickel oxide and nickel sulfate; canned foods; tires; and machinery. By early 1985, three years after approval of Law-decree No. 50, only one foreign firm had registered a direct investment project in Cuba, a Spanish firm recycling metal products (Domínguez 1989, 211), and apparently not a single manufacturing facility offered by Cuba for equity joint venturing had managed to snare a foreign partner.

Tourism. Equity joint venture activity began to pick up after 1987. In that year, the Cuban government established the enterprise Cubanacán expressly for the purpose of developing the international tourism industry through joint ventures. The first such tourism agreement was executed by Cubanacán and the Spanish hotel chain Grupo Sol in 1987 or 1988; the initial tangible result of this agreement was the Sol Palmeras Hotel, in Varadero, which opened for business in May 1990.

Since the joint venture with Grupo Sol was concluded, Cuba has entered into numerous joint venture arrangements related to international tourism. Table 9-1 records eleven tourism joint ventures with Canada, Chile, Finland, Ireland, Jamaica, Spain, and Switzerland. Considering the high degree of interest from foreign investors in developing Cuba's tourism resources, there probably are other similar arrangements in this area that have not been publicized. According to a recent study (Kaplowitz and Kaplowitz 1992, 23), tourism joint ventures have also been established with German, Austrian, French, and Mexican investors.

In early 1992, joint ventures reportedly accounted for over 20 percent of hotel rooms under construction in the island (Business International 1992, 24). Pedro Ross Leal, secretary of the Confederation of Cuban Workers, has stated that over an 18-month period ending in spring 1992, tourism joint ventures generated 30,000 new jobs; the number of new jobs generated by tourism joint ventures was projected to grow to 50,000 to 70,000 by the end of 1992 ("Se reactiva" 1992).

Manufacturing. The more flexible application of Law-decree No. 50 and the statutory changes regarding the role of private property seem to have had a favorable effect in attracting joint venture investment in the manufacturing sector, although the majority of such joint ventures appear to be small.

An exception is the International Textile Corporation (ITC), a joint venture formed in October 1992 between Mexican investors from Monterrey and Cuban textile enterprises. It was originally reported that the ITC would be a $1.1 billion joint venture, with Mexican entrepreneurs investing $611 million (55 percent ownership share) while the Cuban state contributed 15 textile plants located throughout the island ("Mexicans launch" 1992). Subsequent reporting ("Negociantes" 1992) has clarified that the initial Mexican investment is $50 million.

Another significant investment is a joint venture arrangement to produce meningitis B vaccine, expected to result in an investment by Brazil of around $50 million. Because production is to take place in Brazil, however, the impact on the Cuban economy will be less than if production took place in the island. The remaining joint ventures in the manufacturing sector—production of egg cartons, furniture, chemical cleansers, fertilizers, and laser medical equipment—all appear to involve small amounts of investment.

Services. The most significant joint venture in this area is between

Table 9-1. Partial List of Foreign Joint Ventures with Cuban Partners

Foreign entity	Cuban entity	Project	Status	Value of Foreign Investment	Comments
Brazil		Manufacture of meningitis-B vaccine	Signed in 1991	$50 million	Manufacturing to take place in Brazil.
Canada SM Diesel	Cubanacán	Tourism (refurbishing of buses)	Approved in 1991		JV called Caribbean Diesel, S.A. Buses to be used by tourists.
Emery International		Biodegradable egg trays			
Chile Santa Ana/Latinexim Carlos Cardoen		Tourism Shoe manufacturing			Food for international tourism industry Footwear for export and sale in dollar stores
Curaçao Curaçao Dry Dock	Astillero Casablanca	Ship Repair	Signed in 1991		Ship repair in Curaçao. Pending approval by Curaçao Island Council.
Finland	Cubanacán	Tourism	Signed in 1990		Build hotel and 50 cabañas in Santiago de Cuba.
India Cimmco International		Textiles production	Expected to be signed in 1991		JV with Santa Clara textile mill.
Ireland Aer Rianta	Cubanacán	Tourism (Airport management and aircraft maintenance)			
Italy Italcable, S.A.	Ministerio de Comunicaciones	International Communications		$35-$50 million	JV will replace enterprise Intertel.
Benetton	Cubanacán	Tourism (8 stores for tourists)	First store opened in 1993		Also participating is Connolly, a Bahamas-based corporation owned by Benetton.

Foreign Partner	Cuban Partner	Sector	Date	Value	Notes
Jamaica					
Super Clubs	Cubanacán	Tourism	Signed in 1990		Expansion of Villa los Cactos Hotel, Varadero. New construction, Cuba-Cuba Hotel, Varadero.
Lithuania					
Various Monterrey businessmen		Electricity meters	Started November 1991		JV called Teven, S.A.
Mexico					
		Cotton fabric and apparel	Signed October 1992	$50 million; up to $611 million	JV called International Textile Corporation (ITC).
Spain					
Mármoles de San Marino	Empresa Nacional de Mármoles	Marble	Signed October 1991		JV called Marmolex, S.A.
Unidiamond Española	Empresa Nacional de Mármoles	Production of disks to cut marble	Signed October 1991		JV called Cardiamond, S.A.
Miesa, S.A.	Tecenergo	Energy-saving projects	Signed November 1991	$150,000	JV called Cuvastec.
Asturcoex	Emidict (Academia de Ciencias)	Laser medical equipment	Signed November 1991		JV called Tece, S.A.
Asturcoex	Emidict (Academia de Ciencias)	Industrial systems	Signed November 1991		JV called Tumi, S.A.
Esfera 2000	Cubanacán	Tourism	Signed in 1987 or 1988		Build Tuxpán Hotel in Varadero.
Grupo Sol	Cubanacán	Tourism		$150 million	Build Sol Palmeras and Meliá Varadero Hotels; 3 others planned.
Ibercusa	Cubanacán	Tourism	Signed in 1988 or 1989		Build Cohiba Hotel, Havana. JV called Hocusa.
Oasis Corporation	Cubanacán	Tourism			Build 1920 Hotel in Varadero; build facilities in Cayo Largo.
Grupo Havana	Cubanacán	Tourism	Started May 1991	$1 million	Discotheque in Comodoro Hotel, Havana. JV called Havana Club.
Gruexva	Cubanacán	Tourism	Signed November 1991	$120 million over 8 years	Build 3250-room complex in Isle of Youth. JV called Cuvasa.
Switzerland					
Suidol	Cubanacán	Tourism	Signed in 1988 or 1989		Build a 40-yacht marina in Jucaro.
United Kingdom					
Technical and Manufacturing Services	Quimimport	Chemical cleanser			Debt-for-equity swap

Sources: Information culled from *Cuba Business* and from other trade journals and newspapers.

Italcable and the Ministerio de Comunicaciones to modernize the international telecommunications system. Pursuant to the agreement, Italcable plans to invest $30–50 million in Cuba. Two other smaller services joint ventures are also listed in table 9-1: an arrangement to repair ships in Curaçao and an agreement with Spanish investors to develop energy-saving projects in Cuba.

Mining. Another area in which there has been substantial foreign investor interest is mineral exploration and mining. A joint venture to produce marble blocks with a Spanish investor was concluded in October 1991. As is discussed below, foreign investor participation in mining seems to have centered on production partnerships rather than equity joint ventures.

Debt-for-Equity Swaps

Cuba suspended amortization and interest payments on its hard currency debt in 1986. One of the results of this action is that Cuba has not been able to borrow "fresh" money from Western credit institutions since the mid-1980s.

In an attempt to regain access to international financing, Cuba has approached several of its Western creditors offering to renegotiate the outstanding debt and arrears either through purchases of Cuban goods or through debt-for-equity swaps. Cuba's offers reportedly have been aimed primarily at Japan, the United Kingdom, and Mexico (Business International 1992, 24–25; Kaplowitz and Kaplowitz 1992, 46; "Debt-Equity" 1991; "Mexico Considers" 1990). This is not surprising, since these nations are among Cuba's largest creditors.[5] Available information suggests that only one debt-for-equity swap has materialized, a joint venture with the British firm Technical and Marketing Services to produce a chemical cleanser.

Oil and Mineral Production Partnerships

In 1990, Cuba began to permit production partnership agreements in the mining sector. In December 1990, Cuba's Unión del Petróleo and a French consortium consisting of Total, the French oil major, and Compagnie Européenne des Petroles, a subsidiary of the trading group Interagra, signed a production partnership agreement whereby the French consortium was granted the right to search for oil offshore in a 2,000-square-kilometer block; the consortium would also carry out seismographic surveys and drill four exploratory wells in the Bay of Santa Clara, off Cuba's northern coast, over a six-year period. The French companies were to supply capital, specialized equipment, technology, and personnel for the exploration activities and share any production with Unión del Petróleo ("Franceses bajo" 1990; Coone 1991).

According to press reports ("Licenses" 1993), Canada North West Energy and Taurus (Sweden) have also signed agreements to explore for oil in Cuba. Canada North West has reportedly signed several contracts, dealing with exploration and production operations at commercial fields. Taurus holds exploration rights in a large stretch of territory in the southern region of Camagüey province. Several rounds of discussions on exploration rights and production partnerships have been held with Braspetro, the overseas subsidiary of Brazil's national oil company Petrobras ("Brasileños" 1991; "Brazil Negotiates" 1991) and with British Petroleum, but so far there is no evidence that agreements have been signed. Similar discussions with the Mexican state-owned corporation PEMEX have also been reported.

In February 1993, Cuba launched the first round of open bidding for oil exploration and production rights in the island, making presentations to prospective investors in London and Calgary (Brogan 1993; "Cuba Opens" 1993; "Licences" 1993). Eleven onshore and offshore tracts, ranging in size from 560 to 2,400 square miles, were offered to bidders; bidding was to have closed on August 1, 1993.

Cuba has also been discussing with an unnamed foreign company, widely believed to be the Canadian company Sheritt Gordon Ltd., regarding a large investment—reportedly on the order of $1.2 billion— to develop nickel and cobalt mining. Some conversations reportedly have taken place also with the Swiss trading company Marc Rich to develop zinc and lead deposits in Pinar del Río province.

Other Arrangements

Cuba is also actively pursuing other forms of association with foreign entities. One of the most popular is *comercio compensado*, a type of countertrade arrangement that promotes domestic production and exports while minimizing hard-currency outlays. These arrangements generally share most of the following elements: (1) the foreign partner provides raw materials and know-how; (2) the Cuban partner provides manufacturing facilities and labor; (3) the foreign partner is paid by taking back all or a portion of the finished (assembled) product or another commodity; and (4) the Cuban partner gets paid either by keeping a portion of the finished product or receiving another commodity (Pozo 1989). Cuba has also been promoting cooperative processing arrangements, very similar to the *maquiladora* plants operating in Mexico, Central America, and the Caribbean, as well as marketing arrangements and third-country associations.

Information on these arrangements with foreign entities is also very scanty (table 9-2). According to available information, Cuba has entered into at least 20 such arrangements. Most of them are cooperative processing deals, whereby Cuba transforms foreign raw materials or assembles components into goods that can be exported to the market of the foreign partner or to a third country.

There are at least two marketing arrangements with Chilean companies, one to provide technology for marketing Cuban fresh fruits and the other to sell Cuban citrus products in Western Europe through a company established in Rotterdam. Finally, Cuba's Ministerio de la Industria Básica has entered into an association with a Venezuelan state entity to bring together Venezuelan phosphate resources and Cuban technology to produce fertilizers for sale in third markets.

Foreign Investment as a Development Strategy

Cuba's all-out efforts to promote incoming foreign investment have had partial success. Cuba has attracted some foreign capital, raw materials, and technology and has gained access to markets of capitalist countries. In order to assess the viability of a foreign investment–led development strategy for Cuba, however, some broader questions need to be considered. Are current or projected incoming investment flows likely to be sufficient to offset the loss of external financing that Cuba has suffered? What has been the experience so far of foreign investors in Cuba, and what does this experience mean for the foreign investment climate, a critical variable in attracting additional investment? And, more generally, can foreign investment and a socialist, centrally planned economy coexist?

Foreign Investment and External Financing Needs

The disappearance of the socialist economies of Eastern Europe and the breakup of the Soviet Union have had severe repercussions on the

Table 9-2. Other Arrangements with Foreign Entities

Foreign entity	Cuban entity	Project	Status	Comments
Chile				
Agrícola Las Araucarias and Oceánica Chilena	Ministerio de Agricultura	Technology for marketing fruits and vegetables		Marketing agreement.
New World Fruit		Marketing of citrus fruits		Marketing agreement. Sale into Western Europe. New World is located in Rotterdam.
France				
Maestra Energía	Energoimport	Assembly of electric generators		Cooperative processing.
Pompes Guinard		Assembly of deep well pumps		Pumps assembled at the Planta Mecánica, Santa Clara.
Italy				
San Marco Inter-Canada	Profiel	Furniture		Cooperative processing. San Marco will provide Canadian hides.
San Marco Inter-Canada	Profiel	Furniture (minibars)		
Fiatallis		Fork lifts	Signed in 1989	
Mexico		Soap and detergent production		
Netherlands				
Castrol-Holanda	ECIMACT	Production of lubricants	Agreement signed in February 1983	
Spain				
Creaciones Meta	Profiel	Wooden toys		Cooperative processing.
Girabu		Assembly of washing machines	Signed in 1988	Cooperative processing.
Industria Sevillana de Automoción		Assembly of transmission systems		Cooperative processing.

Table 9-2. (Continued)

Foreign entity	Cuban entity	Project	Status	Comments
ENASA	Transimport and truck factory "Narciso López Roselló"	Assembly of light trucks		
Lebrero		Assembly of ground compactor	Signed in 1989	
Grupo Barreiro/Pegaso		Assembly of Taíno EB V8 gasoline engine		
Pegaso		Assembly of buses		
M.Z. Imer		Assembly of cement mixer		
Betico		Assembly of portable compressor		
USSR		Assembly of apparel and footwear	Signed in April 1989	Cooperative processing.
Venezuela				
Corporación Regional del Sudoeste	Ministerio de la Industria Básica	Fertilizer production	Probably signed in 1992	Third country association. Will use Venezuelan phosphates and Cuban nitrogenizing technology.

Sources: Information culled from *Cuba Foreign Trade*, *Cuba Business*, and from other trade journals and newspapers.

Cuban economy. Over the three-year period 1989–91, Cuba essentially lost its main sources of merchandise trade, technology, and development financing. It is not an overstatement to say that in the 1990s, Cuba's socialist economy faces its most difficult external sector challenge ever. In this context, the ability to attract foreign investment from capitalist countries and to generate hard currency revenues has taken on a new importance.

For three decades, socialist Cuba relied heavily on the Soviet Union and Eastern Europe for merchandise trade transactions (Pérez-López 1991). Over the period 1985–89, well over four-fifths of Cuba's merchandise exchanges were with these countries; by comparison, capitalist countries accounted for about 10 percent of exports and imports, and developing countries accounted for the rest (4 to 6 percent). Over 90 percent (by value) of Cuban exports of food products (for example, sugar and citrus), cigarettes, and nickel sulfide and very high shares (over 50 percent) of other exports such as alcoholic beverages, nickel oxide, and nickel sinter were exported to the Soviet Union and Eastern Europe. These countries also provided all or nearly all of Cuba's imports of condensed milk, butter, cheese, wheat flour, industrial raw materials (lumber, railroad ties, and cotton), fuels, and machinery and transport equipment (buses, cane lifters, diesel engines, and tractors). Cuban analysts (Rodríguez 1992, 6) have estimated that 80 to 85 percent of all imports consumed directly or indirectly by the population originated from the socialist countries.

Cuba's exports of sugar to the Soviet Union and Eastern Europe were subject to preferential treatment. In the case of the Soviet Union, this meant a price for Cuban sugar exports that was severalfold higher than that which prevailed in the world market. Although reasonable analysts may disagree about the precise size of the subsidy that the Soviet Union bestowed on Cuba via higher-than-market prices for sugar exports, it is clear that it was substantial, amounting from $1 to $2.8 billion per annum in the 1980s. The insistence on the part of the former Soviet Union that trade with Cuba—including sugar trade—beginning in mid-1991 be conducted on the basis of world market prices and convertible currency eliminated price subsidies in Cuban-Soviet trade and sharply reduced Cuban export revenues.

Another important feature of Cuban trade with the Soviet Union and Eastern European nations was the tendency for such trade to be unbalanced, with the Soviet Union and the Eastern European countries routinely extending credits to Cuba to finance merchandise trade deficits. With the end of this practice in the early 1990s, Cuba's ability to finance imports has been severely trimmed. According to Cuban official Carlos Lage ("Estamos decididos" 1992), Cuba's import capacity in 1991 was 50 percent lower than in 1989; for 1992, the situation was projected to be worse, with import capacity estimated to be 58 percent lower than in 1989.

A further example of the negative impact on Cuba of the changes in economic relations with the former Soviet Union comes from the oil exploration industry. In justifying the opening of oil exploration to foreign companies, a Cuban official noted that Cuba had lost Soviet assistance in oil exploration that amounted to 60 million rubles per annum during the 1980s ("Foreign Investment" 1993, 8).

As discussed above, Cuba does not regularly make available information on the number of foreign investment projects or on the volume of foreign investment. On occasion, however, Cuban officials do release such information, generally in presentations at seminars or meetings promoting investment in the island. Although the information is not very precise and is at times contradictory, it does suggest general trends and permit some inferences regarding the contribution of foreign investment to the Cuban economy.

Number of investment projects. Table 9-3 culls available information on the number of "joint ventures" between Cuban entities and foreign investors. The table contains information on investments that have been consummated (and presumably are either operating already or likely to be in operation in the very near future) and those that are under discussion. An unknown percentage of the joint ventures under discussion at a given time might materialize into joint ventures at a future time.

An important caveat is that the information in table 9-3 probably combines equity joint ventures and all other forms of arrangements with foreign entities (for example, production participation arrangements and cooperative production arrangements). Similarly, it is not clear whether it refers strictly to one arrangement per project or investor or multiple arrangements. For example, if a tourism joint venture relates to the modernization or construction of several sites (hotels), is this covered by only one agreement or by several?

Data in table 9-3 confirm that, since 1990, Cuba has had success in attracting foreign investment in the form of joint ventures. The number of joint ventures concluded rose from fewer than 20 in Decem-

Table 9-3. Number of Cuban Joint Ventures with Foreign Investors, 1990–92

Date	Number of Joint Ventures			Cuban Source
	Concluded	Under Discussion	Total	
December 1990			20	Chamber of Commerce
April 1991	55	100	155	
June 1991			70	J. García Oliveras, Chamber of Commerce
July 1991	40	110	150	J. García Oliveras, Chamber of Commerce
October 1991	50	100	150	J. García Oliveras, Chamber of Commerce
December 1991a	50+	140	190+	Chamber of Commerce
December 1991b	60	150	210	J. García Oliveras, Chamber of Commerce
March 1992	200	150	350	J. García Oliveras, Chamber of Commerce
June 1992a	60	100	160	H. Rodríguez Llompart, Cuban National Bank
June 1992b	250	Several Thousand	Several Thousand	O. Alfonso Montalván, State Committee for Economic Cooperation
November 1992	76			C. Lage, Politburo member

Sources: December 1990: *Cuba Business*, no. 6 (December 1990): p. 11; April 1991: Whitefield (1991a); June 1991: Whitefield (1991b); July 1991: Main (1991); October 1991: Cuba Aggressively (1991), 4A; December 1991a: Jenkins (1991), 11A; December 1991b: *Cuba Business*, no. 6 (December 1991): 15; March 1992: Business International (1992), 24; June 1992a: Sevcec (1992), 5A; June 1992b: Thurston (1992), 10A; November 1992: Carlos Lage (1992), 8.

ber 1990 to about 50 by October 1991 and 76 in late 1992. Throughout 1991 and early 1992, Cuba has reported more than 100 potential joint venture opportunities in the more ill-defined category of joint ventures "under discussion."

The fragility of the data on the number of joint ventures and the need to be cautious in using them are illustrated by two different reports offered by high-level Cuban officials during the June 1992 conference on investment in Cuba sponsored by Euromoney (see table 9-3). While Cuban National Bank president Héctor Rodríguez Llompart indicated that 60 joint ventures had been concluded and 100 were under discussion, State Committee on Economic Cooperation official Oscar Alfonso Montalván stated that 250 joint ventures had been concluded and "several thousand" were under discussion.

Value of investments. Cuban officials have reported very optimistic figures on incoming investment. For example, in October 1991, Julio García Oliveras, chairman of the Cuban Chamber of Commerce, reported that negotiations were ongoing with investors representing potential investments of $1.2 billion (Business International 1992, 24). President Castro has stated that foreigners could provide a significant share of the $20 billion to be invested in the tourism industry in the next few years (*Cuba Business* 1990a, 11).

Actual foreign investments in the island are much more modest. The fragmentary data in table 9-1 suggest that the amount of investment varies significantly from project to project. Thus, while Italcable's investment is expected to be in the range of $35 to $50 million and Grupo Sol and Gruexva have committed over $100 million each over a number of years, there are also many small joint ventures, such as Cuvastec, in which the foreign contribution is about $150,000. Other forms of association with foreign entities (production partnerships, cooperative processing) generally result in lower levels of foreign investment than joint ventures; debt-for-equity swaps essentially do not generate any new capital flows, although some deals may involve infusions of new money as working capital.

Clearly, the bulk of the foreign investment has been in the tourism industry, specifically in the construction of new hotels. According to Cubanacán director general Abraham Maciques, each of the five major investment projects that had been concluded in early 1991 translated into an investment of about $100 million, with about one-half of the investment attributable to the foreign partner).[6] Another way to gauge foreign investment in tourism is to examine it from the perspective of investment per room. Cuban officials have estimated the cost of new rooms at about $60,000 each, with the hard-currency cost—normally contributed by the foreign partner—at about $25,000 (*Cuba Business* 1990a, 10; 1991a, 3). Thus, the approximately 5,000 rooms suitable for international tourism operated by Cubanacán probably represent about $125 million in foreign capital.

It is reasonable to posit, then, that foreign investment in Cuba has been in the hundreds of millions of dollars rather than in the billions and that most of the investment has occurred very recently and in the tourism industry. Not all of the investment that has been committed has actually been realized, since multiyear plans are involved in some cases. Based on discussions with foreign executives, a journalist ("Mr. Castro" 1992, 46) estimated that in 1991, foreign investors plowed

$500 million into the island's economy. Cuban economist José Luis Rodríguez has estimated that foreign investment in the island amounted to $400 to $500 million by the end of 1991 (*Cuba Business* 1992, 7).

To be sure, foreign investment flows have a salutary effect on the balance of payments and provide Cuba with external financing not available from loans and other sources. In addition, investment projects have the potential to generate additional hard currency in the future, with similar salutary effects. The positive contribution of foreign investment, however, is dwarfed by the negative effects of the demise of trade and economic relations with Eastern Europe and the former Soviet Union. Zimbalist (1992, 413) has assessed the situation regarding international tourism as follows: "The gross revenue from the tourist trade in 1991 was approximately $300 million; since foreign inputs needed to be purchased to service this sector and since profits were shared with Cuba's foreign partners, the net foreign exchange earned from this activity probably did not exceed $100 to $120 million. Even if Cuba's most optimistic predictions are realised, gross tourist income will reach . . . $600 million in 1992. . . . Every little bit helps, but Cuba lost approximately $4 billion in imports from the CMEA between 1989 and 1991."

Experiences of Foreign Investors

There are no statistics to support a systematic assessment of the performance of foreign entities operating in Cuba. President Castro (1991a, 48) has stated that the payback period for foreign investments in tourism facilities is as short as three years. Other Cuban sources have reported the payback period for tourism investments as being three and one-half years (Pozo 1992, 38) or four to five years (Kaplowitz and Kaplowitz 1992, 23). These very short payback periods suggest that Cuba is offering quite high levels of investment incentives and therefore that foreign investors have been able to negotiate very lucrative deals with Cuban authorities.

There is, nevertheless, evidence that the relationship between foreign investors and Cuban entities has not been entirely without rough spots: important investments have failed to materialize or have been delayed, disputes have erupted over the performance of Cuban enterprises, and there have been allegations of contract breaches and nationalization. In addition, preliminary results of risk ventures have been disappointing.

- In the spring of 1991, the Canhedo Group, the majority owner of Vasp Brazilian Airlines, was reportedly close to acquiring 60 percent of Cubana de Aviación at a cost of $800 million (Whitefield 1992). The deal has not been consummated, however.
- The Spanish tobacco monopoly Tabacalera pulled out of a massive scheme to develop tourism facilities in Cayo Coco. Since Tabacalera pulled out (in fall 1991), Cuba has been trying to find another foreign partner for the project, which is currently being developed by Cubanacán and INTUR (*Cuba Business* 1990b, 14; 1991b, 2).
- Italcable's negotiations with Cuba have been much delayed. Although a preliminary joint venture agreement was signed in late 1991, Italcable had not received a firm contract from the Cuban side by April 1992 ("Mr. Castro" 1992, 47).
- Construction of the Cohiba Hotel, a joint venture between Cubanacán and the Spanish consortium Ibercusa, has run into several delays. Reportedly, Cuban officials suspended the project, claiming that the Spanish partners failed to make payments for supplies, while the Spanish partners claimed that the Cuban side failed to make deliveries (Business International 1992, 64–65).
- Cuba "nationalized" the very successful Havana Club discotheque, located at the Hotel Comodoro in Havana. Cubanacán, the majority stockholder (80 percent of investment), reportedly bought out Spanish partner Grupo Havana (20 percent equity), changing the discotheque to cater to a domestic clientele. The rationale for taking over the joint venture was that it created social problems because it appealed to certain segments of Cuban youth ("Cuba interviene" 1992; Terre Morell 1992).
- Reports on the data from the Total consortium's seismographic work, and what those data might portend for a significant oil strike off Cuba's northern shore, are contradictory. In late 1991 or early 1992, Cuban officials stated that seismographic studies showed very positive results and that the consortium would begin drilling in the spring 1992 ("Regional Oil" 1992). Based on reports from oil industry insiders, however, a U.S.-based journalist (de Córdoba 1992) reported that the seismographic data suggest the existence "of a very thick oil/bitumen sludge, that would be very difficult to refine and will bring about $6/barrel on the world market."

More generally, the ability of the Cuban government to furnish goods and services to joint ventures and other foreign investment projects is questionable in the light of the overall deterioration of the Cuban economy and generalized shortages of goods and services. The economic deterioration is probably felt most acutely in areas outside of tourism. Fuel and electricity shortages take their toll on the investment climate. They affect tourism facilities even if the latter are given special treatment, such as permission to import goods that are needed, or are equipped with their own electricity generation systems; the more Cuba has to import from hard-currency areas to support tourism enclaves, the less hard-currency net revenue is realized.

Other constraints continue to affect Cuba's investment climate. The concern by foreign investors regarding the lack of convertibility of the peso and the effect this can have on the repatriation of profits affects the type of investment in the island. Thus, investors have concentrated on joint ventures in industries in which the investor receives hard currency for its services or export products, such as tourism (Recio 1991, 29).

The lack of commitment by Cuban officials to private enterprise surely does not provide comfort to foreign investors concerned about potential nationalizations. Although the July 1992 amendments to the Constitution recognizing some forms of private property are positive steps, nevertheless it is clear that foreign investment is accepted because other options are not available rather than because there is a commitment to such a concept. For example, the confidence of investors is not likely to be boosted by statements such as the one attributed to Deputy Foreign Minister Ramón Sánchez Parodi, but believed to reflect views broadly held by the leadership, that "if there were loans available, we wouldn't be looking for capital through investment by foreign companies" (Whitefield 1991). As President Castro told a visiting U.S. scholar (Gunn 1992, 60) in November 1991,

> I am disposed to . . . admit [that there are] elements—I would not call them small islands—of capitalism in certain areas of our socialist system. [But] in no book of Marx, Engels, or Lenin is it said that it is possible to construct socialism without capital, without technology, and without markets. . . . In the case of a small island like Cuba . . . it is especially difficult to develop using only one's own resources. It is for this reason that we have no alternative but to associate ourselves with

foreign companies that can bring capital, technology, and markets. . . . [W]e are dealing with . . . a world where a large part of the socialist system has collapsed.

Foreign Investment and Socialism

Cuba's current drive to attract foreign investment is similar in many respects to the "open door" policy that China began to pursue in 1978. In July 1979, China passed a joint venture law to encourage foreign participation in that country's modernization program, thereby bringing about a break with the rhetoric and practices of the thirty years immediately following the establishment of the People's Republic, when China condemned foreign investment in the developing world as a form of exploitation. The fourth People's Republic constitution, promulgated in 1982, reinforced the open door policy by promising to protect "the lawful rights and interests of foreign investors" (Feinerman 1991, 829–30; Ho 1990).

As Pearson (1991) has noted, the "open" policy of the late 1970s did not reject the view that foreign direct investment could have potential negative effects. Rather, it was premised on the assumption that China could use its strengths (a centrally planned economy, state ownership of the means of production, lack of foreign influence and of a private business class in the country, and so on) to reap the benefits of foreign investment while preventing its problems. That is, the post-Mao leadership believed that China could "selectively absorb the good things and boycott the bad things from abroad" (Pearson 1991, 3).

As Cuba is currently doing, China chose the joint-equity joint venture as the preferred form to attract foreign investment. The Chinese leadership favored this form of direct investment because it believed that partial state ownership would give China additional means of control. They also believed that, as part owners of equity joint ventures, foreign investors would have a higher stake in their success and therefore would be more likely to supply joint ventures with advanced technology and management.

Pearson's analysis shows that China's efforts to control foreign investment at the same time that it attempted to derive substantial benefits from it had mixed results. China encountered major difficulties in implementing controls and gradually liberalizing them to be able to gain the benefits of foreign investment. While socialism helped China in controlling foreign investment—the Chinese state had a well-developed bureaucracy and a monopoly over finance and foreign trade activities, and so on—it also had a disincentive effect. China's socialist economic organization created problems in attracting capital: lack of horizontal or market links between economic units and regions, relatively low worker productivity, and a cumbersome planning bureaucracy.

The most important source of China's effectiveness in maintaining controls was unrelated to socialism; this was its large domestic market. According to Pearson (1991, 219), "the fact that most investors were willing to tolerate the difficult investment conditions and poor access to domestic markets during the 1980s suggests the importance of this belief on the potential for a great payoff, if and when domestic market access could be realized. The need of many transnational corporations to preempt their competitors from capturing the China market first was another impetus for investors that was unconnected to China's socialism. The 'carrot' of China's domestic market, therefore, undoubtedly was crucial to China's capacities to control foreign investment."

In the view of some analysts (for example, Gunn 1992, 60), Cuba's efforts to attract foreign investment are part of a broader strategy to create a "semi-mixed economy based on a variation of the Chinese model." Carlos Lage has been quite explicit in stating that although foreign investment from capitalists is being sought, the primacy of socialism is not in question. He told prospective foreign investors during a June 1992 Euromoney conference (Sevcec 1992, 1A) that "it is natural to use a few good things from capitalism. We believe that socialism and capitalism can coexist." Is such coexistence possible, particularly in the context of a small economy such as Cuba's?

Pearson's analysis of the Chinese experience suggests that the answer is negative. First, regardless of the form of political organization, host countries cannot totally control the investment environment and are forced to liberalize their domestic regime or suffer the consequences of lower investment. Second, smaller socialist economies, once they undertake a development strategy that calls for engagement with the international economy, will find it more difficult to limit their exposure to external forces. Thus, "smaller countries are more likely to find that use of foreign capital will make them more vulnerable to outside forces than larger countries; it will be difficult for smaller countries to turn away investors, for the costs will be higher. Any investment of significant size also will tend to constitute a larger proportion of total investment in that sector" (Pearson 1991, 222). And third, Cuba, like most countries, is in a less favorable position than China to carry out a strategy of simultaneously absorbing and controlling investment because it lacks China's powerful lure of a domestic market.

Conclusions

Although Cuba passed legislation permitting foreign investment in February 1982, Western businessmen were initially very lukewarm toward the opening. Since around 1989, however, there has been a decided upturn in foreign interest, and there is evidence that a number of significant deals have been consummated, particularly in the form of joint ventures in tourism.

Socialist Cuba's conception of the role that foreign investment would play in its economy has evolved over time in response to investor reaction and changes in economic conditions. Initially, the emphasis was on attracting foreign investment that would supply capital, raw materials, and know-how to keep factories running and provide access to foreign markets to export their output. Lack of investor interest and deteriorating economic conditions have forced Cuba to broaden the scope for foreign participation in the economy. At present, there appear to be few restrictions on foreign investment in Cuba, provided the deal is attractive to Cuban authorities. As Raúl Taladrid, vice-president of the State Committee for Economic Cooperation, has put it, "Cuba will negotiate with the devil to survive" (Fletcher 1991).

Analyses of the magnitude, distribution, and impact of incoming foreign investment are not possible because of the lack of information. Available information on the number of foreign investments and their value originates from statements by Cuban government officials and is often not consistent. Since these statements are generally made in the context of seminars or conferences seeking to attract foreign investment, there is the potential for overstatement in order to improve the investment climate. A reasonable estimate is that, by the end of 1992, Cuba had entered into more than 75 joint ventures and was negotiating on another 100; foreign investment probably amounted to about $500–600 million. While this inflow of investment is significant, it is dwarfed by the severe losses in trade and financing that Cuba has suffered as a result of the loss of economic relations with Eastern Europe and the former Soviet Union.

Like the post-Mao Chinese leadership, Cuban authorities express the conviction that they can reap the benefits of foreign investment without having to make changes to Cuba's socialist system. To be sure, socialist economies have a high capacity for bargaining, regulation, and oversight that would permit them to have effective control over foreign investment. The Chinese experience with foreign investment suggests, however, that these advantages are offset by systemic and other problems and the impossibility of controlling the external investment environment. The most significant factor influencing foreign investment in China was the lure of a huge domestic market. It remains to be seen whether foreign investment and socialism can coexist and prosper in a small economy such as Cuba's.

Notes

1. Legal analyses of the 1982 joint venture law include Zorn and Mayerson (1982), Schmidt (1983), McGilvray-Saltzman (1984), and Fiszman (1985). See also Chamber of Commerce (1982), Pérez-López (1985), and Comité Ejecutivo (1991).
2. Business International (1992, 63–64). The foreign investor is identified as John Issa, chairman of Jamaica's Super Clubs resorts.
3. Quote attributed to Abeledo Larrinaga, Vice President of the Cuban Chamber of Commerce, cited in Kaplowitz and Kaplowitz (1992, 4).
4. Business International Corporation (1992, 24, 64). The quote is attributed to John Issa, chairman of Jamaica's Super Clubs resorts.
5. There are no recent official statistics on the distribution of Cuba's hard currency debt by creditor country. In 1983, Cuba's debt with Japan and the United Kingdom amounted to $323 and $215 million, respectively, and these countries were Cuba's third- and fourth-largest creditors (Banco Nacional de Cuba [BNC] 1984, 14). Cuba's debt to Mexico, of more recent vintage, is estimated at about $300 million.
6. See *Cuba Business* (1991a, 3). For example, the foreign investment in the Sol Palmeras Hotel has been reported as either $40 million (Kaplowitz and Kaplowitz 1992, 22) or $60 million (Business International 1992, 62).

References

Banco Nacional de Cuba (BNC). 1984. *Informe seleccionado de la economía Cubana*. Havana. March.

"Brasileños buscan petróleo en la isla." 1991. *El Nuevo Herald*, March 19, 3A.
"Brazil Negotiates Cuba Exploration Pact." 1991. *Journal of Commerce*, November 18, 7B.
Brogan, Chris. 1993. "Energy: Cuba Steps Up Drive for Foreign Investment." Inter Press Service, London (February 19).
Business International Corporation. 1992. *Developing Business Strategies for Cuba*. New York: Business International Corporation.
"Carlos Lage Comments on Economy." 1992. Havana Tele Rebelde and Cuba Vision (November 7), as reproduced in *FBIS-LAT-92-219*, November 12, 2–14.
Castro, Fidel. 1991a. *Independientes hasta siempre*. Havana: Editora Política.
———. 1991b. "Speech to inaugurate the Ninth International Fair in Havana, on November 3, 1991," as reproduced in *FBIS-LAT-91-215*, November 6, 1991.
"Chamber of Commerce Invites Foreign Investment." 1991. Notimex (January 9), as reproduced in *FBIS-LAT-91-007*, January 10, 1991, 3.
Chamber of Commerce of the Republic of Cuba. 1982. *Possibility of Joint Ventures in Cuba*. Havana. February.
Comité Ejecutivo del Consejo de Ministros. 1991. *Possibility of Joint Ventures in Cuba*. Havana. March.
Comité Estatal de Trabajo y Seguridad Social (CETSS). 1990a. "Resolución No. 14/90." *Gaceta Oficial*, September 15, 579–84.
———. 1990b. "Resolución No. 15/90." *Gaceta Oficial*, September 15, 584–88.
Consejo de Estado. 1982. "Decreto-ley No. 50: Sobre asociaciones económicas entre entidades cubanas y extranjeras." *Gaceta Oficial*, February 15, 11–15.
———. 1990. "Decreto-ley No. 122: Sobre regulaciones laborales especiales para los trabajadores del Sistema de Turismo Internacional." *Gaceta Oficial*, August 13, 27–29.
Coone, Tim. 1991. "Cuba opens its oil fields to foreign prospectors." *Financial Times*, March 8, 29.
de Córdoba, José. 1992. "Cuba's Search for Offshore Oil to Replace Soviet Crude Supplies Appears to Falter." *Wall Street Journal*, April 15, A17.
"Cuba Aggressively Pursuing Foreign Investment Ventures." *Journal of Commerce*, October 30, 4A.
Cuba Business. 1990a. No. 3 (June).
———. 1990b. No. 6 (December).
———. 1991a. No. 2 (April).
———. 1991b. No. 6 (December).
———. 1992. No. 2 (June).

"Cuba interviene discoteca hecha con capital español. 1992. *Diario las Américas*, January 12, 1A, 11A.
"Cuba Opens Oil Projects to Western Bidding." 1993. *Journal of Commerce*, February 12, 6B.
"Debt-Equity Plan Mulled to Pay Cuba's Debt to UK." 1991. *Journal of Commerce*, October 28, 3A.
"Dictan regulaciones especiales para trabajadores del turismo." *Trabajadores*, September 26, 2.
Domínguez, Jorge I. 1989. *To Make a World Safe for Revolution*. Cambridge: Harvard University Press.
"Estamos decididos no solo a luchar sino tambien a vencer." 1992. *Granma*, May 6, 6.
Feinerman, James V. 1991. "Chinese Law Relating to Foreign Investment and Trade: The Decade of Reform in Retrospect." In Joint Economic Committee, *China's Economic Dilemmas in the 1990s: The Problems of Reforms, Modernization, and Interdependence*. Washington: U.S. Government Printing Office.
Fiszman, Sula. 1985. "Foreign Investment Law: Encouragement Versus Restraint—Mexico, Cuba, and the Caribbean Basin Initiative." *Hastings International and Comparative Law Review* 8, no. 2 (Winter): 147–83.
Fletcher, Pascal. 1991. "Communist Cuba Will 'Negotiate with the Devil' to Survive." Reuters News Service, August 15.
"Foreign Investment in Oil Exploration Discussed." 1993. *Bohemia*, February 12, 1993, as reproduced in *FBIS-LAT-93-063*, April 5, 8-11.
"Franceses bajo contrato petrolero con Cuba." 1990. *Nuevo Herald*, December 24, 4A.
Fraser, Damian. 1991. "Cuba considers swaps to ease debt." *Financial Times*, September 19, 17.
French, Howard W. 1990. "Cuba Flirts with Capitalism to Avoid Collapse." *New York Times*, December 5, A18.
Gil, María Elena. 1991. "A la búsqueda de nuevos mercados." *Cuba Internacional*, June 1991, 42.
Gunn, Gillian. 1992. "Cuba's Search for New Alternatives." *Current History* 91, no. 562 (February): 59-63.
Ho, Alfred K. 1990. *Joint Ventures in the People's Republic of China: Can Capitalism and Communism Coexist?* New York: Praeger.
Instituto Nacional del Turismo (INTUR). 1990. "Resolución No. 85." *Gaceta Oficial*, September 28, 621–22.
Jenkins, Gareth. 1991. "Cuba, in Need of Cash, Throws Door Open to Investors." *Journal of Commerce*, December 2, 11A.
Kaplowitz, Donna Rich, and Michael Kaplowitz. 1992. *New Opportunities for U.S.-Cuba Business*. Washington, D.C.: Cuban Studies Program, Paul H. Nitze School of Advanced International Studies.

"Licences on Offer." 1993. *Cuba Business* 7, no. 1 (January-February): 7.
Main, Jeremy. 1991. "Cuba: Pushing for Change." *Fortune*, August 26.
McGilvray-Saltzman, Lynn. 1984. "Cuba's Joint Venture Associations: Cuba Reopens Its Doors to Foreign Investment." *Florida International Law Journal* 1, no. 1 (Fall): 45–60.
"Mexicans Launch US$1bn Venture." 1992. *Latin America Weekly Report*, November 12, 88.
"Mexico Considers Debt-for-Equity Swaps." 1990. Notimex News Service, November 13, as reproduced in *FBIS-LAT-90-231*, November 30, 7.
"Minerals Joint Venture?" 1991. *Cuba Business* 5, no. 3 (June 1991): 12.
"Mr. Castro Goes to Market." 1992. *Business Week*, April 20, 6–47.
"Negociantes de México crearán empresa textil." 1992. *El Nuevo Herald*, October 29, 3A.
"Ofensiva de Cuba para atraer inversiones y encontrar petróleo." 1992. *Nuevo Herald*, May 21, 5B.
Pearson, Margaret M. 1991. *Joint Ventures in the People's Republic of China: The Control of Foreign Direct Investment Under Socialism*. Princeton: Princeton University Press.
Pérez-López, Jorge F. 1985. *The 1982 Cuban Joint Venture Law: Context, Assessment, and Prospects*. Coral Gables: North-South Center, University of Miami.
———. 1991. "Swimming Against the Tide: Implications for Cuba of Soviet and Eastern European Economic Reforms." *Journal of Interamerican and World Affairs* 33, no. 2 (Summer): 81–139.
———. 1993. "Cuba's Thrust to Attract Foreign Investment: A Special Labor Regime for Joint Ventures in International Tourism." *Interamerican Law Review* 24, no. 2 (Winter): 221–79.
Pozo, Alberto. 1989. "Comercio compensado: Intercambio sin divisas." *Bohemia*, 81, no. 5 (February 3): 47–53.
———. 1992. "Turismo: Razón de peso." *Bohemia*, 84, no. 2 (January 10): 38.
Recio, Irene. 1991. "Caveat Emptor." *Latin Finance* 33 (December): 33.
"Regional Oil Manoeuvres." 1992. *Cuba Business* 6, no. 1 (February): 6.
"Resolución sobre el desarrollo económico del pais." 1991. *Granma*, October 17, 3.
Reyes, Jannice. 1992. "Firma canadiense hará fuerte inversión en Cuba." *El Nuevo Herald*, May 13, 4A.
Rodríguez, José Luis. 1992. "La economía de Cuba ante la cambiante coyunta internacional." *Boletín de Información sobre Economía Cubana* 1, no. 2 (February): 3–6.
Rua, Manuel, and Pedro Monreal. 1993. "La apertura Economía cubana." *Cuba Foreign Trade*, no. 1, 1–11.

Schmidt, Patrick L. 1983. "Foreign Investment in Cuba: A Preliminary Analysis." *Law and Policy in International Business* 15, no. 2, 689–710.
"Se reactiva el sector turístico de Cuba." 1992. *Novedades* (Mexico), April 29, B7.
Sevcec, Pedro. 1992. "Castro firme en negativa a apertura." *El Nuevo Herald*, June 11, 1A, 5A.
Terre Morell, Claribel. 1992. "No me considero un fracasado." *Bohemia* 84, no. 16 (April 17): B12-B14.
Thurston, Charles W. 1992. "Foreigners Invited to Invest in Cuba at Trade Conference in Mexico." *Journal of Commerce*, June 10, 10A.
Whitefield, Mimi. 1991a. "Cuba: The Struggle Intensifies." *Miami Herald*, April 21.
———. 1991b. "Cuba's Capitalist Comrades." *Miami Herald*, June 23.
———. 1992. "Brazilians May Acquire 60% of Cuban Airline." *Miami Herald*, April 11, 1A, 17A.
Zimbalist, Andrew. 1992. "Teetering on the Brink: Cuba's Current Economic and Political Crisis." *Journal of Latin American Studies* 24, no. 2 (May): 407–18.
Zorn, Jean, and Harold Mayerson. 1983. "Cuba's Joint Venture Law: New Rules for Foreign Investment." *Columbia Journal of Transnational Law* 21, no. 2, 273–303.
Zorn, Stephen. 1984. "Cuba's Cautious Moves to Attract Foreign Investment." *Multinational Monitor* 4, no. 3 (March).

TEN

Reforming Cuba's Economic System from Within
ANDREW ZIMBALIST

The emergence and survival of Cuba's socialist revolution depended on the political and economic support of a larger socialist bloc. When that bloc collapsed in 1989, the collapse of Cuba's socialist economic structure was only a matter of time. The Cuban economy has been in a slow, albeit accelerating, transition toward a mixed economy over the last four years. The new approach announced at the Fourth Party Congress in October 1991 represented a formal recognition of this process of economic structural change, although it understated its necessary magnitude, dressing it in the garb of perfecting socialism. Nevertheless, the pronouncements of the party congress acknowledged more explicitly the process of institutional and policy change that began with Cuba's "special period in time of peace."

One of the prongs of Cuba's strategy of the special period in time of peace, as implemented since the fall of 1990, is to facilitate the economy's reinsertion into world markets by undertaking management and selective structural reforms. The commitment to management and organizational reform is clearly recorded in the documents of the Fourth Party Congress in October 1991:

> The new workstyle established by the Executive Committee of the Council of Ministers; the excellent results of the contingents, the Ministry of the Revolutionary Armed Forces management experiments, and many other initiatives, introduced new and positive work concepts in the coun-

try's economic management. Nevertheless, the current circumstances demand that we search for and apply, in specific activities and in a flexible way, new forms of organization and economic management. These will also be applied to the structure and functioning of agencies and enterprises, so as to achieve maximum effectiveness.

Although economic reform in Cuba during 1989–93 takes on a fundamentally different meaning from previous reform efforts because it is taking Cuba out of a socialist economy, Cuba's ability to make the necessary changes in a stable political framework is enhanced by the revolution's identification with continual efforts at pragmatic reform. Whether or not the entire economic transition can be accomplished peacefully in Cuba is questionable, but the resilience of Cuba's political regime in contrast to the fragility of those in the former Soviet bloc is in part a testimony to the flexible and experimental nature of Cuba's revolutionary culture.

Early Reform Efforts

Cuba did not have stable institutions of economic planning until the latter half of the 1970s. Indeed, the country's first five-year plan did not come until 1976–80. The gradual introduction of Cuba's new planning system, the Sistema de Dirección y Planificación de la Economía (SDPE), was begun in 1977.[1] The SDPE was basically modeled after the 1965 Soviet reforms. It sought to (1) put enterprises on an economic accounting basis; (2) introduce a profitability criterion with its corresponding incentives; and (3) promote decentralization, organizational coherence, and efficiency. Like the earlier Soviet reform, it met with the obstacles of bureaucratic resistance, pervasive shortages, and an irrational price structure. Possibilities for decentralized decision making in Cuba have also been constrained by the inadequate supply of skilled managerial and technical labor. Moreover, Cuba confronted additional difficulties in adapting the Soviet-style reform to Cuban political culture. The Cubans began tinkering with their new system almost from the outset.[2]

A central theme of the SDPE was decentralization. Putting enterprises on an economic accounting scheme and introducing profit sharing was supposed to give them increasing autonomy from the center, and this in turn was to promote efficiency. Nominal economic accounting and profit sharing by themselves, however, did little if anything to enhance the scope of enterprise decision making. In the context of centrally fixed prices, centrally determined investments, and extensive input shortages, these mechanisms did not alter the basic mode of operation of Cuban planning. Being centrally set every five or more years, prices were not a reliable rational guide to production or allocation choices; nor could they systematically identify well-managed enterprises through a profitability index. With shortages commonplace, otherwise efficient enterprises were often thwarted in their production efforts because of nondelivery, untimely delivery, or delivery of improperly specified, poor quality inputs. Bottlenecks and planning imperfections in turn necessitated amendments to the plan after the beginning of the year, often raising an enterprise's output target without increasing its supply of raw materials (Ayala and Ferrer 1989).

Behaving rationally in this environment, enterprises hoarded inputs, thereby aggravating the shortage and supply problem. Since the behavior of profits was fickle because of these and other factors, the planning authorities were compelled on equity grounds to limit the extent of profit retention and distribution, thus weakening the incentive effect. And since profits boomed in certain enterprises despite the absence of properly specified, high-quality production, the planners devised new administrative regulations to control this behavior. In the end the profitability algorithm became hopelessly complicated, and the incentive mechanism was debilitated. Since the center decided upon what investment projects were to be undertaken, the fact that enterprises paid for increasing shares of investment costs out of their bank funds rather than state budget funds (the share of enterprise-financed investments in total investment financing in Cuba rose from 1 per cent in 1981 to 30 per cent in 1985) did not imply a substantive decentralization of capital allocation (Banco Nacional de Cuba [BNC] 1986, 6).

To be sure, in at least one important respect the SDPE represented further centralization of the planning system. Prior to 1976, the system of material supplies was carried out by consolidated enterprises; subsequently, most material balances came to be implemented by the Central Planning Board (Junta Central de Planificación, JUCEPLAN) or the State Committee on Technical-Material Supplies (Comité Estatal de Abastecimiento Técnico-Material, CEATM).[3]

The SDPE, then, like the 1965 Soviet economic reforms, did not bring a significant change in the underlying centralization of decision making in the economic mechanism. There were, however, peripheral changes that accompanied the SDPE, many introduced in an effort to adapt the Soviet centralized model to Cuban conditions, that did increase the flexibility of the system and allow for some decentralization of decision making. Among these new policies was the post-1976 system of Popular Power, which controlled the management of locally oriented service and production enterprises. In the mid-1980s, such enterprises amounted to 34 per cent of all Cuban enterprises.[4] The local budgets of Popular Power grew from 21 per cent of the total state budget in 1978 to 26 per cent in 1980 to 30 percent in 1982 and to 33 per cent in 1984. The local budget share in the Soviet Union in 1980 was 17.1 per cent (Mata 1986, 56).

Another policy allowed for enterprises to make their own contracts for products that were not centrally balanced. There was also encouragement for the development of "secondary" (above-plan) production. Further, the realization that there were growing stocks of unused inputs within enterprises led to the practice of "resource fairs," in which enterprises traded freely and directly with each other. These fairs were first organized by the CEATM in 1979. At the fairs of 1979 and 1980 there were sales of 40 million pesos of inputs. Inventory sales of production inputs by enterprises have continued to grow. In October 1982 the president of JUCEPLAN reported that some 500 million pesos of such resources had already been identified (*Granma* 1982; Echevarría et al. 1986). In May 1985, at the conclusion of the Fourth Plenary on the SDPE, the judgment was reached that the CEATM was still allocating too many products and the number should be significantly reduced, allowing enterprises to contract directly with each other for these products (JUCEPLAN 1985, 25). In fact, the degree of centralization contemplated in the Soviet-designed system was never approached in Cuba, as it was resisted by sectoral and provincial planning bodies.

Other measures of decentralization included the strengthening of the Cuban Institute of Internal Demand, the introduction of free labor contracting in 1980, and an increasing acceptance of private productive and service activity (most notably housing construction cooperatives and free farmers' markets).[5] There was also some light manufacturing by artisans, and enterprises were permitted to use up to 30 per cent of their profits to make input purchases from the private sector.

Free farmers' markets were opened in 1980. Sales of fresh vegetables and fruits grew rapidly until the February 1982 government crackdown on "abuses" (exorbitant prices, excessive middleman profits, and resource diversion from the state sector). Sales began to grow again after the promulgation of new regulations in May 1983 (a 20 percent sales tax, a progressive income tax on private farmer income from 5 to 20 percent, and the expansion of the state-controlled parallel market to compete with the farmers' markets). But new abuses, more serious diversion of resources from state uses, and reported incomes above 50,000 pesos for truckers, wholesalers, and some farmers led to the permanent closing of these markets in May 1986. Although such free market sales of produce were permitted in the other socialist countries before perestroika, private plots tended to be no larger than one-quarter or one-half a hectare (except in Poland and Yugoslavia, where private farming was predominant). In Cuba private plots typically range from 20 to more than 60 hectares. Although private farmers are required to deliver a share of their output to the state, actual deliveries are often modest relative to output, leaving substantial produce to be consumed locally or marketed independently. Castro, for instance, charged that some private farmers delivered no more than 10 per cent of their output to the state (Mesa-Lago 1988, 71). Thus, the potential for economic and political disruption emerging from the private agricultural sector in Cuba prima facie was greater than elsewhere in the Soviet-trade bloc, the Council for Mutual Economic Assistance (CMEA).

Nevertheless, these decentralizing measures taken together did not alter the key dynamic of Cuban planning. Prior to the beginning of the rectification process inaugurated in April 1986, it was apparent from various government documents and speeches that the need for further decentralization and greater worker participation was clearly perceived. The documents of the May 1985 Fourth Plenary evaluating the SDPE, in particular, laid out a series of decentralizing measures that the Cubans intended to carry out. With the severe foreign exchange difficulties that Cuba began to experience around that time, along with the growing excess of uncompleted investments projects, however, resources became too scarce to sustain the momentum toward decentralization, and the state tightened its grip on the economy to economize on the use of foreign exchange as well as to bring existing investment projects to successful completion.

Unintended or profligate use of resources in both the private and public spheres came under increasing scrutiny, as did the lack of coordination among sectoral ministries of the economy and among state planning institutions (for example, the State Committee on Finances, the State Committee on Prices, the National Bank, and JUCEPLAN). These problems and the difficulties of an increasing indiscipline among labor (exacerbated by shortages of inputs and consumer goods), enterprise overstaffing, corruption among officials, and ideological concerns brought on the rectification campaign in early 1986. Market-oriented decentralization was put on hold, although efforts at administrative decentralization were continued.

The Rectification Process

There is no question that the rectification process brought a halt to the previous trend toward both liberalization and increased emphasis on material incentives. Many prominent interpreters of Cuban reality (including Domínguez 1988; Pérez-López 1986; Mesa-Lago 1988), however, have exaggerated the nature and meaning of this shift, either by misapprehending the substance of the SDPE or by misconstruing the new policies. In reality, the SDPE did not approach market socialism. Worker productivity bonuses were never as prominent in Cuba as in other socialist countries in the CMEA, yet they were still very much in evidence during rectification. Urban private sector activity came under increasing regulation but was still permitted. None of the salient characteristics of the late 1960s economy were present in the rectification process, although one could readily observe the strong hand of Fidel Castro in each period.

The rectification process is more usefully understood as a phase in the typical reform cycle of a centrally planned economy (CPE). Periods of liberalization, prompted by the quest for greater efficiency, in CPEs inevitably generate economic, political, and social tensions as well as outcomes that are antithetical to the stated goals of socialist society, such as growing income differentials, inflation, investment diverging from plan, and increased corruption. It is natural if not inevitable that liberalization policies provoke periods of reassessment and retrenchment, as experienced in Hungary and China. Of course, the nature, timing, and intensity of the cycle depend on factors peculiar to each country and to the international political and economic climate. Further, in Cuba's case the emphasis on moral incentives reflects the home-grown revolutionary process and the consequent ideological formation of the leadership.

Balancing Material and Moral Incentives

Material incentives are problematic in centrally planned, shortage-type economies. Not only are there ideological concerns with inequality and attitude, but also there are limits to motivating workers and managers with more money if there are not desirable goods available for purchase. These limits are more severe for CPEs with lower levels of economic development, especially during times of severe foreign exchange constraints. Another difficulty with material incentives at the workplace affects market and planned economies alike: measuring individual contribution to the quantity and quality of output is never straightforward. Each of these problems was pertinent to the Cuban situation in the mid-1980s.

Three types of material incentives for workers were used during rectification: *normas* (piece rates), *primas* (bonuses), and *premios* (profit sharing). Normas were applied to 1.2 million workers (37.2 per cent of the labor force) at the end of 1985. Three-quarters of the normas were "elementary"—that is, not determined by a time-and-motion study. Income paid for overfulfillment of normas grew from 121.7 million pesos (3.9 per cent of worker income on average in 1980) to 274.5 million pesos (6.0 per cent of worker income in 1985). Primas were introduced experimentally in 1979 and then gradually applied throughout the economy the following year. Varieties of primas abounded in Cuba, but most involved giving a bonus to a group of workers for increasing exports, saving raw materials or energy, overfulfilling quality or quantity targets, or developing new products. The value of primas paid out grew steadily from 14 million pesos in 1980 to 90.7 million in 1985, the latter figure still only representing 1.9 per cent of the basic wage. Premios were introduced experimentally in 1979. By 1985 total premio payments amounted to 71.1 million pesos or 1.6 per cent of the basic wage. Among other things, the extension of premios was frustrated by Cuba's system of administered prices, making the meaning of profit or any financial indicator dubious. Taken together, the three material incentives grew rapidly during the early 1980s but still accounted for only 10.6 percent on average of the basic wage in 1985, considerably below elsewhere in the CMEA.[6]

Table 10-1. Application of Material Incentives, 1985–90 (millions of pesos)

Year	(a) Total wages	(b) Norm overfulfil.	(c) Primas	(b)/(a)	(c)/(a)	(d)*	(e)**
1985	7139	275	91	3.85%	1.27%	11.2%	67.0%
1986	7359	251	88	3.40%	1.19%	11.1%	68.0%
1987	7290	188	52	2.58%	0.72%	10.9%	68.3%
1988	7641	186	45	2.44%	0.59%	11.9%	67.5%
1989	7971	188	47	2.36%	0.59%	12.3%⁺	66.98⁺
1990⁺⁺	2058	45	10	2.18%	0.50%	n.a.	n.a.

* absenteeism
** index of worker efficiency (*aprovechamiento en hombres días*)
⁺ January through September only
⁺⁺ January through March only
Source: Comité Estatal (1990), 120–21; Zimbalist and Brundenius (1989), 131–38.

In addition to the problems discussed above, it was discovered that often the three incentives overlapped, paying the worker two or three times for the same work; for example, sugar mill workers were paid for exceeding their norma, working overtime, and increasing exports. To avoid this duplication, many primas, especially those related to export production, were curtailed. In other cases, incentives were applied that had little justification, such as paying mechanics five times for repairing the same piece of machinery or having radio announcers work on piece rates. In yet other cases, elementary normas, set with the participation of the affected workers, were too low. In 1986 more than one-third of all workers with normas produced over 130 percent of their rate (*Granma* 1987, 5). In these instances, the design of certain incentives and output goals were reevaluated.

As shown in table 10-1, rectification brought a gradual reduction in the application of both normas and primas. No data were available to the author on the use of premios after 1985, but interviews with enterprise directors confirmed that there was also a move away from this incentive. The last two columns in table 10-1 support the case prima facie that the diminished use of material incentives after 1985 did not have a deleterious effect on worker effort. In particular, one can detect little if any significant change in the rates of worker absenteeism and worker efficiency between 1985 and 1989. Indeed, effort seems to have improved between 1985 and 1987 and then deteriorated between 1987 and 1989. One might attribute the decline in the latter period to

(1) moral incentives' wearing thin over time; (2) more worker time off for shopping and waiting in lines; and/or (3) increased shortage of raw materials for production and a corresponding increase in absenteeism or decrease in efficiency. In any event, considering the entire four-year period, it does not appear that the effort to rebalance moral and material incentives had a direct, discernible impact on productivity.

Reducing the Scope of Private Sector Activity

The most important policy of rectification regarding private activity was the abolition of the free peasant markets on May 15, 1986. As noted above, the leadership perceived a plethora of threats from these markets. With rectification, the state attempted to replace these markets, which accounted for less than 5 percent of food sales, according to official figures, by expanding the state-run parallel markets. Also, a new distribution enterprise, Frutas Selectas, was set up, and farmers were offered higher prices for sales to this state facility. To say the least, the new arrangement created considerable inconvenience for large numbers of consumers who were forced to locate new sources of supply for many food items.

Another significant measure was to regulate the sale of private housing. The 1984 housing law provided for converting all tenants into homeowners within 20 years (over 60 per cent already owned their homes). The state had already sanctioned private home construction and greatly eased private access to building materials. The result was twofold: a construction boom with private construction accounting for one-third of new houses in the 1980s and a speculation boom with skyrocketing prices for real estate. To curb the latter and its beneficiaries, the state decreed that all housing sales would have to pass through a state agency that would regulate prices. The 1984 housing law itself was left intact.

Other private sector activity came under tighter state regulation, and the scope of some activities was thus reduced. The principal new restriction since 1986 was that private service workers (such as plumbers, electricians, and mechanics), artisans, street vendors, taxi drivers, and so on had to be licensed and had to receive all materials through a state-issued certificate. The number of private wage workers and workers for their own account fell from 52,100 in 1985 to 43,200 in 1987 as private nonfarm income fell from 102.5 million pesos to 67.8 million pesos, but private nonfarm income began to recover in 1988, rising to 80.7 million pesos.[7] Thus urban private sector activity was reduced, but it was hardly obliterated.

Despite the closing of the peasant markets, officially reported private farm income actually increased from 495.6 million pesos in 1985 to 528.9 million pesos in 1988. Within the private agricultural sector, incomes of workers in producer cooperatives fell from 161.8 million pesos in 1985 to 152.5 million in 1988, while the incomes of individual private farmers expanded from 333.8 million pesos to 376.4 million (Comité Estatal 1989a, 21). The greatest difficulty, however, was with respect to the wholesale and retail distribution of this output, not the production itself. The shortage of trucks and the inadequacy of storage, refrigeration, and packaging facilities, as well as the poor internal organization of the state distribution network, often led to the wastage of 25 to 35 percent of certain crops such as potatoes, tomatoes, and onions.

Efforts at Administrative Decentralization

Although market-oriented decentralization was eschewed during rectification, the Cuban government actively pursued policies aimed at administrative decentralization. Even though the main architect of the 1975–85 liberalization policies, Humberto Pérez, was replaced in early 1985 as head of JUCEPLAN, the perception of a torpid, overcentralized system remained and was widespread among government economic functionaries and managers. The momentum toward decentralization, though slowed and redirected, was not broken.

Several ongoing efforts were made, including the formation of production brigades in agricultural and industrial enterprises and the formation of *uniónes de empresas* (industrial associations), to which planning functions were transferred. Production brigades are subunits of an enterprise that operate as separate accounting units. Enterprises contract out a production plan to a brigade, and the brigade receives bonuses according to its performance. Brigades were allowed to organize their own work as well as hire (after considering suggestions from enterprise management) and fire their own brigade chief (Ghai et al. 1986). The brigades began experimentally in agriculture in 1981 and in industry in 1983. By 1986, there were 2,500 brigades in some 300 enterprises, 120 state farms and 180 enterprises outside agriculture; agricultural brigades averaged about 75 workers each. Early indications suggested that the brigades were stimulating both increased worker involvement in decision making and increased productivity (Kay 1987; Meurs 1987; Ministerio de Agricultura 1985, 1986).

Another way enterprise flexibility or autonomy may be increased is through amalgamation. Since 1977 Cuban enterprises have been joined together with other horizontally or vertically related enterprises to form *uniónes de empresas* (Díaz Martínez 1983). It was hoped that the new larger units would be able to carry out more functions (such as research and development, materials supply, maintenance and repair) and become less dependent on the center.

Two reports (Comisión Nacional de Perfeccionamiento 1989; Comisión Nacional del SDE 1989) detailed the ongoing amalgamation of industrial enterprises into uniónes. The number of economic units (either enterprises or uniónes) directed by the ministries of transport, food, basic industry, metallurgy, and light industry was reduced from 155 in 1988 to 88 in 1989, or 43.2 percent. This apparently simplified the tasks of management sufficiently to allow for the reduction of administrative personnel in these ministries from 5,600 to 3,636, or by 37.3 percent.

Other initiatives during rectification were new. In 1988, following the recommendations of a special commission to study the SDPE, several new procedures were adopted in the planning process (JUCEPLAN 1988): (1) the number of commodities and commodity groups subject to central planning was to be reduced from 2,300 to 800; (2) the number of directive indicators to the enterprise was to be cut from an average of 28 to 18; (3) the system of material balances was to be decentralized by "extending direct ties in order to eliminate intermediaries in the process of elaborating and executing the plan of material and technical supplies"; and (4) the number of material balances drawn up by CEATM was to be reduced by 382 (31 per cent) and passed down to the level of the industrial association or the enterprise. Further, direct supplies contracting was established between enterprises for 518 different products during 1988 (Comisión Nacional del SDE 1989; Echevarría and Trueba 1990; Hernández and Riverón 1989).

Experiments were also carried out in central planning methods. In 1988 experimentation was begun in 33 enterprises in "continuous planning." This method called upon the enterprise to draw up a production and input plan, based on the previous year's levels and its expectations for the coming year, prior to receiving the plan control figures from the national ministry. That is, the enterprise was supposed to begin annual planning before it received instructions from the planning hierarchy. Under traditional procedures, plan control figures often arrived at the enterprise too late for a serious discussion or for any meaningful amendments to be made to the the plan (Ayala and Ferrer 1989). In its conception, continuous planning avoided the last-minute-rush syndrome and allowed for some greater initiative at the enterprise level. It never progressed beyond the experimental stage, however (by mid-1990 it had been extended to approximately one-third of Cuba's productive enterprises), because the traditional central planning framework ceased to exist during the special period.

Experiments with pricing policy were also essayed during rectification. Some foreign trade enterprises were using international prices. Other enterprises that were the sole producers of a given product were allowed to set the product's price, subject to issued guidelines and subsequent review by the State Committee on Prices.

The planning process itself was radically altered in practice by the supply disruptions and transformations originating in Eastern Europe and the former Soviet Union after 1989. Although annual plans continued to be produced, they were regarded more as hortatory than as mandatory. The central government itself seemed to have implicitly admitted the impossibility of global planning in the new context by changing its top-level planning organization and by placing clear focus on priority sectoral, as opposed to global, plans.[8]

The Special Period, 1989–93

Although many aspects of the present special period reforms have their roots in policies from the early and mid-1980s, the severity of Cuba's economic crisis and the necessity to better integrate its system with the world economy have forced more fundamental and irreversible reforms.

Enterprise Management

One prominent arena for reform has been enterprise management. The initiative for serious changes in Cuba's enterprise management system came, oddly enough, from the Ministry of the Armed Forces. In July 1987 the decision was taken to begin sweeping experiments in the management of a number of military enterprises. These experiments involved a variety of modern management techniques, such as management by consensus, group work, quality control circles, job rotation, and participatory decision making. The experimentation began in the machine shop of the Che Guevara military products factory during September and October 1987. Over the next production period, quality indicators rose by 20 to 60 per cent despite a reduction in quality control personnel of 33 per cent (Grupo de Perfeccionamiento 1989, 198; Pérez and González 1990; Casas Regueiro 1990).

The success of these experiments led to the decision to generalize the techniques throughout the economy. A national management training system (SUTCER) was set up in 1988 to help introduce and disseminate these methods. Western experts have been called upon to help design course modules, give specialized seminars to enterprise directors and union leaders, build a curriculum for a new master's program in management, and engage directly in enterprise consulting. More than 1,000 administrators have already taken short courses, and several industrial sectors have successfully introduced management reforms.

More than a dozen enterprises under the Ministry of Basic Industry have introduced Japanese-style quality control circles. Initial reports suggest impressive quality and productivity gains. It appears that one of the important reasons for these gains is the absence of a rigid quantity plan; the uncertain planning environment liberates ministries and enterprises from the quantity fetishism of conventional central planning. The more rational and democratic methods are being applied because of the space created by aberrant conditions in the macroeconomy. One interesting result of these reforms is that a larger constituency is being built at the base for greater decentralization in the economic mechanism.

In addition to its efforts to promote democratic management practices, SUTCER also worked with the United Nations Development Program to develop instruction in market-oriented management. Seminars were conducted in negotiation, marketing, accounting and finance, intellectual property, and business strategy; and Cuban managers were sent for internships in multinational companies and foreign business schools.

SUTCER gathered so much momentum as a force of enterprise reform that in May 1992 it was abolished. It appears that once again the Cuban government decided control was more important than efficiency. The management and structural reform concepts promoted by SUTCER continue to be promulgated, but without the growth of an independent organizational base pushing its own agenda.

Organizational Reforms

A second reform arena has been Cuba's foreign trade structures. Several corporations have been established—among them Cubanacán, Gaviota, Cimex, Uneca, Consa, Banco Financiero Internacional, and Cubalse—that for most purposes are allowed to operate independently of the central state apparatus. They behave as profit-maximizing entities and engage in joint ventures inside and outside of Cuba. In part to facilitate trade insurance and to diminish the perceived foreign exchange payment risk to trading partners, the Cuban state has arranged for most of these corporations to be owned privately by individual Cubans. Privately funded and operated nongovernmental organizations (NGOs) have also begun to appear.

Foreign trade increasingly is conducted by decentralized entities rather than the Ministry of Foreign Trade. In 1989, there were 300 Cuban enterprises and other economic entities involved in foreign trade; at the end of 1991 there were some 500. In 1991, the number of trading companies independent of central authorities rose from 30 to 72. In the case of an increasing number of several large undertakings, such as Antillana de Acero, the enterprises are largely handling their own foreign trade, and they are allowed to retain up to 70 percent of their foreign exchange earnings to purchase needed foreign inputs. That is, bureaucratic procedures for allocations via the Ministry of Foreign Trade have been reduced or in many cases obviated. As of October 1992, 500 Cuban enterprises were self-financing in foreign exchange.

The promotion of joint ventures and production sharing arrangements is part of the transformation of Cuba's foreign sector. The experience with this growing and important part of the Cuban economy is discussed at length in chapter 7 in this book. Here it remains only to say that several reforms have permitted these joint ventures to operate with increasing independence from the Cuban state. Among other things, mixed enterprises in Cuba are permitted to make their own provisioning contracts with Cuban enterprises, and they are allowed to set up their own warehousing facilities.

Concomitant to the reorganization of the state sector of the economy, a vibrant informal market has blossomed. In 1992, the average Cuban spent well over half of his or her income on informal or black market purchases, including food, clothing, household appliances, and services. The approximately $200 million sent by Miami relatives and the additional tens of millions of dollars circulating from expenditures by foreign travelers have spawned a widespread underground economy with prices paralleling those at dollar shops, converted at the going black market exchange rate (roughly 40 pesos to the dollar in November 1992). Except in the most egregious cases, the Cuban government seems to have accepted these new marketing networks as a necessary component of the population's efforts to survive. Although a black market always existed in Cuba and has been growing over the last ten years, its present dimensions are unique and contribute to a thoroughly overhauled economic landscape on the island. According to one estimate from Cuba's Center for the Study of the Americas, the value of black market transactions in Cuba rose from roughly two billion pesos in 1990 to an annual rate of over 10 billion pesos in 1993. The pervasiveness of the black market establishes a dynamic that sucks human and other resources away from the official economy and progressively compels Cuban officials to relax controls in the economic mechanism.

Conclusion

The official management reforms are congruent with the endeavor to attract foreign investment and reincorporate Cuba into the world market. They are welcome developments, but they will not extricate Cuba from its economic stranglehold. A broader commitment to an internal market mechanism and privatization of small and some medium-size activities are necessary both to bring greater efficiency to Cuba's internal economic mechanism and to convey the positive vision of a new economic model adapted to the realities of the post-CMEA world.[9] The extensive demoralization of the Cuban people can be shaken by nothing less.

Notes

1. The adoption of the SDPE occurred in 1976, but this year was designated as a year of study and preparation. The gradual implementation of the system began in 1977. Since mid-1986, it has been more commonly referred to as simply the SDE (Sistema de Dirección de la Economía).

2. In the mid- and late 1970s, as Cuba was introducing the Soviet-style SDPE, the model came under continual criticism in Cuba for being too centralized. At the time, Cuba pioneered in establishing its system of Popular Power with contested local elections and in turning over the management of

local enterprises to the newly elected municipal bodies. Miguel Figueras, vice-president of the JUCEPLAN at the time, commented to the author that between 1977 and 1981 the Cubans "were decentralizing 15 percent" of the Soviet-style planning institutions each year.

3. The Cuban phrase for consolidated enterprises is *empresas consolidadas*. They were an earlier and generally smaller incarnation of *unións de empresas*, or industrial associations.

4. The share contributed to output by local enterprises was, of course, considerably less than 34 per cent, since these enterprises were generally quite small.

5. The system of free labor contracting was actually begun on an experimental basis in 1979 in the province of Pinar del Río but was not implemented until 1986 in Havana. The Soviet Union had this system for many years. There, as in Cuba, free contracting denoted the right to hire freely within plan-stipulated limits but not to fire.

6. In the mid-1970s, for instance, the variable part of the basic wage ranged from 15.2 percent in Hungary to 55.2 percent in the German Democratic Republic, with Bulgaria at 39.8 percent, Poland at 31.7 percent, the USSR at 36.4 percent, and Czechoslovakia at 43.8 percent. See Acosta (1982, 291).

7. Indications are that it continued to increase in the first half of 1989, when total private sector incomes increased 4.7 per cent. See Comité Estatal (1987, 193; 1989a, 21; 1989b, 3).

8. Since September 1988 the Central Group (Grupo Central) has been replaced by a smaller body, the Executive Committee of the Council of Ministers, as the primary state organ responsible for orienting the economic plan. It is not apparent what, if any, influence this has had on the degree of centralization or decentralization in the planning process. The Executive Committee reports meeting biweekly to discuss a broad range of sectoral and administrative issues, usually with representatives from enterprises or administrative bodies in the affected areas. See *Granma* (1989).

9. The Fourth Congress of the Cuban Communist Party of October 1991 did affirm the party's intention to expand the very limited private service sector (including mechanical and electrical repair, carpentry, plumbing, artisanry, and other trades), but the implementation of this new policy seems to have gotten off to a slow start.

References

Acosta, José. 1982. *Teoría y práctica de los mecanismos de dirección de la economía*. Havana: Editorial de Ciencias Sociales.

Ayala Castro, Héctor, and Pedro Ferrer. 1989. "Tendencias organizativas de las empresas cubanas." *Economía y Desarrollo*, no. 3.

Banco Nacional de Cuba. 1986. *Informe Económico* (March): 6.
Casas Regueiro, José. 1990. *A problemas viejos, soluciones nuevas.* Havana: Editora Política.
Codina, Alexis. 1987. "Worker Incentives in Cuba." *World Development* (January).
Comisión Nacional del SDE. 1989. *Balance de las tareas para el perfeccionamiento del sistema de dirección de la economía, febrero 1988-enero 1989.* Havana (February).
Comisión Nacional de Perfeccionamiento del SDE. 1989. "Reorganización de las entidades económicas de los organismos centrales." *Cuba: Economía Planificada* 4 (July-September).
Comité Estatal de Estadísticas. 1987. *Anuario estadístico de Cuba.* Havana.
———. 1989a. *Balance de Ingresos y Egresos Monetarios de la Población* (July).
———. 1989b. *Balance de Ingresos y Egresos Monetarios de la Población* (August).
———. 1990. *Boletín estadístico de Cuba* (January-June).
Cuba: Economía Planificada 3, no. 3 (1988); 4, no. 1 (1989).
Domínguez, Jorge. 1985. "Cuba: Charismatic Communism." *Problems of Communism* (September-October).
———. 1988. "Blaming Itself, Not Himself: Cuba's Political Regime after the Third Party Congress." In *Socialist Cuba: Past Interpretations and Future Challenges*, edited by Sergio G. Roca. Boulder, Colo.: Westview Press.
Echevarría, Oscar, Lázaro Ramos, and Abilio Díaz. 1986. "Consideraciones metodológicas para el cálculo de la demanda de piezas de repuesto." *Cuba: Economía Planificada* 1, no. 2.
———, and Gerardo Trueba. 1990. "Algunas reflexiones sobre la planificación en Cuba." *Cuba: Economía Planificada* 5, (January-March).
Ghai, Dharam, Cristóbal Kay, and Peter Peek. 1988. *Labour and Development in Rural Cuba.* London: Macmillan.
Granma. 1982. (October 5).
———. 1987. (January 14).
———. 1989. (September 25).
Grupo de Perfeccionamiento de las Organizaciones Empresariales e Instituciones del MINFAR. 1989. *Bases generales del perfeccionamiento en el MINFAR.* Havana (September).
Hernández, Alma, and Nilda Riverón. 1989. "La planificación empresarial: Problemas y perspectivas." *Economía y Desarrollo*, no. 2.
JUCEPLAN (Junta Central de Planificación). 1985. *Dictámenes de la IV Plenaria.* Havana.
———. 1988. *Decisiones adoptadas sobre algunos elementos del Sistema de Dirección de la Economía.* Havana (March).

Kay, Cristóbal. 1987. "New Developments in Cuban Agriculture: Economic Reforms and Collectivization." Occasional paper no. 1, Centre for Development Studies, University of Glasgow.

Kim, Ilpyong, and Jane S. Zacek, eds. 1990. *Reform and Transformation in Communist Systems: Comparative Perspectives.* Washington, D.C.: Washington Institute.

Mata, Nelson. 1986. "Los gastos de presupuesto de los órganos locales del poder popular." *Finanzas y Crédito,* no. 5, p. 56.

Mesa-Lago, Carmelo. 1988. "The Cuban Economy in the 1980s." In *Socialist Cuba: Past Interpretations and Future Challenges,* edited by Sergio G. Roca. Boulder, Colo.: Westview Press.

Meurs, Mieke. 1988. "Planning, Participation and Incentives in Socialism: The Case of Cuban Agriculture." Ph.D. dissertation. University of Massachusetts, Amherst.

Ministerio de Agricultura. 1985. *Evaluación de la experiencia sobre la introducción de las brigadas permanentes de producción y el cálculo económico interno en las empresas del Ministerio de la Agricultura.* Havana (November).

———. 1986. *Informe: resultados económicos de las empresas constituídas en BPP.* Havana.

Pérez, Armando, and Berto González. 1990. "La organización de la producción en el perfeccionamiento empresarial de las FAR." *Cuba Socialista,* no. 44 (April-June).

Pérez-López, Jorge. 1986. "Cuban Economy in the 1980s." *Problems of Communism* (September-October).

Rabkin, Rhoda. 1988. "Cuba: The Aging of a Revolution." In *Socialist Cuba: Past Interpretations and Future Challenges,* edited by Sergio G. Roca. Boulder, Colo.: Westview Press.

Roca, Sergio G., ed. 1988. *Socialist Cuba: Past Interpretations and Future Challenges.* Boulder, Colo.: Westview Press.

Staff of Radio José Martí. 1986. *Cuba Quarterly Situation Report* 3, no. 3, section 3.

Treaster, Joseph. 1987. "Castro Recoils at a Hint of Wealth." *New York Times,* February 8.

Zimbalist, Andrew. "Incentives and Planning in Cuba." *Latin American Research Review* 24, no. 1 (January).

———, and Claes Brundenius. 1989. *The Cuban Economy: Measurement and Analysis of Socialist Performance.* Baltimore: Johns Hopkins University Press.

———, and Wayne Smith. 1990. "Reform in Cuba." In *Reform and Transformation in Communist Systems: Comparative Perspectives,* edited by I. Kim and J. S. Zacek. Washington, D.C.: Washington Institute.

ELEVEN

Economic Reform in Cuba
Lessons from Eastern Europe
JORGE F. PÉREZ-LÓPEZ

For reasons related to efficiency and practicality, Cuba will reform its economy in the near future to create a market economy. To be sure, a decision to marketize the economy will not come easily to Cuba's leadership, adamant about staying the course with socialism despite a crumbling economy and isolation from world markets. A demonstration effect associated with reforms in the former socialist countries, however, combined with deepening domestic economic hardships, will eventually bring marketization to the island.

In this chapter, starting from the premise that Cuba will create a market economy in the near future, I examine reform experiences in other socialist countries to identify policy lessons that might be applicable to Cuba. Although the reform experiences of each socialist country are different, there are sufficient systemic similarities among these countries, and between them and Cuba, to justify a comparative analysis.

The chapter begins with a very brief historical review of reform efforts in socialist countries and the evolution of thinking about the feasibility of perfecting socialist economies through reforms. Based primarily on the marketization experiences of three Eastern European countries—Poland, Hungary, and Czechoslovakia—I identify in the second part of the chapter a number of issues that most likely would have to be addressed in creating a market economy in Cuba: stabilizing the economy; creating an institutional framework for the market; privatizing; transforming government structures; and establishing a viable social safety net. The chapter concludes with some general observations regarding the process of economic reform in Cuba.

Socialist Economic Reforms in Perspective

The history of efforts by socialist countries to reform their economies is long and has been well documented (for example, by Montias 1969; Wilczynski 1972; Hare 1987). The earliest attempts to reform a centrally planned economy (CPE) by restoring some measure of capitalism to key sectors, particularly agriculture and trade, was probably Lenin's New Economic Policy (NEP) of March 1921, instituted only a few years after the triumph of the Bolsheviks (Campbell 1974, 5). In the 1950s and 1960s, all Eastern European socialist nations and the Soviet Union underwent, or at least attempted, some form of economic reform. Although many of the efforts were stillborn, the reform movement continued, preparing the ground for the very comprehensive reforms of the 1990s.

The preoccupation of socialist leaders with reforming their economic system is rooted in economics rather than in ideology or politics. Analyzing the reforms of the 1960s, Wilczynski (1972, 240) has argued that "the reforms . . . [were not] . . . an accidental byproduct of political de-Stalinization or a return to 'capitalism,' but a logical and necessary evolutionary process to meet the needs of higher stages of economic development." Over time, reforms evolved from modest efforts to "perfect" or fine-tune socialist economies to the current comprehensive attempts to set aside the basic tenets of central planning and create a market economy.

The Reform Imperative

After World War II, reconstruction of the war-torn Soviet Union and Eastern Europe channeled abundant unutilized resources into their economies and supported high growth rates. As these reserves began to be depleted, growth rates slowed down considerably. The growth slowdown that began in the mid-1950s and intensified in subsequent years suggested that the strategy of extensive development followed by

CPEs had run its course. Other weaknesses of the CPE economic model also became apparent.

Inefficient resource allocation. Bureaucratic allocation of resources created inefficiency and waste. Enterprise managers typically understated productive capacities to be able to qualify for the largest possible allocation of resources and to be assigned the lowest possible output targets. Aware of these practices, central planners imposed higher targets than warranted. Because the objective function of enterprises consisted only of maximization of output, cost minimization (consistent with efficient resource allocation) was largely ignored.

Generalized shortages. Shortages of consumer goods, intermediate products, and factors of production (such as labor resources) were commonplace. Initially, these shortages were believed to be transitory and attributable to errors in the planning process (overambitious or taut planning, for example). However, Kornai (1986) has argued that chronic shortages are intrinsic to CPEs because of the impossibility of restraining demand in the face of a so-called soft-budget constraint, whereby investment or operating failures do not result in severe consequences (such as shutdowns or bankruptcies) and are instead rewarded with subsidies from the central government.

Lack of international competitiveness. CPEs were singularly unsuccessful in increasing exports of manufactured goods to Western markets. To some extent, this was a reflection of the autarkic policies they pursued, but it also reflected poor quality in production, design, and marketing; inefficient production; and lack of incentives.

Types of Reforms

Hare (1987) surveyed Eastern European and Soviet economic reforms through the mid-1980s and classified them into two types: (a) cautious reforms—that is, those carried out within the traditional CPE model; and (b) "radical" reforms—those attempting to change the traditional CPE model. While this typology has been overtaken by events—the "radical" reforms of the past pale by comparison with the wholesale scuttling of the CPE model that has occurred in the former socialist countries—it nevertheless is useful in laying out the range of policy instruments that reformers within CPEs attempted to manipulate to improve the efficiency of their economies. Specifically, the following are among the elements identified by Hare (1987, 35) as associated with each type of reform:

Cautious Reforms

a. Partial reforms to improve planning
   Change the number and type of plan indicators at the enterprise level;
   Bonus compensation system for workers and managers;
   Price reform;
   Relaxation of foreign trade controls;
   Greater tolerance of small-scale private sector.
b. Organizational changes to facilitate central planning
   Formation of associations or trusts;
   Combination of branch ministries into larger units.
c. Computerization of plan calculations, and economic calculation in general.

"Radical" Reforms

a. Reform central planning
   Abolish the administrative allocation of productive inputs;
   Use profit maximization as an indicator of enterprise performance;
   Use modeling and other techniques to compute plan variants.
b. Decentralize economic management, e.g., in the following areas:
   Price formation;
   Investment decisions;
   Foreign trade (especially hard currency).
c. Reform the organizational structure
   Break up large enterprises, associations, trusts;
   Move from branch to functional management;
   Facilitate formation of new enterprises of all sizes;
   Create a bankruptcy law.
d. Reform factor markets (i.e., capital and labor markets)
e. Institute political reforms, such as economic democracy, relaxation of one-party control, and depoliticization of the economy.

Examples of cautious reforms include those in the 1950s in Hungary (1953–54), Czechoslovakia (1953–54), the German Democratic Republic (1954–55), and Poland (1956–57). Also in this category are the reforms introduced in the Soviet Union in 1965 (the so-called Kosygin reforms). In 1975, Cuba began to implement an Economic Planning and Management System (Sistema de Dirección y Planificación de la Economía, SDPE) that was inspired by the Kosygin reforms; this very modest effort at reform was reversed by the rectification process that began in 1986.

In contrast, the Yugoslavian reforms of 1950–52, which resulted in departures from command central economy and planning (for example, largely discontinuing directive annual plans, partly restoring the price mechanism, introducing worker self-management, and decollectivizing land), are considered radical reforms. Another example of broad-based radical reform is the New Economic Mechanism (NEM), introduced in Hungary in 1968 (Kramer and Danylyk 1981, 554; Marer 1989, 10), which devolved decision-making authority onto enterprises for investment, production, and price decisions.

Market versus Plan

In the last decade, a school of thought emerged that questioned whether market forces could lead to an efficient allocation of resources within CPEs. Proponents of this line of thought argued that inserting market-oriented elements into a socialist economy was tantamount to "grafting a branch of an apple tree onto a telephone pole." According to this line of reasoning, efficient allocation of resources requires extensive private ownership of the means of production, which runs counter to one of the basic tenets of CPEs.

For example, Soviet economist Popkova-Pijasheva (1990) argued that there are basic incompatibilities between central planning and market economy institutions. One of the incompatibilities is related to valuation. In CPEs, planned output is valuable by virtue of being part of the plan, whether or not it is useful to society; in market economies, output has value only if it is sold to a willing purchaser and then at the price the purchaser is willing to pay. Second, mandatory input and output norms are antithetical to the economic freedom required by the market system. And third, if permitted to compete, private capital would displace less efficient state capital. Popkova-Pijasheva (1990, 83–84) concluded that no in-between construct of a socialist market system is viable: "It is either the plan or the market. Just as a plan cannot be a little bit a market plan, a market cannot be a little bit planned or an enterprise a little bit free. Either prices call the tune—that is, credits, taxes, and monetary privileges, or sanctions are used by the state as levers of regulation—or the State Planning Committee shapes our economic life according to its science-based conceptions, planning our needs and demands as well as bringing them into correlation with actual possibilities. There is no third way."

Ickes (1990) expressed skepticism about the feasibility of reaping the benefits of markets within CPEs. In his view, markets inserted into CPEs tend to be seen as independent of other elements in the economic system, especially price formation and the entry and exit of enterprises. In the absence of these other elements, markets will not perform as expected and retrenchment will ensue, giving rise to incomplete reforms. In some cases, reforms may be counterproductive—they may create inflationary pressures and other macroeconomic disequilibria.

Hinds (1990) made a strong case in support of the argument that market forces cannot lead to an efficient allocation of resources without extensive private ownership of the means of production. Because private ownership of the means of production is forbidden in CPEs, there are no capital markets and there is no market for labor. This gives rise to at least three difficult problems: (1) how to ensure that investment in the right amounts and in the right places occurs; (2) how to deal with substandard performance by workers or enterprises, given the inability to turn to bankruptcies or firings; and (3) how to avoid wide divergences in the wage level for similar activities and skills in different enterprises.

Supporting the key role of private ownership, Winiecki (1990) has posited that CPE economic reforms failed because members of the ruling stratum benefited from the institutional status quo. Bureaucrats and party apparatchiks who drew economic benefits from the existing system of property rights had an incentive for maintaining that system. Since the advice of these same individuals was sought by the leadership in designing and implementing reforms, their chances for preventing, distorting, and/or aborting reforms were great.

More generally, Kornai (1990) has characterized the relationship between state ownership and market organization, or between private ownership and bureaucratic organization, as weak linkages. Attempts in CPEs to guide activities of the state sector via market instruments—the cornerstone of market socialism—failed because it was not possible to reduce the dominant influence of the bureaucracy (and the apparatchiks). Similarly, attempts to impose bureaucratic control over the private sector also failed because of basic incongruities between the two. Kornai concludes that market socialism and other "third ways" between classical socialism and contemporary capitalism are not economically feasible.

Although the preponderance of the evidence suggests that "hybrid" models that introduce selected market-oriented elements into socialist models and "third ways" are not economically feasible, the Cuban leadership has not accepted this conclusion. Despite the deteriorating economic situation, the Fourth Congress of the Cuban Communist Party ("Resolución" 1991) was willing to consider only very modest reforms (for example, encouragement of foreign investment from capitalist countries in the form of joint ventures) *within the context of a socialist economy:* "These programs and measures are part of the supreme goal of saving the fatherland, the revolution and socialism, to continue advancing in the rectification process under the conditions of the special period, to achieve economic independence, and to continue moving forward in the construction of a Cuban socialist society, on the basis of our concepts and in response to our realities."

Cuban analysts (including González 1992 and Rodríguez 1992) write with conviction about positive factors within the nation that could permit overcoming the current economic crisis and eventually reestablishing of economic growth through gradual insertion into the capitalist world economic system. In this regard, Cardoso and Helwege's (1992, 55) evaluation of the prospects for a hybrid economic model in Cuba is instructive:

> A hybrid model cannot work. It may sound like the path to a smoother transition, compared to a full-fledged shift to free markets. Bureaucrats may prefer this option, believing that it allows them to control the economy. But whom would such a system benefit? Not the ordinary Cuban worker, whose wage must remain low for the country to achieve any degree of international competitiveness. Nor will it benefit the extraordinary worker, with a willingness to hustle, for she will find that credit rationing, import controls, and bureaucracy stand in the way of setting up a small business.
>
> A hybrid system yields the worst of both systems: little foreign investment because the state fiddles too freely with the rules of the game, and glaring inequities that are excused as necessary incentives to attract elusive capital. Latin America experimented with hybrid models throughout the 1950s and 1960s. The result was persistent poverty and corruption.

Creating a Market Economy in Cuba

Strategies for the transformation of Eastern European CPEs into market economies differ across countries in terms of scope, pace, and sequencing of specific policy actions. These differences, in turn, reflect each individual country's pace of political reforms, degree of consensus for marketization, and severity of the economic situation. There are, nevertheless, remarkable similarities with regard to policies that are being implemented or considered.

Drawing primarily on the recent reform experiences of Poland, Hungary, and Czechoslovakia, I identify in this section of the chapter some of the policy initiatives likely to be needed to create a market economy in Cuba.[1] Many of the specific actions examined below are interlinked, and progress on one front depends on the successful implementation of changes in others. Nevertheless, they are treated separately here for ease of exposition. The identification of policy initiatives in this section of the chapter is not exhaustive but is merely an effort to put forward the key areas in which action would be needed to transform Cuba into a market economy.[2]

Stabilize the Economy

The Cuban economy is, and has been for some time, facing severe internal and external macroeconomic disequilibria. Internal disequilibria manifest themselves in a growing budget deficit, the inability to produce the goods and services the population wants to consume, and the persistence—and in recent years, expansion—of a physical rationing system. External disequilibria reveal themselves most clearly in persistent balance of payments problems and a very large foreign debt. A prerequisite for a marketization program in Cuba is to achieve macroeconomic stability.

Budget Deficit. Table 11-1 presents available data on the Cuban state budget for the period 1985–90. While government revenues remained essentially unchanged, expenditures rose by over 15 percent. As a result, the budget deficit widened from about 2 percent of revenues in 1985–86 to 13.6 percent and 15.9 percent, respectively, in 1989 and 1990.

In a departure from practice, Cuba has not published a state budget since 1990. For 1991, the National Assembly of People's Power approved rolling over the 1990 budget and authorized the Executive Committee of the Council of Ministers to modify the budget as needed to meet any contingencies (Pérez-López 1992). In view of the economic crisis of the 1990s, it is reasonable to assume that the budget deficit increased significantly. On the revenue side, the drop in economic activity would have reduced revenues: turnover taxes, payments by

Table 11-1. Cuban State Budget, 1985–90 (millions of pesos)

	1985	1986	1987	1988	1989	1990[a]
Revenues	12,294	11,699	11,272	11,386	11,904	12,463
Expenditures	12,547	11,887	11,881	12,532	13,528	14,448
Productive sphere	4,941	4,420	4,475	4,713	4,975	5,443
Housing and community services	734	718	680	787	860	870
Education and public health	2,548	2,693	2,725	2,857	2,906	2,953
Other social and cultural activities	1,965	1,830	1,850	2,060	2,301	2,506
Administration	643	639	565	561	525	503
Defense and domestic order	1,336	1,268	1,242	1,274	1,377	1,380
Other	381	319	244	280	305	245
Reserves	—	—	—	—	279	549
Surplus/(deficit)	(253)	(188)	(609)	(1146)	(1624)	(1985)

Sources: 1989-90: "La economía" (1989), 26; 1985-88: BNC (1985, 1986).
[a] Approved by the National Assembly of People's Power.

enterprises out of profits, and foreign trade differentials. On the expenditure side, payments to workers dislocated by the shutdown of plants associated with shortages of energy and raw materials would have boomed.

Inflation. Although the purchasing power of Cuba's population is very high relative to the volume of goods available for purchase, it has not resulted in open inflation because of the government's tight control of prices. The rationing system for consumer products, in place since March 1962, has created massive pent-up demand for consumer goods. Prices of certain consumer products under the rationing system are reportedly still heavily subsidized, although the government has made efforts to cut back on these subsidies.

The relative stability of Cuban prices differs significantly from the situation that prevailed, for example, in prereform Poland and Yugoslavia, where prices essentially had been deregulated (with the exception of those for staple food products and energy) and open inflation was rampant. However, the combination in Cuba of regulated prices that bear little relation to costs of production, pent-up demand, and a large monetary overhang create the potential for rapid open inflation when prices are deregulated as part of a marketization effort.

External Imbalances. Cuba does not publish statistics on the balance of payments, but in the context of the renegotiation of the hard-currency debt with Western creditors that began in the early 1980s, some information on the hard-currency balance of payments has been released.

Cuba's hard-currency current account deteriorated severely in the second half of the 1980s, requiring the drawing down of reserves. The situation improved in 1988 as a result of severe cutbacks on hard-currency imports; this reduction of imports, in turn, severely disrupted production in many areas of the economy that depended on imported raw materials and capital goods. In the first three quarters of 1989, the most recent period for which data are available (Banco Nacional de Cuba [BNC]–Comité Estatal de Estadísticas [CEE] 1989), the hard-currency balance of payments improved somewhat as hard-currency imports were severely cut back. As discussed in chapter 9, since around 1989 Cuba has received some foreign capital in the form of investments in joint ventures with Cuban enterprises, a positive development from a balance-of-payments perspective.

Foreign Debt. According to the most recent information (BNC-CEE 1989), Cuba's hard-currency debt amounted to the equivalent of 6.45 billion pesos in 1988 and 6.20 billion pesos in September 1989. In early 1990 Soviet and Eastern European officials released information on the magnitude of the debt owed by Cuba. According to former Soviet Premier Ryzhkov, Cuba's debt to the Soviet Union amounted to 15.4 billion rubles at the end of 1989, while the debt to Eastern European nations was reported at about 900 million rubles.[3] Based on these figures, it can be estimated that Cuba's total foreign debt (to the Soviet Union, Eastern Europe, and Western creditors) at the end of 1989 was about $32.0 billion.[4]

Cuba's external indebtedness is very high both in per capita terms (population of about 10.6 million in 1989) and in comparison with national product (global social product was about 27 billion pesos in 1988) and export capacity (merchandise exports amounted to 5.5 billion pesos in 1988), even by Latin American standards (World Bank 1990).

- Cuba's per capita debt of about $3020 was the highest in the region.
- Cuba does not publish statistics on gross national product (GNP) comparable with those produced by other market economies. Using the global social product as a very rough estimate of the overall value of goods and services produced by the economy, one can

calculate that the external debt in 1988 exceeded the value of output produced by the economy. In 1988, only six Latin American countries (Bolivia, Costa Rica, Ecuador, Guyana, Jamaica, and Panama) had foreign debt exceeding GNP. Mexico and Brazil, two countries usually considered to be heavily indebted, had foreign debt-to-GNP ratios of 0.57 and 0.33 respectively.
- Cuba's foreign debt-to-exports ratio of about 5.5 was among the highest in the region, with only Bolivia having a higher ratio.

Within the reforming socialist economies, the Cuban external debt problems are similar to those faced on the eve of reform by heavily indebted Poland and, to a lesser extent, Hungary.

External Competitiveness. In 1989, manufactured products accounted for 3.3 percent of the value of Cuba's total exports (*Anuario estadístico de Cuba* [AEC] 1988, 262). Products of the sugar industry accounted for 73.2 percent of exports, mining (mostly nickel) for about 9 percent, tobacco for about 1.6 percent, fisheries for 2.4 percent, and agricultural products for 3.9 percent. Cuba's inability to penetrate world markets with manufactured products is evidence of the lack of international competitiveness of Cuban producers. This reflects a variety of factors, including a deliberate policy of import substitution, concentration on sugar production to conform to the role assigned to Cuba within the "socialist division of labor" dictated by the former Council for Mutual Economic Assistance, low quality of manufactured products, and an overvalued currency.

The adoption of appropriate macroeconomic policies is a prerequisite for creating an operating market economy in Cuba. While it is necessary at the outset to create a macroeconomic environment that supports systemic changes, it is also critical that such a supportive macroeconomic environment continue to exist once marketization initiatives are begun. This calls for close coordination between macroeconomic policies and the implementation of marketization initiatives.

Development of concrete proposals for a comprehensive macroeconomic stabilization plan would require detailed information on the performance and capabilities of the Cuban economy that are not currently available and would go beyond the scope of this paper. A short-term macroeconomic stabilization plan at a minimum would need to deal with the following issues:

- *Restoration of fiscal discipline.* Adopt tight monetary and fiscal policies. For instance, reduce money supply by capping credits

(subsidies) to enterprises; reduce the budget deficit through a severe cutback on military expenditures.
- *External financing.* Seek the renewal of external financing through loans from governments and international financial institutions and lines of credit from suppliers.
- *Exchange rate.* Devalue the peso and set an exchange rate that will make Cuban goods competitive in international markets.
- *Trade policy.* Liberalize foreign trade to permit the importation of goods consumers want to purchase and to introduce domestic competition.

The longer-term agenda would include elimination of subsidies to enterprises and consumers, creation of a tax system that will not make budget balance dependent on enterprise profitability, introduction of market-based credit and monetary controls, review of laws and regulations dealing with incoming foreign investment, and convertibility of the peso.

Create an Institutional Framework for the Market

In order for a market economy to operate efficiently, a number of legal, economic, and financial institutions must be in place. Paradoxically, although central authority will play a much smaller role in a market economy than in a CPE, the central authority must be very active during the transition period to ensure the creation of the appropriate institutions that support a free market.

After more than thirty years of socialism, Cuba is ill-equipped to support a market economy. Unlike Poland, Hungary, and other Eastern European nations that have permitted substantial market-oriented behavior (private ownership of businesses, farmers' markets, self-employment in certain service occupations, and the like) alongside the centrally planned economy, Cuba has shied away from doing so. As part of the rectification process, moreover, small-scale market-oriented experiments that were permitted in the early 1980s (such as farmers' free markets to dispose of agricultural output beyond procurement quotas) were eliminated. In order to transform the economy to a market-oriented one, the Cuban government must develop a legal framework that supports market behavior, pursue procompetitive policies, and encourage the development of the private sector.

Promote competition. Like other CPEs, the Cuban economy is

Table 11-2. Number of Industrial Enterprises According to Value of Output, 1988

	Total	Output in million pesos				
		Up to 1	1 to 30	30 to 60	60 to 90	Over 90
Total	836	52	733	37	8	6
Electricity	14		8	3	3	
Fuels	5	1	2			2
Ferrous mining & metallurgy	10	1	7	1		1
Nonferrous mining & metallurgy	14	2	8	3	1	
Nonelectrical machinery	145	13	132			
Electrical & electronic machinery	22	4	18			
Metal products	29	1	28			
Chemicals	36	2	31	3		
Paper & cellulose	10	1	8	1		
Printing	17	2	14	1		
Forestry & wood products	16	1	15			
Construction materials	52	5	47			
Glass and ceramics	7		7			
Textiles	16		11	5		
Apparel	16		16			
Leather products	16	1	15			
Sugar	148	2	141	4	1	
Food products	141	5	121	12	2	1
Fishing	23	1	21			1
Beverages & tobacco	41	5	33	2	1	
Other industrial activities	49	4	42	2		1
Irrigation	9	1	8			

Source: AEC (1988), 238.

characterized by a high degree of economic concentration. This is in part the result of the socialist fascination with bigness and the preference on the part of central planners to deal with as few enterprises as possible (Pryor 1973; Ehrlich 1985).

In 1988, the Cuban industrial sector consisted of 836 enterprises, many of which tended to be very large and were the only domestic producers of specific items (table 11-2). The degree of concentration varied across industries and was very high in some in which it does not appear that natural monopoly conditions were present (for example, only seven enterprises nationwide in the glass and ceramics industry, 17 in printing). Each of the six largest industrial enterprises accounted for more than one percent of the value of industrial sector output, a very different industrial structure from the one that prevailed in prerevolutionary Cuba (Monzón Cepero 1984).

A procompetitive policy would require the following:

- Breaking up monopolies and encouraging the establishment of small- and medium-sized enterprises.
- Establishing legal procedures for bankruptcies.
- Establishing and enforcing rules regarding anticompetitive behavior, such as monopolies, predatory behavior, and unfair competition.
- Adopting trade policies that open the domestic market to import competition.
- Engaging in a national campaign to educate the public about the operation of a market economy.
- Educating consumers about the benefits of competition and encourage the formation of consumer organizations.

Liberalize prices. The Cuban government has set prices in Cuba since the mid-1960s. A very elaborate price-setting apparatus is in place. Zimbalist and Brundenius (1989, 14) describe this mechanism, presumably as it existed around 1987-88, as follows:

> The State Price Committee was formed in 1976.... The committee is divided into groups that deal with different types of products and other functions of the committee. One group in charge of price setting for most nonperishable consumer goods has fourteen employees. It is responsible for 250,000 individual products, each having at least two prices—one wholesale and one retail. Each year the group will consider adjusting approximately 15,000 prices as cost conditions and inventory levels change. Such adjustments, however, are generally minor. The large and comprehensive adjustments are saved for periodic price reforms.

Unregulated prices are an essential ingredient of market behavior, and price liberalization should proceed as rapidly as marketization begins to take hold. Allowing prices to be established essentially through the interaction of supply and demand ought to stimulate production (particularly agricultural and artisan production). It would also obviate the need for consumer subsidies and have a salutary effect on the budget deficit. State intervention in price formation may be justified in the areas of public utilities and natural monopolies or, during a transition period, in situations where compelling economic or social reasons require it.

Create factor markets. As a result of Cuba's full-employment policy and the centrally planned nature of investment, there are no operating markets for labor and capital in the island. As a result, labor and capital resources are misallocated, creating the paradoxical situation in which there have been surpluses of resources in some areas (underemployed or redundant workers) at the same time that there were severe shortages in others.

The establishment of a functioning labor market in Cuba will require a basic policy shift that recognizes as the objective in the employment area the attainment of a high level of *productive* employment but not necessarily *full* employment. The overriding preoccupation with protecting existing jobs must give way to a deep commitment to creating new, productive ones. In practical terms, the creation of an operating labor market may require the following actions:

- Revitalizing free trade unions and restoring their role as legitimate representatives of workers in collective bargaining over economic and work-related issues.
- Reviewing the existing labor code with a view to ensuring that workers are afforded basic rights (including freedom of association, right to bargain collectively, workplace standards such as occupational safety and health, limits on hours of work, and so on).
- Considering changes to the labor code that promote labor market flexibility and respond to the collective-bargaining situation that will prevail in small- and medium-sized firms and in privatized large enterprises.
- Granting enterprises the authority to determine the optimal number of workers that should be employed and at which level of wages and the authority to release redundant workers.
- Removing factors that act as incentives for enterprises to hoard labor; encouraging the movement of redundant workers to productive activities.
- Providing training for dislocated workers and new entrants into the labor force.

The Cuban financial system is severely underdeveloped, with the BNC holding a virtual monopoly. Unlike other centrally planned economies such as Poland and Hungary, Cuba has no commercial banking system, with the BNC performing commercial banking roles as well. There are few savings institutions, and interest rates do not attract significant volumes of deposits.

Marketization would require operating domestic financial markets that direct domestic savings into productive investment opportunities.

- A prerequisite for the creation of financial markets may be the establishment of a private commercial banking system and a central bank.
- Eventually, markets should be created for equity and debt of newly established and privatized firms.
- There is a legitimate role for the government in establishing the legal framework for financial markets and regulating them, including setting accounting, disclosure, and reporting standards; determining conditions and legal requirements for entry into financial markets (including entry by foreign institutions); and supervising capital markets and banks.

Environment. The lifting of the Iron Curtain revealed the severe environmental decay that had occurred in Eastern Europe and the Soviet Union (noted by Feshbach and Friendly 1992 among others). Disregard for pollution controls, coupled with a government-controlled media and restrictions on the ability of citizens to protest against environmental degradation, created an environmental crisis in these countries. The pervasiveness of this environmental decay suggests that socialism, as an economic system, either could not deal with or did not give a sufficiently high priority to externalities.

While the extent of environmental decay in Cuba is not well documented at this time,[5] it is reasonable to expect that there will be areas in which substantial environment cleanup will be necessary (for example, bays, which reportedly are heavily polluted, and the areas surrounding open-pit nickel mining and processing operations). As the economy is transformed, the emerging legal framework must ensure that proper account is taken of environmental costs.

Privatize

Experience with piecemeal reforms in socialist countries has demonstrated that private ownership is a sine qua non for obtaining the efficiencies of the market system. In economies in transition, private ownership could and should be promoted through the encouragement of entrepreneurship, but it is clear that this approach alone will not deal with the crux of the problem: the overwhelming ownership of resources by the state.

The process of collectivization that occurred in Cuba is well documented and need not be revisited here. Suffice it to say that prior to the revolutionary takeover of January 1, 1959, the Cuban economy was predominantly capitalistic; with some notable exceptions, such as passenger railroads, the means of production were owned by either domestic or foreign individuals or corporations. It has been estimated, however, that by 1968 the Cuban state controlled 100 percent of resources in industry, construction, transportation (except cargo handling), retail, wholesale and international trade, banking, and education; and 70 percent of the agricultural sector (Mesa-Lago 1970, 204). The state's share of resources in agriculture has increased steadily over the years as the state has taken over land operated by private farmers who died or retired and private farmers have been encouraged to turn land over to the state. As a result, by 1988, 92 percent of the agricultural sector was under state control (Rodríguez 1990, 61). Collectivization levels in Cuba most likely exceed those of Eastern Europe, where significant shares of agricultural property remained in private hands and other forms of private property were permitted (Dallago 1988).

The interest in privatization—contracting with or selling to private parties the functions or firms previously controlled or owned by governments—is not only the purview of socialist economies in transition. Developed and developing countries alike have shown an interest in privatizing as a way to reduce government expenditures, increase efficiency, and for other purposes. As a student of privatization puts it,

> The popularity of privatization has different origins, reflecting different hopes that its proponents have for it. Many proponents emphasize efficiency. They see privatization as a means to increase output, improve quality, and reduce unit costs. Others hope it will curb the growth of public spending and raise cash to reduce government debt. Others like its general emphasis on private initiative and private markets as the most successful route to economic growth and human development. Finally, a large group sees in privatization a way to broaden the base of ownership and participation in a society—encouraging larger numbers to feel they have a stake in the system. (Hanke 1987, 4)

While there is general consensus on the desirability of privatizing state property in socialist countries, there is no agreement as to how it should be done, or how quickly. The following approaches have been suggested (Luis 1991):

- Reconstitute enterprises as limited-liability stock-issuing companies and sell the stock. This approach would raise revenue for the state, but might favor the *nomenklatura*, as they may be those in the best position to buy stock.
- Turn over ownership of enterprises to workers. This step would be effective in distributing productive assets quickly but would discriminate against the self-employed, the service sector workers, or those outside the labor force. Moreover, workers in economically viable enterprises would obtain more financial benefits than those in enterprises that go bankrupt and shut down.
- Reconstitute enterprises as limited-liability stock-issuing companies and distribute (give away) the stock to all citizens. This would create equity, but dilution of ownership might make management more difficult. If stock in individual enterprises were thus distributed rather than bundled as mutual funds, there might be equity problems depending on the economic viability of specific enterprises.
- Reconstitute enterprises as limited liability stock-issuing companies whose shares are bundled as "citizen shares." In a formulation by Feige (1990), a portion of these shares (half, in one formulation) would be sold at low cost to citizens; another (possibly 10 percent) would be retained by the central government (with the dividends to be used for paying for national defense, government operations, and debt service); another (perhaps 20 percent) would be allocated to regional or local governments; and the rest (perhaps 20 percent) would be unbundled into shares of individual corporations and sold at public auction to foreigners (to raise foreign exchange) or citizens.

Two important issues that would need to be addressed in privatizing state assets in Cuba, regardless of which privatization methodology were used, are 1) how to deal with foreign interest in purchasing state assets and, more specifically, with the possible role that the exile community might play in privatization; and 2) whether some compensation should be paid to those citizens who had property expropriated by the revolutionary regime.

Transform Government Structure

As a result of state ownership of the factors of production and the regimentation of a command economy, the Cuban government is intrusive. Creation of a market economy requires a radical transformation in the role of government from direct participant in the economy to indirect facilitator of economic activity.

Creation of a market economy in Cuba would require transforming the governmental structure through taking at least the following steps:

- Abolishing central planning organizations and structure as well as ministries that serve as advocates for specific industries (such as sugar, steel, and mining). Retaining the capacity of these institutions, however, to gather and process statistical data (industry ministries and central planning organizations, respectively, would carry out these functions).
- Streamlining government management functions in general and those of the military and the party in particular. Releasing human and physical resources into the private sector.
- Redirecting resources into areas that traditionally have been ignored by socialist economies (for example, protection of the environment).

Establish a Viable Social Safety Net

Transformation from a centrally planned economy to a market economy is bound to have adverse short-term impacts on certain segments of the population. Reforms in Eastern Europe (see, for example, Central Intelligence Agency [CIA] 1992) have given rise to substantial unemployment as enterprises reduced their payrolls when faced with a "hard" budget constraint; others were forced to go bankrupt and shut down. At the same time, the liberalization of prices and the elimination of consumer subsidies have reduced the purchasing power of consumers in general, but particularly of those citizens with low or fixed incomes. A social safety net that supports dislocated workers while they find new jobs and guarantees minimum levels of consumption for all citizens reduces the costs to individuals of the transformation to a market economy and makes the changes politically more palatable.

Assistance to unemployed workers. The full employment policies that have been pursued by socialist Cuba have sociopolitical rather than economic objectives.[6] These policies have been very popular with workers. Many benefits received by workers (such as health care, pensions, allocation of housing and consumer goods) have been associated with their jobs.

As has been discussed more thoroughly in chapter 6, since 1977 Cuba has had a safety net to assist workers whose jobs were eliminated for a variety of reasons; such "available" workers were eligible for reassignment to another job, could enroll in retraining programs, and were eligible for compensation for a twelve-month period. Beginning in August 1990, Cuba passed several pieces of legislation aimed at assisting dislocated workers during the current recession coinciding with the special period. Considering the massiveness of dislocations from the industrial sector, the weak condition of the economy, and the lack of productive employment opportunities, these programs are tantamount to transfer payments and are not financially viable.

As the Cuban economy undergoes a process of transformation into a market economy, it could be anticipated that unemployment would rise, following the pattern observed in Eastern Europe. However, the degree of dislocation that has already occurred during the special period (as a result of reductions in work hours and plant shutdowns because of shortages of imported intermediate commodities and fuels) is so significant that unemployment need not rise and may actually decline once a reform program reestablishes the normal flow of imported commodities. In any event, an integral part of an economic reform program for Cuba should include assistance to unemployed workers. This assistance might consist of the following elements:

- an unemployment compensation system that provides income support to workers during temporary periods of unemployment;
- employment services to dislocated workers, including referrals to job openings, counseling services, and mobility assistance;
- programs to provide specialized training and retraining for dislocated workers; and
- (in the longer run) an unemployment insurance fund financed from a payroll tax.

Assistance to the needy. As in Eastern Europe, the elimination of consumer subsidies and the deregulation of prices in Cuba are likely to have an adverse impact on the purchasing power of low-income citizens and those on fixed incomes. A balanced approach to marketization would be sensitive to the needs of these groups and institute safeguards to ensure that their consumption levels are not unduly affected. As in the case of job dislocations, the current Cuban economic crisis has already taken its toll on the Cuban population, reducing allocations of goods and services and heightening the sensitivity of the population to further consumption reductions.

Concluding Observations

Although to date Cuba has rejected any steps to create a market economy, there is no reason to believe that the island will be the exception to the global move toward marketization. Domestically, Cuba is facing the same economic quagmire that prompted marketization in Eastern Europe. Political changes in the East, moreover, have reduced the number of Cuba's allies and patrons, isolating Cuba and sharply reducing inflows of foreign goods and financial aid. The Cuban leadership's ability to freeze potential political reforms has also frozen marketization efforts, but it is a matter of time before a thaw occurs on both fronts.

The marketization experiences of Eastern Europe differ with respect to scope, pace, and sequencing of policy changes, but they nevertheless suggest a number of common themes: stabilizing the economy, creating an institutional framework for the market, privatizing, transforming government structures, and establishing a social safety net. There is much in these foreign experiences that can help analysts in thinking through the mechanics and implications of creating a market economy in Cuba.

Creation of a market economy in a setting where the regime in power has been committed to rooting out market behavior for over 30 years raises complex and challenging issues. A successful strategy for transforming Cuba to a market economy must first tackle the severe macroeconomic imbalances that plague the economy. A macroeconomic stabilization plan would need to restore fiscal balance, reestablish external financing, and develop exchange rate and trade policies that would make Cuban exports competitive in international markets. At about the same time, the painstaking and time-consuming work to create (or rebuild, as the case may be) legal, economic, and financial institutions to support the market must also begin. Unless such an institutional framework is created, stabilization efforts will not be lasting. At a minimum, Cuba must develop institutions that promote and support competition, price liberalization, operating factor markets, and consideration of environmental impacts in economic decision making.

A successful economic reform program must also address the issue of the inordinately high degree of concentration of property in the hands of the government and how to turn it over to the private sector. While it is clear that privatization brings about economic efficiency gains, the mechanics of privatization are complex and politically charged. To succeed, a privatization program must have political support. Closely related to privatization, the reform program must also bring about radical change in the role of government from direct participation in the economy to indirect facilitation of economic activity.

Finally, a comprehensive economic reform program must be sensitive to the needs of those who might be disproportionately disadvantaged by it and must offer them some temporary relief. Two groups that might deserve special attention are workers who become dislocated as a result of economic reform and the needy. These groups have already experienced a great deal of hardship during the current economic crisis, and the prospect of further reductions in consumption levels associated with marketization is bound to be unsettling to them. To the extent that these citizens perceive that their immediate economic needs are being addressed and that economic reforms will improve their living standards, they may become supporters of the reform process.

Notes

1. Particularly useful in drafting this chapter have been Council of Economic Advisers [CEA] (1991), Central Intelligence Agency [CIA] (1992), Lane (1992), Sachs (1990 and 1991), and Wellisz (1991).

2. By now there is a substantial and growing literature on Cuban economic reform. While there tends to be a consensus on the specific issues that must be addressed, there is no such consensus on how they should be addressed or on the sequencing of actions. Among the contributions to this literature are Jorge (1991), Castañeda (1991), Cardoso and Helwege (1992), and Johnson (1992).

3. The debt to the Soviet Union in November 1989, as given by Premier Ryzhkov, was reported in March 1990 in the Soviet newspaper *Izvestia*; Cuba's debt to the Eastern European socialist nations is from Rosenthal (1990).

4. This is a very rough estimate, obtained by combining Cuban debt to Western countries (6.20 billion pesos), to the Soviet Union (15.4 billion rubles or $24.3 billion) and to Eastern Europe (900 million rubles or $1.4 billion) at the end of 1989. Peso and ruble figures have been converted to U.S. dollars using official exchange rates (1 peso = $1.00 and 1 ruble = $1.58) although both of the currencies are severely overvalued.

5. A notable exception is Espino (1992).

6. Article 44 of the Socialist Constitution of 1976 states that "in a socialist society, work is a right, a duty, and a matter of pride for all citizens" (*Constitución* 1976:24).

References

Anuario estadístico de Cuba. 1988. Havana: Comité Estatal de Estadísticas. Annual.

Banco Nacional de Cuba. Various years. *Economic Report*. Havana.

———, and Comité Estatal de Estadísticas. 1989. *Quarterly Economic Report*. Havana (September).

Campbell, Robert W. 1974. *The Soviet-Type Economies*. Boston: Houghton Mifflin.

Cardoso, Eliana, and Ann Helwege. 1992. *Cuba after Communism*. Cambridge: MIT Press.

Castañeda, Rolando H. 1991. "Cuba: Una opción por la libertad, el desarrollo y la paz social." In *Cuba in Transition: Papers and Proceedings of the Association for the Study of the Cuban Economy*, edited by George P. Montalván and Joaquín P. Pujol, pp. 257–308. Miami: Florida International University.

Central Intelligence Agency (CIA). 1992. "Eastern Europe: Struggling to Stay on the Reform Track." Paper submitted to the Subcommittee on Technology and National Security, Joint Economic Committee, U.S. Congress (June 8).

Constitución de la República de Cuba. 1976. Havana: Editorial de Ciencias Sociales.

Council of Economic Advisers. 1991. "Economics in Transition around the World." In *Economic Report of the President 1991*, pp. 193–232. Washington, D.C.: U.S. Government Printing Office.

Dallago, Bruno. 1988. "The Role of the Non-Socialist Sector in Hungary and

Poland." In NATO Economics Directorate. *The Economies of Eastern Europe Under Gorbachev's Influence*, pp. 190–216. Brussels.

La economía cubana en 1989. 1989. Havana: Comité Estatal de Estadísticas.

Ehrlich, Eva. 1985. "The Size Structure of Manufacturing Establishments and Enterprises: An International Comparison." *Journal of Comparative Economics* 9, no. 3 (September): 267–95.

Espino, María Dolores. 1992. "Environmental Deterioration and Protection in Socialist Cuba." In *Cuba in Transition—Volume 2: Papers and Proceedings of the Association for the Study of the Cuban Economy*, edited by George P. Montalván, pp. 327–42. Miami: Florida International University.

Feige, Edgar L. 1990. "A Socialism with Private Property." *Wall Street Journal*, March 9, p. A12.

Feshbach, Murray, and Alfred Friendly. 1992. *Ecocide in the USSR*. New York: Basic Books.

González Núñez, Gerardo. 1992. "Los dilemas de la economía cubana mas allá del corto plazo." Paper presented at the 17th Conference of the Caribbean Studies Association, Saint George's, Grenada (May).

Hanke, Steve H. 1987. *Privatization and Development*. San Francisco: Institute for Contemporary Studies.

Hare, Paul. 1987. "Economic Reform in Eastern Europe." *Journal of Economic Surveys* 1, no. 1 (1987): 25–58.

Hinds, Manuel. 1990. *Issues in the Introduction of Market Forces in Eastern European Socialist Economies*. Washington, D.C.: World Bank.

Ickes, Barry W. 1990. "Obstacles to Economic Reform in Socialism: An Institutional-Choice Approach." *Annals of the American Academy of Political and Social Science* 507 (January): 53–64.

Johnson, Bryan T. 1992. "Preparing for a Market Economy in Cuba." *Heritage Foundation Backgrounder*, no. 890 (April).

Jorge, Antonio. 1991. *A Reconstruction Strategy for Post-Castro Cuba*. Coral Gables: North-South Center, University of Miami.

Kornai, Janos. 1986. "The Soft Budget Constraint." *Kyklos* 39, no. 1, 3–30.

———. 1990. "The Affinity Between Ownership Forms and Coordination Mechanisms: The Common Experience of Reform in Socialist Countries." *Journal of Economic Perspectives* 4, no. 3 (Summer): 131–47.

Kramer, Joseph C., and John T. Danylyk. 1981. "Economic Reform in Eastern Europe: Hungary at the Forefront." In Joint Economic Committee, *East European Economic Assessment*, 1, 549–70. Washington, D.C.: U.S. Government Printing Office.

Lane, Timothy D. 1992. "Transforming Poland's Economy." *Finance and Development* 29, no. 2 (June): 10–13.

Luis, R. Luis. 1991. "Lessons from Privatization in Eastern Europe and Latin

America." In *Cuba in Transition: Papers and Proceedings of the Association for the Study of the Cuban Economy*, edited by George P. Montalván and Joaquín P. Pujol, pp. 105–13. Miami: Florida International University.

Marer, Paul. 1989. "Hungary's Reform and Performance in the Kadar Era (1956–88)." In Joint Economic Committee, *Pressures for Reform in the Eastern European Economies*, 2, 1–15. Washington, D.C.: U.S. Government Printing Office.

Mesa-Lago, Carmelo. 1970. "Ideological Radicalization and Economic Policy in Cuba." *Studies in Comparative International Development* 5, no. 10: 203–16.

Montias, John Michael. 1969. "East European Economic Reforms." In *Comparative Economic Systems*, edited by Morris Bornstein, pp. 324–36. Homewood, Ill.: Irwin.

Monzón Cepero, Antonio. 1984. "Acerca del nivel de concentración y centralización de la producción y el capital en Cuba prerevolucionaria." *Economía y Desarrollo* 83, 98–107.

Pérez-López, Jorge F. 1992. *The Cuban State Budget: Concepts and Measurement*. Coral Gables: North-South Center, University of Miami.

Popkova-Pijasheva, Larissa. 1990. "Why Is the Plan Incompatible with the Market?" *Annals of the American Academy of Political and Social Science* 507 (January): 80–90.

Poznanski, Kazimierz. 1986. "Economic Adjustment and Political Forces: Poland Since 1970." *International Organization* 40, no. 2 (Spring).

Pryor, Frederic L. 1973. *Property and Industrial Organization in Communist and Capitalist Systems*. Bloomington: Indiana University Press.

"Resolución sobre el desarrollo económico del país." 1991. *Granma* (October 17): 3.

Rodríguez, José Luis. 1990. *Estrategia del desarrollo económico en Cuba*. Havana: Editorial de Ciencias Sociales.

———. 1992. "La economía de Cuba ante la cambiante coyuntura internacional." *Boletín de Información sobre la Economía Cubana* 1, no. 1 (January 1992); 1, no. 2 (February 1992).

Rosenthal, Bertrand. 1990. "Revelan por primera vez el monto de la deuda cubana con los comunistas." *Diario las Américas* (June 14): 1A, 11A.

Sachs, Jeffrey D. 1990. "My Plan for Poland." *International Economy* 3, no. 6 (December-January): 28–30.

———. 1991. "Poland's Big Bang: A First Report Card." *International Economy* 5, no. 1 (January-February): 40–43.

Wellisz, Stanislaw. 1991. "The Lessons of Economic Reform: The Polish Case." *Journal of International Affairs* 45, no. 1 (Summer): 165–79.

Wilczynski, J. 1972. *Socialist Economic Development and Reforms*. New York: Praeger.

Winiecki, Jan. 1990. "Obstacles to Economic Reform of Socialism: A Property-Rights Approach." *Annals of the American Academy of Political and Social Science* 507 (January): 65–71.

World Bank. 1990. *World Debt Tables 1989–90*. First Supplement. Washington, D.C.: World Bank.

Zimbalist, Andrew, and Claes Brundenius. 1989. *The Cuban Economy: Measurement and Analysis of Socialist Performance*. Baltimore: Johns Hopkins University Press.

CONTRIBUTORS

Juan M. del Aguila is associate professor of political science at Emory University.

Sergio Díaz-Briquets is senior associate at Casals and Associates, a consulting firm located in Arlington, Virginia.

Jorge I. Domínguez is professor of government at Harvard University and visiting senior fellow (1993–94) at the Inter-American Dialogue in Washington, D.C.

María Dolores Espino is assistant professor of economics at Florida International University.

Julie M. Feinsilver is visiting scholar, School of International Service, American University, and senior research fellow, Council on Hemispheric Affairs.

Damián J. Fernández is associate professor of international relations and director of the Graduate Program in International Studies at Florida International University.

Jorge F. Pérez-López is an international economist with the Bureau of International Labor Affairs, U.S. Department of Labor, Washington, D.C.

Archibald R. M. Ritter is professor of economics in the Norman Patterson School of International Affairs at Carleton University, Ottawa, Canada.

Sergio G. Roca is professor and chair of the Department of Economics at Adelphi University.

Andrew Zimbalist is the Robert A. Woods professor of economics at Smith College.

INDEX

Abrantes, José, 20, 33, 39n.2
Absenteeism, 130, 138, 227, 228
Academy of Sciences, Cuban, 6, 142n.4
Administrators, 135
Africa, 3, 7, 42, 56, 184. *See also* Angola; Congo, People's Republic of the; Ethiopia; South Africa, Republic of
Agriculture, xvi–xvii, 73; biotechnology and, xviii, 168, 169, 171–74; climate and, 186; industrial workers shifted to, 74, 77, 87, 99, 100, 108, 113, 118–19, 121, 123, 125, 136, 138–39, 140–41, 185, 229–30 (*see also* Workers, "mobilized"); labor/production brigades in (*see* Agriculture, industrial workers shifted to); oil consumption by, 143n.7; overfertilized, 104; problems facing, 186; reforms in, xix; state dominance of, 254; supply and demand and, 251; wages in, 135; waste as factor of, 107–8, 111, 229; workforce of, 134 (*see also* Agriculture, industrial workers shifted to). *See also* Chemicals, agricultural; Cooperatives, agricultural; Crops; Drainage; Farmers' markets; Farms; Feeds; Frutas Selectas; Gardens, community; Grazing; Irrigation; Peasants; Seedlings; Seeds; Soils
Aguila, Juan M. del, xv
AIDS, 178, 179

Air Force, Cuban, 33
Alarcón, Ricardo, 43, 57, 61
Alcoholic beverages, 205. *See also* Liquors
Aldana, Carlos, 33, 34, 63; fall of, 4, 39n.3, 110; rise of, 4, 28
Alkaline (enzyme), 175
Allergies, research focus on, 176, 179
Almeida, Juan, 3, 5
Alpha-amylase, 175
Alpha fetoprotein, 179
Alvarez, Luis, 32
Amalgamation, enterprise, 230
Angola, 3, 7, 48
Animals, laboratory, 169, 173, 179. *See also* Livestock
Antibodies, monoclonal, 176, 178
Anticor, 175
Antigua, 160
Antillana de Acero, 233
Apartheid, 7, 45
Apparel industry, 135, 137. *See also* Black market
Arcos, Gustavo, 16
Arcos, Sebastián, 16
Argentina, 49, 51, 84, 150, 178
Artisans, 223, 228, 235n.9, 251. *See also* Trades
Asamblea Nacional del Poder Popular. *See* National Assembly of People's Power
Asia, tourism in, 160
Associación Latinoamericana de Integración (ALADI), 50

Atheism, as PCC tenet, 13
Austria, 150, 197
Azotobacter, 100–101, 174

Bacteria, research on marine, 175
Bacteriacides, 172
Bahamas, 159, 160
Bananas, 96, 112. *See also* Plantains
Banco Financiero Internacional, 233
Bankruptcy: CPE immunity to, 240, 241, 243; in Eastern Europe, 256; as element in market economy of Cuba, 251
Banks, 252–54
Barter, as trade technique, 51, 56, 177, 184
Batteries, production of auto, 196
Bay of Pigs, 82
Bays, pollution of, 253
Beef, xvii, 97, 106, 107, 109
Bermuda, 160
Beta-galactosidase, 175, 186
Beverage industry, 134, 175. *See also* Alcoholic beverages; Soft drinks
Bicycles, xvi, 75
Biofactories, 169, 173–74
Biofertilizers, 168, 172, 174. *See also* Azotobacter; Rhizobium
Biological Pest Control Production Centers, 169, 174
Biology, research in molecular, 169, 176
Biopesticides, 168, 172, 174
Bioremediation, 171, 175
Biotec (biotechnology database), 182
Biotechnology, xvii, xviii–xix, 52, 167–89; agricultural (*see* Agriculture, biotechnology and); as export, xvi, 44, 49, 72, 75, 112, 170, 171, 177–79, 184, 186; industrial, 169, 171, 174–75; internationalization of, 183–84; marine, 169; marketing of, 179–83, 185; medical, 169; pharmaceutical, 169 (*see also* Pharmaceuticals); problems relative to, 72, 179–84; products of, 171–79; spe-

cializations within, 169. *See also* Drugs; Equipment, biotechnological; Fertilizers; Japan, and biotechnology; Pharmaceuticals; United States, and biotechnology
Black market, 15, 78, 233–34
Blacks, 5, 6
Blood, analysis of, 179
Bohemia (mag.), 9
Bolivia, 50, 248
Bonuses, productivity, 241; in Cuba, 225–27, 229
Braspetro (Brazilian oil co.), 201
Brazil: Cuba and, 49–51, 177, 179, 197, 201, 210; foreign debt of, 248; tourists to Cuba from, 150
Brigades: labor/production (*see* Agriculture, industrial workers shifted to); rapid-response, xv, 16; youth, 77
British Petroleum, 201
British Virgin Islands, 160
Bulgaria, 48, 235n.6
Bulldozers, 99
Buses, 76, 205
Bush, George, 51, 60
Businesses, private, 76, 78. *See also* Corporations, private; Farms, private; Privatization; Sociedades anónimas

Cachaza, 173
Camacho, Julio, 30
Campa, Concepción, 32
Campaigning, ban on political, 13
Canada, 46, 51, 53, 149, 152, 197, 201
Canada North West Energy, 201
Cane lifters, imported, 205
Canhedo Group, 210
Capitalism, Cuba vs., 45, 114
Cardet, Luis A., 96
Cardoso, Eliana, 244
Caribbean: Cuban trade in, 44, 46, 49–50; tourism in, 149–52, 155, 157, 159, 160, 163n.1. *See also* Antigua; British Virgin Islands; Carib-

bean Common Market; Cayman Islands; Cuba; Curaçao; Dominica; Dominican Republic; Grenada; Haiti; Jamaica; Puerto Rico; Saint Lucia; Saint Vincent
Caribbean Common Market (CARICOM), 52, 58
Carpenters, 78, 235n.9
Carranza, Julio, 63
Casas, Julio, 31
Casas, Senén, 33
Castings, 196
Castro, Fidel, 3, 26; as agricultural theorist, xvii, 100–102; and Aldana, 28; and biotechnology, 169, 180; on capital, 211–12; delegation of power by, 2; and economic problems, 68, 69, 106, 111, 120; favorites of, 32, 33; and foreign investment, 75, 194, 195, 209; good-will tours of, 50; in 1965–85, 2; opposition to, xv, i, 8–16; on PA, 96, 99–103, 105, 107, 109; Party congresses as forum for, xiv; vs. peasant free enterprise, 17n.5; private farmers scrutinized by, 224; vs. privatization, 110; and rectification, 8–9; revolution abjured by, 59; and scientific revolution, 167; vs. second party, 29, 36–37; Soviet Union praised by, 115n.3; Spain savaged by, 54; strength of, xiv–xv, 1, 5, 6, 17, 62–64, 79, 82–83, 86, 91, 114, 225; and tourism, 208; trade philosophy of, 44–45; and unemployment, 141; and U.S. policies, 82 (*see also* Cuban Democracy Act). *See also* Cuban Communist Party (PCC)
Castro, Raúl, 3, 26, 33, 108
Cattle, 100, 105, 173. *See also* Beef; Milk
Cayman Islands, 160, 194
Cayo Coco, 210
CEATM (Comité Estatal de Abastecimiento Técnico-Material). *See* State Committee on Technical-Material Supplies

Cement, 74, 138
CENIC. *See* National Research Center
Center for Biological Research (CIB), 173
Center for Genetic Engineering and Biotechnology (CIGB), 167, 170–71, 174, 185
Central Committee, PCC, 4, 5, 26–28, 34–35, 38
Centrally planned economies (CPEs), 98, 225–26, 239–44, 249
Central Planning Board (JUCEPLAN), 96, 222, 223, 225, 229, 235n.2
Central State Group, 96, 235n.8
Ceramics, 137, 250
Cereals, 104, 105. *See also* Corn; Grain; Rice
CETSS (Comité Estatal de Trabajo y Seguridad Social). *See* State Committee on Labor and Social Security
CETSS-MINJUS-TSP resolution, 131
Chamber of Commerce, Cuban, 61
Cheese, 175, 205
Chemicals, agricultural, 104. *See also* Bacteriacides; Fertilizers; Herbicides; Pesticides
Chemicals industry, 137
Children, labor status of parents affected by, 124, 132
Chile, 49, 50, 83–84, 197, 202
China, People's Republic of, xix; as biotechnology customer, 177, 186; as CPE, 225; Cuba and, xv, 44, 45, 48, 54–56, 184, 186; joint ventures of, 55, 212–14, 215; "market socialism" of, xiii. *See also* Tiananmen Square
Chromatography, gas, 178
Cienfuegos (prov.), Cuba, 138
Cigarettes, 73, 205
Cigars, 53, 73
CIGB. *See* Center for Genetic Engineering and Biotechnology
Cimex, 233
Cintra Frías, Leopoldo, 33

268 • Index

CIS (Commonwealth of Independent States), 47–48
Citrus, 103, 104, 138; export of, 47, 72, 95, 202, 205; tissue-culture research on, 174
Clearing accounts, 184
Climate, 84. See also Drought; Floods; Hurricanes
Clinton, Bill, 59–60
CMEA. See Council for Mutual Economic Assistance
Cobalt, 201
Coffee, 9, 53, 103, 138
Cohiba Hotel, 210
Cold War, end of, xii, 7. See also Communism, collapse of international; Soviet Union; United States
Collective bargaining, 252
Collectivization, 254
Colombia, 49–51, 176–78
Colomé Ibarra, Abelardo, 33
Colony-stimulating factors, development of, 176
Combines (intercorporate arrangements), 89
Comercio compensado, 201–202
Commerce. See Trade
Commissions for the Selection, Evaluation and Promotion of Workers, 129–31
Commonwealth of Independent States (CIS), 47–48
Communications industry, 134, 135
Communism: collapse of international, xii, 7, 17, 19, 48, 50, 60, 103, 113, 220; Cuba commitment to, xiii, 25, 38; inefficiency inherent in, 27. See also Cuban Communist Party; Eastern Europe, collapse of communism in; Marxism-Leninism; Soviet Union, crumbling/collapse of
Communist Youth Union, 3, 6, 10–11, 15, 26
Compagnie Européenne des Petroles, 200
Components, electronic: imported, 136

Computerization, as economic step forward, 241
Congo, People's Republic of the, 7
Consa, 233
Consolidated enterprises, 222, 235n.3
Constitution, Cuban, 13; and private property, 193–94, 211; revised, 51, 118; and right to work, 118, 142n.1, 260n.6
Construction industry, 135, 138–39, 143n.7, 254. See also Housing
Construction materials, production of, 134, 137, 196
Consumerism, 89
Cooperative processing, 195, 202, 208
Cooperatives: agricultural, 9, 11, 13, 17n.5, 100, 102, 108, 134, 229; housing-construction, 223. See also Cooperative processing
Corn, 110
Corporations, private, xix–xx, 233. See also Businesses, private; Sociedades anónimas
Corruption, official, 3, 20, 22–23, 225; as CPE byproduct, 225; in Latin America, 244; worker-level, 130
Cosmetics industry, 175. See also Perfume
Costa Rica, 83, 248
Cotton, imported, 136, 205
Council for Mutual Economic Assistance (CMEA), xiv, 224; Cuba and, 67, 76, 85, 95, 209, 248; life after, 234; and productivity bonuses, 225; worker incentives in, 226
Council of Ministers, Executive Committee of the, 235n.8
Counterreform, PCC and, 21–39
Countertrade, 184. See also *Comercio compensado*
CPE. See Centrally planned economies
Crime, tourism in prerevolutionary Cuba linked with, 148
Crops, rotation of, 107. See also Food(stuffs); Tobacco

Cruz, María Elena, 16
Cuba: as a U.S. state, 87; international military operations of, 3, 7, 142n.2; marketization of, 245, 248–49, 251–53, 255–59; and mixed-market economics, 87–92; new image for, 58–61, 63; pre-Castro, 251, 254; Soviet brigade in, 48. *See also* Castro, Fidel; Cuban Communist Party; Guantánamo Bay; Havana; Rectification; Santiago; "Special period in time of peace"
Cubalse, 233
Cubanacán, 148, 149, 153–55, 163n.3, 196, 208, 210, 233
Cubana de Aviación, 210
Cuban-American National Foundation, 49, 59
Cuban Communist Party (PCC), 20; congresses of, xiii–xiv, 19, 22, 26 (*see also* Cuban Communist Party, Third Congress of; Fourth Congress, Cuban Communist Party); and counterreform, 21–39; Cuban criticism of, 13; decline of, xiv, 1, 10–11; Department of the Americas of, 61; Fourth Congress of (*see* Fourth Congress, Cuban Communist Party); personnel reshuffling in, 61; streamlining of, 256; Third Party Congress of, 22, 23, 30. *See also* Aldana, Carlos; Castro, Fidel; Castro, Raúl; Central Committee, PCC; Machado, José R.; Political Bureau, PCC; Secretariat, PCC
Cuban Democracy Act, 49, 51, 59, 183
Cuban Democratic Convergence, 16
Cuban–Dominican Republic Enterprise Group, 52
Cuban Institute of Internal Demand, 223
Cuban National Bank (BNC), 225, 252–53
Cuban Revolutionary Armed Forces (FAR), 48
Cuban Sugar Research Institute, 172
Cuban tourism, xvi–xix, 13–15, 34, 43, 44, 46, 48, 64, 72–73, 75, 77–78, 82, 147–66; accounting for, 155–59, 160, 163n.4; Castro hopes for, 208; "costs" of, 158–59; Cuban Revolution and, 148; Cubans excluded from, 15, 78; development of, 209–11, 214; dollar fallout from, 233–34; as export industry, 112, 158; foreign investment in, 14, 34 (*see also* Cuban tourism, joint ventures in); government control of, 14; income multipliers, 160–63; indirect revenue from, 159; Israel and, 56; joint ventures in, 73, 139–40, 148, 154–55, 159, 193, 194, 196–97; local economies and, 160; pre-Castro, 147–48, 150, 152; problems of, 72–73; promotion of, 58; Spain and, 53; vs. sugarcane harvest, 140; U.S. potential for, 57; wages in, 135; workers in, 139–40, 193. *See also* Cubanacán; Hotels, resort; INTUR
Cuban Workers' Confederation, 3
Cubasoy, 23, 172
Curaçao, 200
Cuvastec, 208
Czechoslovakia, xx, 7, 48, 235n.6, 238, 241, 245
Czech Republic, 83, 91

Dairy products, 175. *See also* Butter; Cheese; Eggs; Milk
Dams, irrigation, 105
Debt, foreign, xii, 72, 200, 215n.5, 245, 247–48, 260n.4
Debt-for-equity swaps, 200, 208
Decentralization: as CPE tactic, 241; Cuban government efforts at, 221–25, 229–31, 232. *See also* Industrial associations
Declaration of Santiago, 50
De la Guardia, Antonio and Patricio (brothers), 3
Democracy, single-party, 37
Detergents, production of, 196, 197, 200
Dextranase, 175

Diagnostics, human, 171, 172, 176, 178
Díaz, Adolfo, 96–97, 100
Díaz-Briquets, Sergio, xvii
Discipline, on-job, 130–31, 142
Discotheques, 210
Disease, Cuban biotechnology vs. 173, 176, 178, 179. *See also* AIDS; Hepatitis; Meningitis; Syphilis
DNA molecular weight markers, 178
Domínguez, Jorge I., xiv–xv
Domínguez, Luis Orlando, 3
Dominica, 160
Dominican Republic, 51, 52
Drainage, agricultural, 101–102, 105, 109
Drought, 84
Drugs: narcotic, 3, 20, 148; pharmaceutical, 72
Duties, import, 159, 192

Eastern Europe: collapse of communism in, 11, 19, 20, 45, 48, 79, 83, 90, 202; Communist Party congresses in, xiii; Cuba and, xii, 46–48, 104, 141, 205–206, 209, 214; Cuban debt to, 247, 260n.4; Cuban defectors in, 17n.3; Cuban students in, 48; Cuban trade with, xv, 74; Cuban vaccines in, 176; Cuban workers in, 7, 48; economic lessons from, 238–63; environmentalism in, 253; farmers' markets in, 224; imports of, 90; private property in prereform, 254; socioeconomic reforms in, xiii, 46–48, 90–91, 120, 190, 231, 239, 240, 244–45, 249, 256–58; unemployment in, 256, 257; wage variables in, 235n.6; after World War II, 239. *See also* Bulgaria; Czechoslovakia; German Democratic Republic; Hungary; Poland; Yugoslavia
East Germany. *See* German Democratic Republic
Economic Planning and Management System. *See* Sistema de Dirección y Planificación de la Economía
Economy, xv–xvi, xix, xx; decline of, xi–xii, 7–9, 14, 17, 24, 63, 67–84, 87, 94, 118, 120–21, 126, 132, 147, 167, 178, 183, 190, 202–205, 211, 214, 231, 234, 238, 244–49, 257, 258; future of, 83–92; planning of (*see* Sistema de Dirección y Planificación de la Economía); pre-Castro, 254; reform of, xx, 230–63 (*see also* Sistema de Dirección y Planificación de la Economía); socialistic element of, 78; tiers of, 77–79; tourism and, xviii. *See also* Centrally planned economies; Debt, foreign; Inflation; Investment; Lage, Carlos; Peso, shakiness of; Poverty; Privatization; Recession; Rectification; "Special period in time of peace"; Sugar; Trade
Ecuador, 50, 248
Education, 11, 79, 88, 89, 120–21; decline of, xii; salaries in, 135; state control of, 254; workforce of, 134. *See also* Students; Training
Eggs, 97, 107
Elections, 10–11, 13, 36, 37, 234n.2
Electricians, 78, 228
Electricity: generation of, 75, 135, 137; shortage of, xii, 74, 211
Electrocardiography, 179
Electromyography, 179
Electronics industry, 136
Electrophoresis, 178
ELISA (enzyme-linked immunosorbent assay), 179. *See also* SUMA
Embargo(es): UN condemnation of, 57; U.S. Cuban, 3, 46, 51, 57, 60, 82, 85, 113, 148, 152, 180, 183
Employment, 133–37. *See also* Unemployment; Workers
Endonucleases, restriction, 176, 178, 186
Energy: conservation of, xvi; imported, xii; joint venture, 200; short-

age of, xv, xvii, 74, 126, 127, 246. *See also* Electricity; Fuels; Nuclear Power; Oil
Environmentalism, 89, 253, 256, 259
Enzymes, industrial, 168, 171, 175, 176, 186. *See also* ELISA
Epidermal growth factor, recombinant, 176, 186
Equipment: biotechnological, 178–79; medical, 196, 197. *See also* Farm equipment; Machinery
Escalona, Juan, 26, 60
Espín, Vilma, 3, 30, 32
Espino, María Dolores, xvii–xviii
Ethiopia, 7
Europe: Cuban biotechnology and, 178, 182, 186; Cuban overtures to, 44. *See also* Eastern Europe; European Community; Western Europe
European Community, 53, 177
Excursionists, and tourists contrasted, 149
Exiles. *See* United States, Cuban emigrants in
Expanded Immunization Programs (EPI), 176
Exports, xv, 70–75, 82, 84, 95–96, 112, 136, 140, 158, 167–68, 202, 205, 247, 248, 258; to Canada, 46; to China, 54–55; *comercio compensado* and, 201–202; decline in, xii; development of new, 75; inflated value of, 69 (*see also* Sugar, Soviet subsidization of); raw materials as, xix; to Soviet Union, 47 (*see also* Sugar, Soviet subsidization of); to Spain, 53; stress on, xvi; tourism among, 155. *See also* Biotechnology; Citrus; Nickel; Oil, as Cuban export; Seafood; Sugar; Tobacco
Extractive industries, 89. *See also* Mining; Oil

Factories, Sino-Cuban, 55
FAR. *See* Cuban Revolutionary Armed Forces

Farm equipment, 99. *See also* Bulldozers; Cane lifters; Graders; Tractors
Farmers' markets: in Cuba (*see* Mercados libres campesinos); in Eastern Europe, 249
Farms, private, 78, 87, 100, 102, 134, 224; decline of, 254; income from, 229. *See also* Cooperatives, agricultural; Gardens, community; Peasants
Feeds, animal, 101, 105, 111, 173. *See also* Cereals; Soybeans
Feinsilver, Julie M., xviii
Fernández, Damián J., xv
Fertilizers, xviii, 100–101, 104; imported, 174, 186; joint ventures in production of, 197, 202; for legumes, 173; shortage of, 140; state-supplied, 102; for sugarcane, 173. *See also* Agriculture, overfertilized; Biofertilizers
Figueras, Miguel, 235n.2
Fiji, 160
Finance, 135. *See also* Banks
Finland, 197
Fish, 97, 107, 112–13, 158, 248; transgenesis of, 173
Floods, 186
Fodder. *See* Feeds, animal
Food(stuffs), 7, 88, 196; on black market, 233; crisis in, xv, 11, 77; emphasis on producing, xvi–xvii, 72, 87; export of, xvi, 248; imported, xii, 74, 75, 96, 97, 136, 205; processing of, 134; Sino-Cuban joint ventures in, 55. *See also* Coffee; Dairy products; Fruits; Nutrition; PA (*programa alimentario*); Vegetables; Yuca
Foreign policy, xv, 41–65. *See also* Africa; Canada; Castro, Fidel; China, People's Republic of; Europe; Latin America; Middle East
Forestry, 135, 169. *See also* Lumber
Fourth Congress, Cuban Communist Party, xiii, xiv–xv, 1, 24–39; and

agriculture, 14; and biotechnology, 97, 167, 168–69, 172, 180, 186; and Cuban life, 14, 110; democracy rejected by, 24; economic recommendations of, xvi, 14, 67, 75, 94, 97, 106, 147, 190, 194–95, 220–21, 235n.9, 244; and elections, 14; and international relations, 43, 45, 94; and labor, 119, 130; organization of, 26; and Party reform, 14, 27–38; and religion, 14; and Third World, 25
France, 52, 150, 197, 200–201
Franco, Francisco, 45
Frentismo, 27
Fringe benefits, worker, 130. *See also* Bonuses, productivity; Overtime; Profit Sharing; Vacations
Fruit(s), 74, 96–98, 106, 107, 110, 111, 138; in farmers' markets, 224; marketing of, 202; tissue-culture research on, 174. *See also* Bananas; Citrus; Pineapples
Frutas Selectas, 228
Fuels: imported, 73–75, 123, 205; shortage of, 131, 132, 136–38, 140, 142, 211, 257. *See also* Gasoline; Oil
Fuerzas Armadas Revolucionarias (FAR), 20
Furniture, production of, 137, 197

Gambling, as tourism element, 148
García, Guillermo, 2
García, María de los Angeles, 32
García, Yadira, 32
García Oliveras, Julio, 194, 208
Gardeners, private, 78
Gardens, community, xvii, 110
Gasoline, 74
Gaviota, 148, 233
Genentech (biotechnology co.), 181
Genetic engineering, 167–68, 169, 178
Genetics, animal, 172. *See also* Transgenesis

German Democratic Republic, 7, 87, 235n.6, 241
Germany, Federal Republic of, 87, 150, 154, 197
Ghana, 48
Glass industry, 137, 196, 250
Goldstein, Daniel J., 171
González, Felipe, 54
González, Gerardo, 104
Gorbachev, Mikhail, 45
Graders, mechanical, 99
Grain(s), 107; imported, 49, 104, 205. *See also* Cereals; Rice; Sugarcane
Granma, 21, 43, 111–12
Grasses, research on, 174
Great Britain. *See* United Kingdom
Grenada, 52
Gruexva, 208
Grupo Havana, 210
Grupo Sol, 154, 196–97, 208
Guantánamo, U.S. naval base, 48
Gulf War, 45, 57
Guyana, 248
Guzmán, Arturo, 112

Haiti, 51
Hardware, production of, 196
Hart, Armando, 3, 30
Havana, Cuba, 98, 108, 110, 126, 138, 153
Havana, University of, 12
Havana Club, 210
Havana Foreign Trade Fair, 49
Hawaii, tourism in, 160
Health care, 11, 79, 88, 89, 121, 169; decline of, xii; wages for workers in, 135; of workers, 141, 257. *See also* Hospitals; Vaccines
Heber Biotec, 177–78, 182, 185
Helwege, Ann, 244
Hepatitis, 176, 178, 179
Hepatitis B, 176
Hepatitis B vaccine, recombinant, 176–77, 178, 186
Herbicides, xviii, 104, 140, 174
Herrera, Luis, 177

Hidalgo, Alcibiades, 61
Hinds, Manuel, 243
HIV, research focus on, 176, 179. *See also* AIDS
Hoffman-LaRoche (pharmaceutical co.), 178, 181
Hogs, 105, 110. *See also* Pork
Homologuismo, 27
Hondal, Alfredo, 32
Hong Kong, 160
Hospitals, 120
Hotels, resort, 14, 148, 152–55, 196, 197, 208. *See also* Motels; Sol Palmeras Hotel
Housing, 78, 79, 88, 140–41, 223, 228, 257. *See also* Construction industry; Cooperatives, housing-construction
Human rights: Cuba and, 14, 16, 44, 48, 49, 53, 55, 57, 58; internationalization of, 46; Spain and Cuban, 53; UN focus on Cuban, 48, 49
Human transfer factor, 176
Hungary, xx, 48; banking system of, 253; as CPE, 225; Cuban workers in, 7; economic reforms in, 83, 241, 242; foreign debt of prereform, 248; and marketization, 238, 245, 249; wage variables in, 235n.6
Hurricanes, 84, 85
Hydrosulfuric acid, production of, 196
Hyperthyroidism, 179

Ibercusa (Spanish consortium), 210
Ickes, Barry W., 243
Ifopol, 172
Imports, xii, 67, 70–77, 82, 84, 86, 96, 97, 104, 105, 112, 136, 174, 186, 205–206, 209; from China, 54; Cuban Democracy Act and, 183; curtailing of, 132, 136–38, 140, 167–68, 173, 174, 178, 185, 186, 247; deflated value of, 69; export industries dependence on, 112; miscellaneous, 136; Soviet subsidization of, 69; from Soviet Union, 47

(*see also* Oil, Soviet); from Spain, 53; tourism and, xviii, 72–73. *See also* Cereals; Components, electronic; Feeds; animal; Fuels; Grain; Machinery; Oil, as Cuban import; PA (*Programa alimentario*); Raw materials; Spare parts
Incentives, worker, 226–28. *See also* Fringe benefits
Income, 78, 134–35, 142, 224, 229. *See also* Unemployment compensation
Income taxes: as Cuban possibility, 89; in Eastern Europe, 90
India, 177
Indian Ocean, tourism in islands of, 160
Industrial associations, 229, 230, 235n.3
Industry, xvii, 73; dependence on imported oil of, 136, 143n.7; energy-intensive, 74; makeup of, 250–51; reforms in, xix; state control of, 254; wages of workers in, 135; workforce of, 134. *See also* Biotechnology; Plants, industrial; Tourism
Inflation: in contemporary Eastern Europe, 90–91, 120; as CPE byproduct, 225; in Cuba, 246
Institute of Cuban Studies, 12
Institute of Oceanology, 175
Institutes, research, 169, 185
Insurance industry, 135
Intellectuals, 6. *See also* National Union of Artists and Writers
Interferons, 169, 176, 178, 182–83, 186
Interleukin–2, 176
International Monetary Fund (IMF), 57, 120
International Textile Corporation (ITC), 197
INTUR (Instituto Nacional de Turismo), 148, 149, 153, 160, 193, 210
Invertase, 175
Investment, competition for foreign,

xvi, xix, 13, 43, 44, 46, 48–49, 51, 57, 62, 64, 73, 75, 82, 152, 154–55, 159, 180, 184, 190–96, 200–12, 213–15. See also Cubanacán; INTUR; joint ventures; Tourism, foreign investment in
Iran, 48, 56, 74
Iraq, 48, 56
Ireland, Republic of, 197
Irrigation, 101, 102, 105, 109, 141
Israel, 56
Issa, John, 215nn.2,4
Italcable, 200, 208, 210
Italy, 150

Jail, for opposition leaders, xv
Jamaica, 52, 155, 160, 197, 248
Japan, 53, 168, 177, 181, 182, 200, 215n.5, 232
Job swaps, 125–26, 129
Joint ventures, 48–49, 190–219, 233, 244, 247; In biotechnological research, 181–82; with Brazil, 49; with China, 55, 212–14, 215 (see also China, People's Republic of—joint ventures of); legal framework of, 191–95; shareholders in, 192; with Spain, 53; in tourism, 73, 139–40, 148, 154–55, 159, 194, 196–97. See also Comercio compensado; Cooperative processing; Debt-for-equity swaps; Hotels, resort; International Textile Corporation; Marketing arrangements; Production partnerships; Third country associations.
Jordán, Alfredo, 32
JUCEPLAN (Junta Central de Planificación). See Central Planning Board
Juragúa nuclear power plant, 138
Juventud Rebelde (Newspaper), 12

Karposi's sarcoma, 178
Kornai, Janos, 243
Kosygin reforms, 241

Labor, xvii; foreign influences on, 15; free contracting of, 223, 235n.5; mobilization of (see Agriculture, industrial workers shifted to); during "special period," 118–46. See also Job swaps; Self-employment; State Committee on Labor and Social Security (CETSS); Trades; Unions; Workers
Labor brigades. See Agriculture, industrial workers shifted to
Labor Code, 252
Labor courts, 131
Lactose, intolerance of, 175
Lage, Augustín, 184
Lage, Carlos, 5, 6, 30, 33, 34, 61, 63, 114, 170; capitalism rejected by, 190, 213; on PA, 94, 109
Larrinaga, Abeledo, 215n.3
Latin America: Cuba and, xv, 44–46, 49–50, 184, 186; debt patterns in, 45, 247–48; *maquiladora* plants of, 202; politicoeconomic change in, 89, 91; reform movements in, 83–84, 244; social democracy in, 83–84; Spain and, 53; tourists to Cuba from, 149, 150, 156; unemployment in, 135; U.S. intervention in, 45. See also Argentina; Bolivia; Brazil; Caribbean; Chile; Colombia; Costa Rica; Ecuador; Guyana; Mexico; Nicaragua; Panama; Paraguay; Peru; Uruguay; Venezuela
Latin American Parliament, 50
Lazo, Esteban, 4, 30
Lead, 201
Leather goods, 137
Legumes, 173. See also Beans
Lenin, Vladimir, 20, 239
Leninism. See Marxism-Leninism
Lettuce, 108
Lezcano, Jorge, 30, 138
Liberation theology, 30
Libya, 48
Limonta, Manuel, 171, 178
Lincoln, Abraham, 29
Liquors, Cuban, 175. See also Rum
Livestock, 99, 103, 112, 168, 172. See also Cattle; Hogs; Oxen; Poultry; Sheep

Lugo, Orlando, 108
Lumber, imported, 137, 205

Machado, José, 3, 26, 28, 29
Machinery: Cuban production of, 134, 196; imported, 75, 76, 96, 136, 205. *See also* Farm equipment; Spare parts
Maciques, Abraham, 208
Malformations, research on congenital, 176
Malmierca, Isidoro, 61
Management, training of, 232
Maquiladora plants, 202
Marble, 200
Mariel boatlift, 2
Marketing arrangements, 202
Market economies, 242
Martí, José, 29
Marxism-Leninism, 19, 42, 45, 46, 62, 63
Mas Canosa, Jorge, 49
Masons (tradesmen), 78
Meat, 168. *See also* Beef; Pork
Mechanics (technicians), 78, 228
Media: Cuban, 12, 13, 36, 37, 183; government control of CPE, 253; of socialist countries, xiv. *See also* Press; Radio; Television
Medical schools, 169
Medicine, clinical, 169. *See also* Biotechnology, medical; Health care
Meléndez, Ernesto, 63
Mella, Carlos, 178
Menem, Carlos, 49, 50
Meningitis, 32, 176
Meningitis B vaccine, 197
Mercados libres campesinos, 95–96, 106, 110, 223–24, 249
Merck-Sharpe (pharmaceutical co.), 177
Metallurgy, 137
Metal products industry, 137. *See also* Castings
Metals, 137. *See also* Cobalt; Lead; Mining; Nickel; Zinc
Mexico: Cuba and, 45, 49, 51, 54, 74, 197, 200, 201, 215n.5; and Cuban biotechnology, 177, 178, 180; foreign debt of, 248; political upheaval in, 41; social democracy in, 84; tourists to Cuba from, 150
Michel, Raúl, 32
Microorganisms, oil spills treated with, 171–72
Middle East, 56, 184. *See also* Gulf War; Iran; Iraq; Israel; Syria
Military, xix, 6, 231–32, 249, 256. *See also* Cuban Revolutionary Armed Forces (FAR)
Milk, xvii, 97–99, 103, 107, 109, 168; imported condensed, 205
Mining, 137, 200, 256. *See also* Extractive industries; Metals
MINREX (Ministry of Foreign Relations), 44, 58, 61
Miret, Pedro, 3, 30
MLCs. *See* Mercados libres campesinos
Monopolies: in communist Eastern Europe, 90; as "new Cuba" imperative, 251, 252
Monreal, Pedro, 63
Montalván, Oscar Alfonso, 207
Motels, tourist, 152–54
Multinationals, Cuba and, 64

Namibia, 7
National Assembly of People's Power, 36
Nationalization, investor fear of, 211
National Research Center (CENIC), 173, 174
National Union of Artists and Writers, 6, 16. *See also* Prieto, Abel
New Economic Mechanism (NEM) (Hungary), 242
New Economic Policy (NEP) (Soviet Union), 239
Newsprint, imported, 136–37
Nicaragua, 7
Nickel, 75, 137, 201; compounds of, 196, 205; export of, 47, 73, 84, 95, 112, 205, 248; pollution relative to

mining of, 253; Soviet subsidization of, 69
Nitrogen, production of, 138
Nonaligned Movement (NAM), 50, 56
Normas. *See* Piece rates
North America, tourists to Cuba from, 149. *See also* Canada; United States
Nuclear nonproliferation treaty, 51
Nuclear power, 49, 56, 75, 138
Nutrition, 74, 79, 88

Occupational safety, 141, 252
Ochoa, Arnaldo, 3, 20, 28, 33
Oil: Caribbean, 49; Cuban, xviii, 49, 84, 85, 175, 195, 200–201 (*see also* Unión del Petróleo); as Cuban export, xv, 69, 158; as Cuban import, 73–76, 84, 86, 104, 136, 137, 143n.7, 158; Cuban processing of, 75, 137, 138; drilling for, 206, 210; Iranian, 56, 74; Latin American, 49, 51; Mexican, 74; royalties on Cuban, 195; Soviet/Russian, 45–47, 74, 115n.3; Venezuelan, 49, 74
Oil spills, microorganisms vs., 172, 175
OJLB (Organos de Justicia Laboral de Base). *See* Labor courts
Onions, 229
Organization of American States (OAS), 50
Overtime, 227
Oxen, xvi, 72, 74, 75, 105, 140

PA (*programa alimentario*), xvi–xvii, 75, 94–117, 140–41; future of, 109–15; nature of, 97–99, 113–14; origins of, 95–97; results of, 106–109; successes of, 114
Pacific Ocean, tourism in countries on, 160. *See also* Fiji
Pagés, Raisa, 111
Palestinians, as Cuban cause, 45
Palmero, Cándido, 33

Panama, 248
Pan American Health Organization (PAHO), 171, 176
Paper products, 137, 196, 197; imported, 137. *See also* Newsprint
Paraguay, xi, 49–50
Partido Comunista de Cuba. *See* Cuban Communist Party (PCC)
Parties, ban on political, 13, 25, 37
Patents, as technological industry concern, 72, 177, 180, 182–84
PCC. *See* Cuban Communist Party
Peasants, 4, 5, 9, 13, 17n.5, 95. *See also* Cooperatives, agricultural; Farmers' markets; Farms; Gardeners; Peasants' Association
Peasants' Association, 5
PEMEX (Mexican corp.), 201
Pensions, worker, 113, 120, 257
Pentón Arias, Eduardo, 177
Pérez, Humberto, 2, 96, 229
Pérez Herrero, Antonio, 2
Pérez Lezcano, Sergio, 28
Pérez Lezcano, Sixto, 28
Pérez-López, Jorge V., xvii, xix, xx
Perfume, manufacture of, 175
Período especial en tiempo de paz. *See* "Special period in time of peace"
Permutas. *See* Job swaps
Peru, 50, 51
Peso, shakiness of, 211, 249
Pesticides, xviii, 140, 174, 186. *See also* Biopesticides
Petrobras (Brazilian oil co.), 201
Petroleum. *See* Oil
Pharmaceutical industry, international, 177, 178, 181, 182
Pharmaceuticals, xviii, 168, 169, 171, 176–78, 196. *See also* Interferons; Vaccines
Phosphates, Venezuelan, 202
Piece rates, 226, 227
Pigs. *See* Hogs
Pinar del Río (prov.), Cuba, 138
Pineapples, 174
Pino, Rafael del, 3, 33

Plantains, 106, 110, 173–74, 179
Plant genetics, 172. See also Transgenesis
Plants (flora), 168, 173. See also Cereals; Coffee; Fruits; Grains; Grasses; Seedlings; Seeds; Tobacco; Tubers; Vegetables
Plants, industrial: shutdowns of, 118, 121, 126, 127, 130, 136, 138, 142, 246, 257
Platt Amendment, 42
Playboy, Cuban women in, 15
Plumbers, 78, 228, 235n.9
Poland, xx; agricultural patterns in, 224; banking system of, 253; foreign debt of prereform, 248; inflation in, 246; and marketization, 238, 245, 249; political upheaval in, 41; reforms in contemporary, 83, 241; wage variables in, 235n.6
Political Bureau, PCC: Castro thinning of, 2–5, 26, 28; Central Committee controlled by, 36; makeup of, 4–6; military supervised by, 28; provincial network of, 4; reform of, 30–34, 39; stuffing of, 5. See also Aldana, Carlos; Lage, Carlos
Politics, xiv–xv, 1–18. See also Campaigning; Castro, Fidel; Cuban Communist Party; Elections; Parties; Repression, of political dissidents
Pollution, 253
Popkova-Pijasheva, Larissa, 242
Popular Power, 223, 234n.2
Pork, 97, 106. See also Hogs
Potatoes, 103, 174, 179, 229
Poultry, 97, 105, 106, 173. See also Eggs
Poverty, 79; in Latin America, 84, 244
PRC. See China, People's Republic of
Premios. See Profit sharing
Press, 13, 36, 37. See also *Granma*
Prieto, Abel, 6, 33
Primas. See Bonuses, productivity
Printing industry, 137, 250

Privatization, 252, 258–59; as Castro devil, 110; as Cuban option, xx, 89, 238–39, 253–55; in Eastern Europe, 90; mechanics of, 255, 259; popularity of, 254
Proceso de rectificación de errores y tendencias negativas. See Rectification
Production brigades. See Agriculture, industrial workers shifted to
Production partnerships, 200–201, 208
Profit sharing, 226, 227
Programa alimentario. See PA (*programa alimentario*)
Prostitution, tourism and, 15, 148
Provincial assemblies, 36
Public health. See Health care
Public safety, 89
Public transportation, 11; cutbacks in, xii, 74, 142; imported equipment for, 136; as labor-relocation factor, 125, 126, 131, 132, 138, 140–41; oil consumption by, 143n.7; state control of, 254; wages in, 135. See also Buses; Railroads
Public utilities, 252
Puerto Rico, 157

Radio, 13
Railroads, 254
Rationing, 78, 87, 88, 245, 246
Raw materials: imported, 136–37, 205; shortage of, 142, 196, 228, 246, 247, 257
Reagents, 176, 178, 179, 185, 186
Real estate, speculation in Cuban, 228
Recession, xi–xii; contemporary international, 91
Recreation, 11
Rectification, xi–xii, xv, 46, 47, 64, 224–31, 244; Castro and, 8–9; and counterreform contrasted, 21; economic reforms during, xix, 249; failure of, 21; and PA, 95, 96, 106; and PCC, 22–24; and SDPE, 242

Refrigeration, inadequate, 229
Religion, 13. *See also* Liberation theology; Roman Catholic Church
Rennin, 175, 186
Repairmen, electrical/mechanical, 235n.9
Repression, of political dissidents, 16, 17. *See also* Brigades, rapid-response
Resource fairs, 223
Retirement, worker, 131–32, 142–43n.5
Revolution, Cuban, xi, xiii, 2, 20, 82, 256. *See also* Castro, Fidel
Rhizobium, 173
Rice, 97–99, 101, 103, 105–109, 112, 141
Risquet, Jorge, 3, 28, 30, 61
RIT Belgium (pharmaceutical firm), 177
Ritter, Archibald R. M., xv–xvi
Rizo, Julián, 28, 99
Robaina, Roberto, 6, 30, 44, 57
Roca, Sergio, G., xvi–xvii
Rodríguez, Carlos Rafael, 3, 5, 29
Rodríguez, José Luis, 8–9, 209
Rodríguez Llompart, Héctor, 207
Roman Catholic Church, 16, 30
Rosales del Toro, Ulises, 33
Ross Leal, Pedro, 30, 137, 197
Royalties, oil, 195
Rum, Cuban, 101
Russia, 47, 48, 74, 75, 138, 176, 177, 186. *See also* Soviet Union

Saint Lucia, 52, 159
Saint Vincent, 52
Sánchez, Elizardo, 16
Sánchez Parodi, Ramón, 211
Sanctions, market regulation via, 242
San José Accord, 51
Santa Clara, Bay of, 201
Santa Cruz del Norte, Cuba, 10
Santiago (province), Cuba, 4
Santiago de Cuba, Cuba, 153
Saturdays, work patterns on, 131
Schering-Plough (pharmaceutical co.), 178

Science: Cuban commitment to, 135, 167; mystic appeal of, 168
SDE (Sistema de Dirección de la Economía). *See* Sistema de Dirección y Planificación de la Economía (SDPE)
SDPE. *See* Sistema de Dirección y Planificación de la Economía
Seafood, as Cuban export, 53
Secretariat, PCC, 2, 5, 28, 36
Security Council, UN, 50
Seedlings, 172, 186
Seeds: disease-resistant, 168, 172, 173, 186; misuse of, 107; production of, 169, 174
Self-employment, 78, 110 (*see also* Farms, private); in Eastern Europe, 249
Seminars, management-training, 232
Seniority, job, 129, 130
Services, personal/community, 78, 135
Shanghai, 55
Sheritt Gordon Ltd., 201
Simeón, Rosa Elena, 174
Sistema de Dirección y Planificación de la Economía (SDPE), 114, 221–25, 230, 234nn.1, 2, 241–42. *See also* Central Planning Board (JUCEPLAN); Popular Power; Resource fairs; State Committee on Technical-Material Supplies
Sistema Económico Latinoamericano (SELA), 50
Smith, Wayne, 60
Smith-Kline (pharmaceutical co.), 177
Socialism, Marxist-Leninist. *See* Communism; Marxism-Leninism
Social security, 131, 135, 142n.4, 192
Sociedades anónimas, 48
Soft drinks, 175
Software, biotechnology-related computer, 178–79
Soils: misuse of, 107; zeolite-enriched, 101
Sol Palmeras Hotel, 215n.6
Somalia, 57

South Africa, Republic of, 7, 45
Soviet Union: agricultural production in, 107; crumbling/collapse of, 11, 17, 19, 20, 47, 48, 115n.3, 177, 190, 202, 231 (*see also* Communism, collapse of international); Cuba and, xii, 41, 44–48, 55, 62, 67–72, 76, 79, 91, 95, 103, 104, 137, 171, 177, 184, 205–206, 209, 214 (*see also* Cuba, Soviet brigade in; Sugar, Soviet subsidization of); Cuban debt to, 247, 260n.4; Cuban workers/students in, 7, 48; and de-Stalinization, 239; and environmentalism, 253; foodstuffs of, 46–47; labor contracting in, 235n.5; Party congresses in, xiii; reforms in, 91, 221, 239–41; today, 83 (*see also* Russia); trade with, xv (*see also* Council for Mutual Economic Assistance); wage patterns in, 235n.6; after World War II, 239. *See also* Communism; Russia
Soybeans, 105, 172, 173. *See also* Cubasoy 23
Spain: Cuba and, xv, 45, 49, 51, 53–54, 210; joint ventures with, 154–55, 196, 197, 200; tourists to Cuba from, 150
Spare parts, imported, 76, 136–38
"Special period in time of peace," xii, 244; economic patterns during, 183, 220, 231–34; labor adjustments during, 118–46; recession during, 257; scientific pursuits during, 167, 174, 176–77, 184–85; and tourism, 147
State Committee on Finances, 225
State Committee on Labor and Social Security (CETSS), 118, 119, 121, 123–32, 141
State Committee on Prices, 225, 231, 251
State Committee on Technical-Material Supplies (CEATM), 222, 223, 230
Steel: Cuban, 256; Soviet, 115n.3
Steel wool, production of, 196

Stock (securities), privatization and, 255
Street vendors, 228
Streptokinase, 176–77, 186
Stroessner, Alfredo, xi
Students, 7, 48, 138, 185
Subsidies, xvii, 69, 111–13, 240, 248–49, 251 (*see also* Sugar, Soviet subsidization of); in Eastern Europe, 258
Sugar, 52, 56, 64, 72, 74, 85, 89; animal feeds from, 101; centrality of, xii; and cooperatives, 9; as export, 47, 54–55, 75, 95, 158, 205, 248 (*see also* Sugar, Soviet subsidization of); foreign investment in, 195; milling of, 174–75, 227; ministry of, 256; ox-tended, 74; Soviet subsidization of, 45, 47, 69, 100–103, 205; weather effect on, 84; workers in, 134, 227. *See also Cachaza*
Sugarcane, 101–103, 105, 109, 140, 172–74, 179
SUMA (Ultra-Micro ELISA System), 178, 179, 186
Summit conferences, Iberoamerican, 45, 54
Surfactants, 175
SUTCER (Cuban management training system), 232
Sweden, 201
Switzerland, 197, 201
Syphilis, 179
Syria, 48

Tabacalera (Spanish co.), 210
Taladrid, Raúl, 214
Tariffs, 49, 159
Taurus (Swedish energy co.), 201
Taxes, 159, 249; on farmers, 224; income (*see* Income taxes); joint ventures and, 73, 154, 192, 195; PA and, 105; payroll, 257; peasant resentment of, 13; tourism-related, 154, 159; turnover, 245. *See also* Duties; Tariffs
Taxi drivers, 228

Technology, xviii, 135; U.S., 82. *See also* Biotechnology
Telecommunications, international, 200
Tella, Guido de, 49
Textile industry, 137, 175. *See also* Apparel industry; Cotton; International Textile Corporation
Textilera Hilatex, 137
Therapeutics, human, 171, 172
Third-country associations, 202
Third World: Cuba and, 25, 42, 45, 46, 52, 58, 65, 184; liberation movements of, 20. *See also* Africa; Latin America; Middle East
Tiananmen Square, 55
Tires, production of automobile, 196
Tobacco, 9, 73, 134, 138, 148, 172, 174, 179, 248. *See also* Cigarettes; Cigars
Tomatoes, 103, 229
Torralba, Diocles, 3
Torres, Nelson, 32
Total (French oil company), 200, 210
Tourism: advantages of, 155; Cuban (*see* Cuban tourism); health, 168; Latin American competition in, 52
Tourist (term), 149
Trabajadores disponibles. See Workers, "available"
Trabajadores movilizados. See Workers, "mobilized"
Trabajadores sobrantes. See Workers, "surplus"
Tractors, 102, 105, 140, 205
Trade (commerce), 69–79, 84, 114, 184, 205, 233, 246, 249, 251; reform in foreign, xvii–xviii; state control of, 254; wages of workers in, 135; workforce of, 134. *See also* Barter; Biotechnology; Black market; Clearing accounts; Combines; *Comercio compensado*; Countertrade; Debt-for-equity swaps; Exports; Imports; Marketing arrangements; Monopolies; Multinationals; Nickel; Oil; Production partnerships; Royalties; Sugar; Third-country Associations
Trades (professions), 78, 228, 235n.9. *See also* Artisans
Trading companies, xviii
Training: management, 232; worker, 123, 129, 193, 252, 257
Transgenesis, 171, 173
Transportation. *See* Public transportation
Trinchet, Oscar, 102, 105
Tropical Agricultural Research Institute, 172
Truckdrivers, 224
Trucks, 76, 229
Tubers, xvii, 96–100, 103, 106–11. *See also* Potatoes

Uneca, 233
Unemployment, 185, 257; as Cuban problem, 118, 135–36, 137; in Eastern Europe, 83, 91; frictional vs. long-term, 135
Unemployment compensation, 113, 125, 257. *See also* Workers, compensation for dislocated
UNESCO, 171
UNICEF, 176
Unión del Petróleo, 200–201
Uniónes de empresas. See Industrial associations
Unions, labor, 123, 126, 129, 141, 252. *See also* Collective bargaining
United Kingdom, 200, 201, 215n.5. *See also* Bermuda; British Virgin Islands; Cayman Islands; Hong Kong
United Nations, 48, 49, 56–58, 149, 171. *See also* Security Council
United Nations Development Program (UNDP), 171, 232
United Nations Industrial Development Organization (UNIDO), 171
United States: and Argentina, 49, 50; and Cuba, 29, 45, 47, 57, 59–60, 79, 82, 86, 87, 91, 149, 195 (*see also* Bay of Pigs; Cuban-American National Foundation; Cuban De-

mocracy Act; Embargo U.S. Cuban; Guantánamo Bay; Mariel boatlift; Platt Amendment); vs. Cuban biotechnology, 183 (see also Cuban Democracy Act); Cuban citizen perspective on, 11; Cuban emigrants in, 3, 59–61, 64, 85, 150, 233, 255 (see also Cuban-American National Foundation); and Latin America, 45 (see also United States, and Cuba); socioeconomic system of, 87–88; and technology/biotechnology, 180, 182; tourists to Cuba from, 149–50. See also Hawaii

Uruguay, 50

Vacations, worker, 128–31
Vaccines, 32, 173, 176. See also Hepatitis B vaccine; Meningitis B vaccine
Valdés, Ramiro, 2
Vallee Diagnósticos, 179
Varadero, Cuba, 153–55, 196
Vasp Brazilian Airlines, 210
Vázquez, Lázaro, 32
Vegetables, xvii, 74, 96–100, 103, 106–11, 138; in farmers' markets, 223; research on, 174. See also Beans; Legumes; Lettuce; Onion; Tomatoes; Tubers
Veiga, Roberto, 3
Venezuela, 49–51, 54, 74, 150, 176–78, 202
Vietnam, 41, 60
Villas, tourist, 153

Water, potable, xii
Western Europe: Cuba and, xv, 52–54; Cuban citrus in, 202; tourists to Cuba from, 149, 150, 152. See also European Community; France; Germany; Ireland; Italy; Spain; Sweden; Switzerland; United Kingdom
West Germany. See Germany, Federal Republic of
Wholesalers, 224
Winiecki, Jan, 243

Wire, production of, 196
Women, 6; and Fourth Party Congress, 35; organizing of, 4, 5 (see also Women's Federation); as Playboy models, 15; in Political Bureau, 5–6, 32; as workers, 122, 132, 143n.5. See also Prostitution
Women's Federation, 5, 6
Wood products industry, 137. See also Lumber; Paper
Work, as moral imperative, 11. See also Constitution, Cuban—and right to work
Workers: "available," 123–25, 128, 129, 257; cafeteria benefits of, 128–29; discipline problems with, 108, 225; dislocation of, 118–29, 132, 136–42 (see also Agriculture, industrial workers shifted to); in Europe, 7, 48; and health care, 257; vs. management, 129–31 (see also Commissions for the Selection, Evaluation and Promotion of Workers; Labor courts); "mobilized," 125, 130, 141 (see also Agriculture, industrial workers shifted to); organization of, 4, 5 (see also Cuban Workers' Confederation; Unions, labor); production norms for, 78, 124, 130; redundant, 252; slowdowns by, 8; "surplus," 124–28; and work interruptions, 126. See also Absenteeism; Artisans; Bonuses, productivity; Commissions for the Selection, Evaluation and Promotion of Workers; Employment; Fringe benefits; Job swaps; Labor; Occupational safety; Overtime; Piece rates; Profit sharing; Retirement; Self-employment; Seniority; Trades (professions)
World Bank, 57
World Health Organization (WHO), 176

Yeast, lysine-free, 173
Youth: as Cuban political factor, 6; and tourism, 15. See also Children; Communist Youth Union; Students

Youth brigades, 77
Yuca, 108
Yugoslavia, 48, 224, 242, 246

Zeolite, 101
Zimbalist, Andrew, xix
Zinc, 201
Zionism, 56